LIFE

AND

PUBLIC SERVICES

OF

JOHN QUINCY ADAMS

Engraved from a Painting by A.B. Durand.

JOHN QUINCY ADAMS.

J. Q. Adams

LIFE

AND

PUBLIC SERVICES

OF

JOHN QUINCY ADAMS,

SIXTH PRESIDENT OF THE UNITED STATES.

WITH

THE EULOGY

DELIVERED BEFORE THE LEGISLATURE OF NEW YORK.

BY WILLIAM H. SEWARD.

"THIS IS THE END OF EARTH—I AM CONTENT."

KENNIKAT PRESS
Port Washington, N. Y./London

LIFE AND PUBLIC SERVICES OF JOHN QUINCY ADAMS

First published in 1849
Reissued in 1971 by Kennikat Press
Library of Congress Catalog Card No: 75-137926
ISBN 0-8046-1489-X

Manufactured by Taylor Publishing Company   Dallas, Texas

KENNIKAT SERIES ON AMERICAN HISTORY AND
CULTURE IN THE NINETEENTH CENTURY

TO THE

FRIENDS OF EQUAL LIBERTY

AND HUMAN RIGHTS

THROUGHOUT THE WORLD,

This Volume

IS RESPECTFULLY INSCRIBED.

ADVERTISEMENT.

―――∿∿∿∿∿―――

THE Publishers apologize for the delay in issuing this volume, which was announced by them as in press, more than one year since, shortly after the decease of its illustrious subject. Gov. Seward, in undertaking its preparation, was well aware of the engrossing attention which his professional duties required, but looked constantly for relaxation from his multiplied business engagements, in the hope that he might be able to complete the work commenced by him. It however became necessary for its timely completion, to obtain the literary assistance of an able writer, who has, under his auspices, completed the work. The Publishers confidently believe, that it will in all respects, be received as a faithful and impartial history of the Life of the "Old Man Eloquent," and worthy a place in the library of every friend of liberty and humanity.

AUBURN, April, 1849.

PREFACE.

THE claims of this volume are humble. For more than half a century JOHN QUINCY ADAMS had occupied a prominent position before the American people, and filled a large space in his country's history. His career was protracted to extreme old age. He outlived political enmity and party rancor. His purity of life—his elevated and patriotic principles of action—his love of country, and devotion to its interests—his advocacy of human freedom, and the rights of man—brought all to honor and love him. Admiring legislators hung with rapture on the lips of "the Old Man Eloquent," and millions eagerly perused the sentiments he uttered, as they were scattered by the press in every town and hamlet of the Western Continent. At his decease, there was a general desire expressed for a history of his life and times. A work of this description was understood to be in preparation by his family. It was not probable, however, that this could appear under several years, and when published, would undoubtedly be placed, by its size and cost, beyond the reach of the great mass of readers. In view of these circumstances, there was an evident want of a volume of more limited compass—a book which would come within the means of the people generally,—and adapted not only for libraries, and the higher classes of society, but would find its way into the midst of those moving in the humbler walks of life. To supply this want, the present work has been prepared. The endeavor has been made to compress within a brief compass, the principal events of the life of Mr. Adams, and the scenes in which he participated; and to portray the leading traits of character which distinguished him from his contemporaries. It has been the aim to present such an aspect of the history and principles of this wonderful man, as shall do justice to his memory, and afford an example which the youth of America may profitably imitate in seeking for a model by which to shape their course through life. How far this end has been attained, an intelligent and candid public must determine.

CONTENTS.

CHAPTER I.

CHAPTER XI.

CHAPTER XII.

CHAPTER XIII.

CHAPTER XIV.

CHAPTER XV.

THE LIFE OF JOHN QUINCY ADAMS.

CHAPTER I.

THE ANCESTRY, BIRTH, AND CHILDHOOD, OF JOHN QUINCY
ADAMS.

THE Puritan Pilgrims of the May-Flower landed on
Plymouth Rock, and founded the Colony of Massachusetts, on the 21st day of December, 1620.

HENRY ADAMS, the founder of the Adams family in
America, fled from ecclesiastical oppression in England,
and joined the Colony at a very early period, but at
what precise time is not recorded. He erected his
humble dwelling at a place within the present town of
QUINCY, then known as MOUNT WOLLASTON, and is
believed to have been an inhabitant when the first
Christian Church was gathered there in 1639. On the
organization of the town of Braintree, which com-
prised the place of his residence, he was elected Clerk
of the Town. He died on the eighth day of October,
1646. His memory is preserved by a plain granite
monument, erected in the burial-ground at Quincy,

by JOHN ADAMS, President of the United States, and bearing this inscription:—

In Memory

OF

HENRY ADAMS,

Who took his flight from the Dragon Persecution in Devonshire, in
England, and alighted with eight sons, near Mount Wollaston.
One of the sons returned to England, and after taking time
to explore the country, four removed to Medfield and
the neighboring towns; two to Chelmsford. One
only, Joseph, who lies here at his left. hand,
remained here, who was an original pro-
prietor in the Township of Braintree,
incorporated in the year 1639.

This stone, and several others, have been placed in this yard, by a
great-great-grandson, from a veneration of the piety, humility, simplicity, prudence, patience, temperance, frugality, industry, and perseverance of his ancestors, in hopes of recommending an imitation of their
virtues to their posterity.

Joseph Adams, the son of Henry Adams mentioned in the above inscription, died on the sixth of December, 1694, aged sixty-eight years. Joseph, the next in succession, died February 12th, 1736, at the age of eighty-four years. His son John Adams, was a Deacon of the Church at Quincy, and died May 25th, 1761, aged seventy years. This John Adams was the father of him who was destined to give not only undying fame to his ancient family, but a new and powerful impulse to the cause of Human Freedom throughout the world.

JOHN ADAMS, son of John Adams and Susannah

Boylston Adams, was born at Quincy on the nineteenth day of October (old style), 1735. He received
the honors of Harvard University in 1755, and then,
in pursuance of a good old New England custom,
which made those who had enjoyed the benefits of a
public education, in turn impart those benefits to the
public, he was occupied for a time in teaching.

It ought to encourage all young men in straitened
circumstances, desirous of obtaining a profession and
of rising to eminence, to know that John Adams, who
became so illustrious by talents and achievement as to
lend renown to the office of President of the United
States, pursued the study of the law under the incon-
veniences resulting from his occupation as an instructor in a Grammar School.

John Adams was an eminent and successful lawyer,
but it was not the design of his existence that his talents should be wasted in the contentions of the courts.

The British Parliament, as soon as the Colonies had
attracted their notice, commenced a system of legislation known as the Colonial System, the object of
which was to secure to the mother country a monop-
oly of their trade, and to prevent their rising to a condition of strength and independence. The effect of
this system was to prevent all manufactures in the Colonies, and all trade with foreign countries, and even
with the adjacent plantations.

The Colonies remonstrated in vain against this policy, but owing to popular dissatisfaction, the regula-

tions were not rigidly enforced. At length an Order in Council was passed, which directed the officers of the customs in Massachusetts Bay, to execute the acts of trade. A question arose in the Supreme Court of that province in 1761, upon the constitutional right of the British Parliament to bind the Colonies. The trial produced great excitement. The cause was argued for the Crown by the King's Attorney-General, and against the laws by James Otis.

It will be seen that the question thus involved was the very one that was finally submitted to the arbitrament of arms in the American Revolution. The speech of Otis on the occasion, was an effort of surpassing ability. John Adams was a witness, and he recorded his opinion of it, and his opinion of the magnitude of the question, thus :

"Otis was a flame of fire! With a promptitude of classical allusion, a depth of research, a rapid summary of historical events and dates, a profusion of legal authorities, a prophetic glance of his eyes into futurity, a rapid torrent of impetuous eloquence, he hurried away all before him. AMERICAN INDEPENDENCE was then and there born. Every man of an unusually crowded audience, appeared to me to go away ready to take up arms against Writs of Assistance."

Speaking on the same subject, on another occasion, John Adams said that "James Otis then and there breathed into this nation the breath of life."

From that day John Adams was an enthusiast for the independence of his country.

In 1764 he married Abigail, daughter of the Reverend William Smith, of Weymouth. The mother of John Quincy Adams was a woman of great beauty and high intellectual endowments, and she combined, with the proper accomplishments of her sex, a sweetness of disposition, and a generous sympathy with the patriotic devotion of her illustrious husband.

In 1765, the British Parliament, in contempt of the discontent of the Colonies, presumptuously passed the Stamp Act; a law which directed taxed stamped paper to be used in all legal instruments in the Colonies. The validity of the law was denied; and while Patrick Henry was denouncing it in Virginia, James Otis and John Adams argued against it before the Governor and Council of Massachusetts.

The occasion called forth from John Adams a "Dissertation on the Canon and Feudal Laws,"—a work, which although it was of a general character in regard to government, yet manifested democratic sentiments unusual in those times, and indicated that republican institutions were the proper institutions for the American People.

The resistance to the stamp act throughout the Colonies procured its repeal in 1766. But the British Government accompanied the repeal with an ungracious declaratory act, by which they asserted "that the Parliament had, and of right ought to have, power to bind the Colonies, in all cases whatsoever." In the next year a law was passed, which imposed duties in the Colonies, on glass, paper, paints, and tea. The spirit of insubordination manifested itself throughout the Colonies, and, inasmuch as it radiated from Boston, British ships of war were stationed in its harbor, and two regiments of British troops were thrown in the town, to compel obedience. John Adams had now become known as the most intrepid, zealous, and indefatigable opposer of British usurpation. The Crown tried upon him in vain the royal arts so successful on the other side of the Atlantic. The Governor and Council offered him the place of Advocate General in the Court of Admiralty, an office of great value; he declined it, "decidedly, peremptorily, but respectfully."

At this interesting crisis, JOHN QUINCY ADAMS was born, at Quincy, on the 11th of July, 1767. A lesson, full of instruction concerning the mingled influences of piety and patriotism in New England, at that time, is furnished to us by the education of the younger Adams. Nor can we fail to notice that each of those virtues retained its relative power over him, throughout his long and eventful life. He was brought into the church and baptized on the day after that on which he was born.

John Quincy Adams, in one of his letters, thus mentions the circumstances of his baptism:

"The house at Mount Wollaston has a peculiar interest to me, as the dwelling of my great-grandfather, whose name I bear. The incident which gave rise to this circumstance is not without its moral to my heart. He was dying, when I was baptized ; and his daughter, my grandmother, present at my birth, requested that I might receive his name. The fact, recorded by my father at the time, has connected with that portion of my name, a charm of mingled sensibility and devotion. It was filial tenderness that gave the name. It was the name of one passing from earth to immortality. These have been among the strongest links of my attachment to the name of Quincy, and have been to me, through life, a perpetual admonition to do nothing unworthy of it."

It cannot be doubted that the character of the person from whom, in such affecting circumstances, he derived an honorable patronymic, was an object of emulation. John Quincy was a gentleman of wealth, education, and influence. He was for a long time Speaker of the House of Representatives in Massachusetts, and during many years one of His Majesty's Provincial Council. He was a faithful representative, and throughout his public services, a vigorous defender of the rights and liberties of the Colony. Exemplary in private life, and earnest in piety, he enjoyed the public confidence, through a civil career of forty years' duration.

The American Revolution was rapidly hurrying on during the infancy of John Quincy Adams. In 1769 the citizens of Boston held a meeting in which they instructed their representatives in the Provincial Legislature to resist the usurpations of the British Government. John Adams was chairman of the committee that prepared these instructions, and his associates were Richard Dana and Joseph Warren, the same distinguished patriot who gave up his life as one of the earliest sacrifices to freedom, in the battle of Bunker Hill.

Those instructions were expressed in the bold and decided tone of John Adams, and they increased the public excitement in the province, by the earnestness with which they insisted on the removal of the British troops from Boston.

The popular irritation increased, until on the 5th of March, 1770, a collision occurred between the troops and some of the inhabitants of Boston, in which five citizens were killed, and many wounded. This was called the Bloody Massacre. The exasperated inhabitants were with difficulty restrained from retaliating this severity by an extermination of all the British troops. A public meeting was held, and a committee, of which SAMUEL ADAMS was chairman, was appointed to address the Governor (Gage), and demand that the troops should be withdrawn. John Adams described the excitement, on a later occasion, in these words:

"Not only the immense assemblies of the people from day to day, but military arrangements from night to night, were necessary to keep the people and the soldiers from getting together by the ears. The life of a red-coat would not have been safe in any street or corner of the town. Nor would the lives of the inhabitants have been much more secure. The whole militia of the city was in requisition, and military watches and guards were everywhere placed. We were all upon a level. No man was exempted: our military officers were our only superiors. I had the honor to be summoned in my turn, and attended at the State House with my musket and bayonet, my broadsword and cartridge-box, under the command of the famous Paddock."

The Governor withdrew the troops and sent them to the castle : the commanding officer and some of the soldiers were arrested, and brought to trial for murder.

John Adams, the advocate and leader of the exasperated people, was solicited by the Government to act as counsel for the accused. The people, in the heat of passion, would naturally identify the lawyer with his clients, and both with the odious cause in which they served. John Adams did not hesitate. His principle was fidelity to duty in *all* the relations of life. Adams, together with Josiah Quincy, defended the accused with ability and firmness, and the result crowned not only the advocates, but the jury and the people of Boston with honor. Distinguishing between the Government, upon whom the responsibility rested, and the troops who were its agents, the jury acquitted the accused. The people sustained the verdict ; affording to Great Britain and to the world a noble proof, that they had been well prepared by education for the trust of self-government.

The controversy between the Province of Massachusetts and the British Government continued, and the exasperation of the Colonies became more intense, until the destruction of the imported tea in the harbor, in December, 1773, incensed the Ministry so highly, that they procured an act closing the port of Boston. This act was followed by the convention of the first American Congress at Philadelphia, on the 5th of September, 1774. As John Adams had been the master spirit in the agitation in Massachusetts, he was appointed one of the Delegates to the General Congress. After his election, his friend Sewall, the King's Attorney General, labored earnestly to dissuade him from accepting the appointment.

The Attorney General told the delegate that Great Britain was determined on her system, that her power was irresistible, and that he, and those with him who should persist in their designs of resistance, would be involved in ruin.

John Adams replied, "I know Great Britain has determined on her system, and that very determination determines me on mine. You know I have been constant and uniform in opposition to her measures. The die is now cast. I have passed the Rubicon. Sink or swim, live or die, survive or perish with my country is my unalterable determination."

It was these energetic and resolute expressions which Daniel Webster wrought into so magnificent an imaginary speech, in his glowing Eulogy on John Adams and Thomas Jefferson.

John Adams continued in Congress throughout the sessions of 1775 and 1776, and on all occasions was an intrepid and earnest advocate for Independence. On his motion, George Washington was appointed Commander in Chief of the Army.

John Adams was the mover of Independence in the Congress. On the 6th of May, 1776, he brought the subject before that body, by a resolution expressed as follows :—

"Whereas it appears perfectly irreconcilable to reason and good conscience, for the people of these Colonies now to take the oaths and affirmations necessary for the support of any government under the crown of Great Britain, and it is necessary that the exercise of every kind of authority under the said crown should be totally suppressed, and all the powers of government exerted under the authority of the people of the Colonies for the preservation of internal peace, virtue, and good order, as well as for the defence of their lives, liberties, and properties, against the hostile invasion, and cruel depredations of their enemies :—Therefore, it is recommended to the Colonies to adopt such a government as will, in the opinion of the representatives of the people, best conduce to the happiness and safety of their constituents, and of America."

This resolution was adopted, and was followed by the appointment of a committee, on the motion of Richard Henry Lee, seconded by John Adams, to prepare a Declaration. This committee consisted of Thomas Jefferson, John Adams, Benjamin Franklin, Roger Sherman, and Robert R. Livingston. Jefferson and Adams were a sub-committee, and the former prepared the Declaration, at the urgent request of the latter.

Jefferson bore this testimony to the ability and power of John Adams.—" The great pillar of support to the Declaration of Independence, and its ablest advocate and champion on the floor of the House, was John Adams."

On the day after the Declaration of Independence was adopted, he wrote the memorable letter in which he said with prophetic unction,—" Yesterday the greatest question was decided that ever was debated in America; and greater, perhaps, never was or will be decided among men. A resolution was passed without one dissenting Colony, 'That the United States are, and of right ought to be, free and independent States. The day is passed. The fourth day of July, 1776, will be a memorable epoch in the history of America. I am apt to believe it will be celebrated by succeeding generations as a great anniversary festival. It ought to be commemorated as the day of deliverance, by solemn

acts of devotion to Almighty God.   It ought to be solemnized with pomps, shows, games, sports, guns, bells,
bonfires, and illuminations, from one end of the continent to the other, from this time forward, forever.
You may think me transported with enthusiasm, but I
am not.   I am well aware of the toil, and blood, and
treasure, that it will cost to maintain this Declaration,
and support and defend these States : yet through all
the gloom, I can see that the end is worth all the
means ; and that posterity will triumph, although you
and I may rue, which I hope we shall not."

From this time, until November 1777, John Adams
was incessantly employed in public duties in Congress,
during the session of that body ; and during its recess,
as a member of the State Council in Massachusetts.
During this period, John Quincy was instructed at
home, by her who, in long after years, he was accustomed to call his almost adored mother, who was aided
by a law-student in the office of his father.   EDWARD
EVERETT, in his Eulogy upon John Quincy Adams,
made the very striking and just remark, that there
seemed to be in his life no such stage as that of boyhood.   While yet but nine years old, he wrote to his
father the following letter :

Braintree, June 2nd, 1777.

DEAR SIR,

   I love to receive letters very well ; much better than I love to
write them.   I make but a poor figure at composition.   My head is
much too fickle.   My thoughts are running after bird's eggs, play
and trifles, till I get vexed with myself.   Mamma has a troublesome

task to keep me a studying. I own I am ashamed of myself. I have but just entered the third volume of Rollin's History, but designed to have got half through it by this time. I am determined this week to be more diligent. Mr. Thaxter is absent at Court. I have set myself a stint this week, to read the third volume half out. If I can but keep my resolution, I may again at the end of the week give a better account of myself. I wish, sir, you would give me in writing, some instructions with regard to the use of my time, and advise me how to proportion my studies and play, and I will keep them by me, and endeavor to follow them.

With the present determination of growing·better, I am, dear sir, your son,   JOHN QUINCY ADAMS.

P. S. Sir—If you will be so good as to favor me with a blank book, I will transcribe the most remarkable passages I meet with in my reading, which will serve to fix them upon my mind.

After making all just allowance for precocity of genius, we cannot but see that the early maturity of the younger Adams proves the great advantage of pure and intellectual associations in childhood.

The time soon arrived when John Quincy Adams was to enjoy advantages of education such as were never afforded to any other American youth. Among the earliest acts of the American Congress, was the appointment of Benjamin Franklin, Silas Dean, and Arthur Lee, as Commissioners to France ; they were charged to solicit aid from France, and to negotiate a treaty, by which the Independence of the United States should be acknowledged by Louis Sixteenth, then at the height of his popularity. Silas Dean was recalled in 1776, and John Adams was appointed to fill his place. He embarked on this mission the 13th of February, 1778, in the frigate Boston, commanded by Captain Tucker. John Adams had gone down to Quincy, and the frigate called there to receive him on board. On the eve of embarkation he wrote the following simple and touching letter to Mrs. Adams:

" *Uncle Quincy's,—half after* 11 *o'clock,* 13 *February,* 1778.

" DEAREST OF FRIENDS,

" I had not been twenty minutes in this house, before I had the happiness to see Captain Tucker and a midshipman coming for me. We will be soon on board, and may God prosper our voyage in every stage of it as much as at the beginning, and send to you, my dear children, and all my friends, the choicest blessings!

" So wishes and prays yours, with an ardor that neither absence, nor any other event can abate,

" JOHN ADAMS.

" P. S. Johnny sends his duty to his mamma, and his love to his sisters and brothers. He behaves like a man."

" He behaves like a man!"—Words which gave presage of the future character of John Quincy Adams. His education had now commenced: an education in the principles of heroic action, by John Adams, the colossus of the American Revolution. How devoted he was to this important charge, and with what true philosophy he conducted it, may be seen by the following letter written about that time by him, to Mrs. Adams:

" Human nature, with all its infirmities and depravation, is still capable of great things. It is capable of attaining to degrees of wisdom and of goodness which we have reason to believe appear respectable in the estimation of superior intelligences. Education makes a greater difference between man and man, than nature has made between man and brute. The virtues and powers to which men may be trained, by early education and constant discipline, are truly sublime and astonishing.

"Newton and Locke are examples of the deep sagacity which may be acquired by long habits of thinking and study. Nay, your common mechanics and artisans are proofs of the wonderful dexterity acquired by use ; a watchmaker, finishing his wheels and springs, a pin or needle-maker, &c. I think there is a particular occupation in Europe, which is called paper staining, or linen staining. A man who has long been habituated to it, shall sit for a whole day, and draw upon paper various figures, to be imprinted upon the paper for rooms, as fast as his eye can roll and his fingers move, and no two of his draughts shall be alike. The Saracens, the Knights of Malta, the army and navy in the service of the English Republic, among many others, are instances to show to what an exalted height, valor or bravery or courage may be raised, by artificial means.

"It should be your care therefore, and mine, to elevate the minds of our children, and exalt their courage, to accelerate and animate their industry and activity, to excite in them an habitual contempt of meanness, abhorrence of injustice and inhumanity, and an ambition to excel in every capacity, faculty, and virtue. If we suffer their minds to grovel and creep in infancy, they will grovel and creep all their lives.

"But their bodies must be hardened, as well as their souls exalted. Without strength, and activity and vigor of body, the brightest mental excellencies will be eclipsed and obscured.

" JOHN ADAMS."

No one can read this extraordinary letter, and compare it with the actual character of John Quincy Adams as ultimately developed, without regarding that character as a fulfilment, in all respects, of the prayers and purposes of his illustrious parent.

The voyage of the American Minister was made in a time of great peril. The naval supremacy of Great

Britain was already established.   Her armed ships traversed the ocean in all directions.   Captain Tucker saw a large English ship showing a row of guns, and with the consent of the Minister, engaged her.   When hailed, she answered with a broadside.   John Adams had been requested to retire to the cockpit, but when the engagement had begun, he was found among the marines, with a musket in his hands.

The desired treaty with France had been consummated by Dr. Franklin, before the arrival of John Adams.   After that event, Congress decided to have but one minister in that country, and Dr. Franklin having deservedly received the appointment, John Adams asked and obtained leave to return home, after an absence of a year and a half.   During that period the younger Adams attended a public school in Paris, while his leisure hours were filled with the instructions casually derived from the conversation of John Adams, and Dr. Franklin, and other eminent intellectual persons, by whom his father was surrounded.   The improvement of the son during his sojourn abroad is thus mentioned by John Adams, just before his embarkation on his return to America.

" My son has had a great opportunity to see this country, but this has unavoidably retarded his education in some other things.   He has enjoyed perfect health from first to last, and is respected wherever he goes, for his vigor and vivacity both of mind and body ; for his constant good-humor, and for his rapid progress in French, as well as in general knowledge, which, for his age, is uncommon."

John Adams now regarded his public life as closed. He wrote to Mrs. Adams :

" The Congress, I presume, expect that I should come home, and I shall come accordingly. As they have no business for me in Europe, I must contrive to get some for myself at home. Prepare yourself for removing to Boston, into the old house, for there you shall go, and I will draw writs and deeds, and harangue juries, and be happy."

This calculation was signally erroneous, as all calculations upon personal ease and peace by great and good men always are. He remained at home only three months, and during that time he had other and higher occupations than drawing writs and deeds. He was elected Delegate to the Convention charged with the responsible and novel duty of forming a written constitution for Massachusetts. In that body he labored with untiring assiduity, as in Congress; the constitution thus produced was in a great measure prepared by himself, and it is due to his memory to record the fact, that it was among the most democratic of all the constitutions which were adopted by the new States. The younger Adams having returned to America with his father, had thus the advantage of seeing republican theories brought into successful, practical application.

About this time Congress resolved on sending a

Minister Plenipotentiary to Great Britain, to negotiate, if possible, a treaty of peace. John Adams and John Jay received each an equal number of votes. The result was the appointment of Mr. Jay as Minister to Spain, and of John Adams as Minister to the Court of St. James. He was instructed to insist on the independence of the United States.

The younger Adams again attended the Diplomatist. They embarked in the French frigate *La Sensible*, on the 17th of November, 1779.

The frigate sprang a leak, and was obliged to put into the port nearest at hand, which proved to be Ferrol in Spain. They disembarked on the 11th of December, and traversed the intervening distance to Paris over land, a journey of a thousand miles. This journey was performed through the mountains on mules. Spain, as well as France, was then in alliance with America, and the Minister was everywhere received with respect and kindness. The French officers at Ferrol wore cockades in honor of the Triple Alliance, combining a white ribbon for the French, a red one for the Spanish, and a black one for the Americans.

The United Powers proposed demands which were ominous of disappointment to the Minister.—On the 12th of December he wrote :—" It is said that England is as reluctant to acknowledge the independence of America, as to cede Gibraltar, the last of which is insisted upon, as well as the first."

The travellers reached Paris about the middle of

February, 1780. John Adams mentioned a singular coincidence in his letter announcing their arrival. " I have the honor to be lodged here with no less a personage than the Prince of Hesse-Cassel, who is here upon a visit. We occupy different apartments in the same house, and have no intercourse with each other, to be sure; but some wags are of opinion, that if I were authorised to open a negotiation with him, I might obtain from him as many troops to fight *on our side* of the question, as he has already hired to the English *against us !*"

The American Revolution has wrought wonderful changes since that day. No German Prince could now send a man, or a musket, to war against its principles.

John Adams soon discovered that there was no prospect of success for his mission to England. He remained at Paris until August, 1780, and during the interval his son was kept at an academy in that city.

At the expiration of that period the Minister repaired to Holland, and there received instructions to negotiate a loan, and then a treaty of amity and commerce with the states of that country. The younger Adams while in Holland was placed at school, first at Amsterdam, and afterwards in the University of Leyden.

A letter of the father, dated at Amsterdam, 18th December, 1780, gives us a glimpse of the system of instruction approved by him, and a pleasant view of the principles which he deemed it important to be inculcated.

"I have this morning sent Mr. Thaxter with my two sons to Leyden, there to take up their residence for some time, and there to pursue their studies of Latin and Greek under the excellent masters, and there to attend lectures of the celebrated professors in that University. It is much cheaper there than here. The air is infinitely purer, and the company and conversation are better. It is perhaps as learned a University as any in Europe.

"I should not wish to have children educated in the common schools of this country, where a littleness of soul is notorious. The masters are mean spirited wretches, pinching, kicking, and boxing the children upon every turn. There is, besides, a general littleness, arising from the incessant contemplation of stivers and doits, which pervades the whole people.

"Frugality and industry are virtues everywhere, but avarice and stinginess are not frugality. The Dutch say, that without a habit of thinking of every doit before you spend it, no man can be a good merchant, or conduct trade with success.

"This, I believe, is a just maxim in general; but I would never wish to see a son of mine govern himself by it. It is the sure and certain way for an industrious man to be rich. It is the only possible way for a merchant to become the first merchant, or the richest man in the place. But this is an object that I hope none of my children will ever aim at. It is indeed true everywhere, that those who attend to small expenses are always rich.

"I would have my children attend to doits and farthings as devoutly as the merest Dutchman upon earth, if such attention was necessary to support their independence. A man who discovers a disposition and a design to be independent, seldom succeeds. A jealousy arises against him. The tyrants are alarmed on the one side, lest he should oppose them: the slaves are alarmed on the other, lest he should expose their servility. The cry from all quarters is, '*He is the proudest man in the world : he cannot bear to be under obligation.*'

"I never in my life observed any one endeavoring to lay me under particular obligation to him, but I suspected he had a design to make me his dependent, and to have claims upon my gratitude. This I should have no objection to, because gratitude is always in one's power. But the danger is, that men will expect and require more of us than honor, and innocence, and rectitude will permit us to perform.

"In our country, however, any man, with common industry and prudence, may be independent."

One cannot turn over a page of the domestic history of John Adams, without finding a precept or example, the influence of which is manifested in the character of his illustrious son. Thus he writes to Mrs. Adams, touching certain calumnies which had been propagated against him :—

"Do n't distress yourself about any malicious attempts to injure me in the estimation of my countrymen. Let them take their course, and go the length of their tether. They will never hurt your husband, whose character is fortified with a shield of innocence and honor, ten thousand-fold stronger than brass or iron. The contemptible essays, made by you know whom, will only tend to their own confusion. My letters have shown them their own ignorance, a sight they could not bear. Say as little about it as I do. I laugh, and will laugh before all posterity, at their impotent rage and envy."

In July, 1781, Francis Dana, who had attended John Adams as Secretary of Legation, was appointed Minister to Russia. John Quincy Adams, then fourteen years old, was appointed Private Secretary of this mission. He remained at that post fourteen months, performing its duties with entire satisfaction to the minister. The singular ripeness of the youthful secretary was shown in his travelling alone, on his return from St. Petersburgh, by a journey leisurely made, and filled with observations of Sweden, Denmark, Hamburgh, and Bremen. On arriving in Holland, he resumed his studies at the Hague.

John Adams, having completed his mission in Holland, was charged, with Dr. Franklin, John Jay, and Thomas Jefferson, with the duty of negotiating a definitive treaty of peace with Great Britain. The treaty was executed at Paris on the 3d of September, 1783, and was ratified January 14th, 1784. The younger Adams enjoyed the satisfaction of being pres-, ent at the conclusion of the treaty; and while it was under process of negotiation, he was constantly favored with opportunities of listening to the instructive conversation of Franklin and Jefferson.

The negotiation of the treaty was dilatory in the extreme. It was embarrassed with French intrigues, great carelessness at home, and greater reluctance on the part of England. The wearied Minister wrote to Mrs. Adams on the 30th of May, 1783: "Our son is at the Hague, pursuing his studies with great ardor. They give him a good character wherever he has been, and I hope he will make a good man." On the 9th of June he wrote in these homely, but manly words: "I am weary, worn, and disgusted to death. I had rather chop wood, dig ditches, and make fence upon my poor little farm. Alas, poor farm! and poorer family! what have you lost that your country might be free! and that others might catch fish and hunt deer and bears at their ease!

"There will be as few of the tears of gratitude, or the smiles of admiration, or the sighs of pity for us, as for the army. But all this should not hinder me from going over the same scenes again, upon the same occasions—scenes which I would not encounter for all the wealth, pomp, and power of the world. Boys! if you ever say one word, or utter one complaint, I will disinherit you. Work! you rogues, and be free. You

will never have so hard work to do as papa has had.
Daughter! get you an honest man for a husband, and
keep him honest. No matter whether he is rich, provided he be independent. Regard the honor and the
moral character of the man, more than all circumstances. Think of no other greatness but that of the
soul, no other riches but those of the heart."

After concluding the treaty of peace, John Adams,
together with Franklin and Jay, was charged with the
duty of negotiating a treaty of commerce with Great
Britain, and John Adams, taking his son John Quincy
with him, proceeded to London, and took up his residence at the British Court. Mrs. Adams embarked in
June, 1784, to join her husband.

John Adams was appointed Minister Plenipotentiary
to the same Court in 1785, and thus he, who ten years
before, when a subject, in the province of Massachusetts, had said, " *I know that Great Britain has determined upon her system, and that very determination
determines me on mine,*"—was the first Representative
of his independent country admitted to an audience
by the discomfited majesty of the Imperial States.
The occasion was adapted to excite profound emotions,
though of different kinds, in each party. John Adams
addressed the King thus :—

" The United States of America have appointed me
their Minister Plenipotentiary to your Majesty, and
have directed me to deliver to your Majesty this letter,
which contains the evidence of it. It is in obedience

to their express commands, that I have the honor to assure your Majesty of their unanimous disposition and desire to cultivate the most liberal and friendly intercourse between your Majesty's subjects and their citizens ; and of their best wishes for your Majesty's health and happiness, and for that of your royal family.

"The appointment of a Minister from the United States to your Majesty's Court, will form an epoch in the history of England, and of America. I think myself more fortunate than all my fellow citizens, in having the distinguished honor to be the first to stand in your Majesty's royal presence, in a diplomatic character; and I shall esteem myself the happiest of men, if I can be instrumental in recommending my country more and more, to your Majesty's royal benevolence, and of restoring an entire esteem, confidence and affection, or in better words, 'the old good nature, and the old good harmony,' between people, who, though separated by an ocean, and under different governments, have the same language, a similar religion, and kindred blood. I beg your Majesty's permission to add, that although I have sometimes before been intrusted by my country, it was never, in my whole life, in a manner so agreeable to myself."

George III. replied with dignity, but not without some manifestations of excitement :—

"The circumstances of this audience are so extraordinary, the language you have now held is so extremely proper, and the feelings you have discovered so justly adapted to the occasion, that I must say that I not only receive with pleasure the assurances of the friendly disposition of the People of the United States, but I am very glad the choice has fallen upon you to be their Minister. I wish you, sir, to believe, and that it may be understood in America, that I have done nothing in the late contest, but what I thought myself indispensably bound to do, by the duty which I owed my people. I will be frank with you—I was the last to conform to the separation, but the separation having been made, and having become inevitable, I have always said, as I say now, that I would be the first to meet the friendship of the United States, as an independent power.

" The moment I see such sentiments and language as yours prevail, and a disposition to give this country the preference, that moment I shall say, let the circumstances of language, religion and blood have their natural and full effect."

The kindly feelings expressed by the King, were, however, comparatively, only the language of ceremony, for the British Ministry, and the British people, did not regard the new republic with favor. But they could not withhold the exhibition of reluctant respect.

It was at such a time as this, and in such circumstances, that John Quincy Adams surveyed, from a new position, the colossal structure of British power, and the workings of its combined systems of conservative aristocracy, and progressive democracy. It was here that he imbibed new veneration for Russell, Sidney, Hampden, and Milton, its republican patriots; for Shakspeare, Dryden, and Pope, its immortal poets; and for Addison and Johnson, its moralists; here he learned from Wilberforce the principles of political philanthropy, as well as the patience and perseverance to defend them, and studied eloquence by the living models of Pitt, Fox, Erskine, Burke, and Sheridan.

This, indeed, was a fitting conclusion to a precocious education by the patriots and philosophers of his own country, with practical observations in the courts of Spain and the Netherlands, of the weak but amiable Louis XVI., and the accomplished, but depraved, Catharine II.

John Quincy Adams now became fearful that the duties of manhood would devolve upon him without his having completed the necessary academic studies. He therefore obtained leave to return home in 1785, at the age of eighteen years, and entered Cambridge University, at an advanced standing, in 1786. He graduated in 1788 with deserved honors.

CHAPTER II.

JOHN QUINCY ADAMS STUDIES LAW—HIS PRACTICE—ENGAGES
IN PUBLIC LIFE—APPOINTED MINISTER TO THE HAGUE.

AFTER leaving the University, young Adams entered the office of Theophilus Parsons, who was then in the practice of law at Newburyport, and who afterwards for so many years filled with dignity and ability the office of Chief Justice of Massachusetts.

Adams completed the usual term of professional study, and then commenced the practice of the law in Boston. It may encourage some who are oppressed by the difficulties attending initiation in the profession, to know, that during the first and only four years of John Quincy Adams' practice, he had occasion for despondency.

" I had long and lingering anxieties, (he afterwards said,) in looking forward, doubtful even of my prospects of comfortable subsistence, but acquiring more and more the means of it, till in the last of the four years, the business of my profession yielded me an income more than equal to my expenditures."

But the country and the age had claims on John Quincy Adams, as well as on his father, for higher

duties than "making writs," and "haranguing juries,"
and "being happy."

The American Revolution, which had been brought
to a successful close, had inspired, throughout Europe,
a desire to renovate the institutions of government.
The officers and citizens of France who had mingled
in the contest, had carried home the seeds of freedom,
and had scattered them abroad upon soil quick to receive them. The flame of Liberty, kindled on the
shores of the Western Continent, was reflected back
upon the Old World. France beheld its beams, and
hailed them as a beacon-light, which should lead the
nations out from the bondage of ages. Inspirited by
the success attending the struggle in the British colonies, the French people, long crushed beneath a grind-
ing despotism, resolved to burst their shackles and
strike for Freedom. It was a noble resolution, but
consummated, alas! amid devastation and the wildest
anarchy. The French Revolution filled the world
with horror. It was the work of a blind giant, urged
to fury by the remembrance of wrongs endured for
generations. The Altar of Liberty was reared amid
seas of blood, and stained with the gore of innocent
victims.

The measurable failure of this struggle in France,
teaches the necessity of due preparation before a
people can advance to the permanent possession and
enjoyment of their rights. The American colonists
had been trained to rational conceptions of freedom, by

lessons of wisdom and sagacity read them by their Puritan fathers, and by the experience in self-government, afforded during a century and a half of enjoyment of a large share of political privileges, granted by the mother country. They were thus prepared to lay deep and strong the foundations of an enlightened government, which, equally removed from the extremes of despotism on the one hand, and anarchy on the other, and granting its subjects the exercise of their right to "life, liberty, and the pursuit of happiness," shall endure through ages to come. But the people of France, shut up in darkness during centuries of misrule, passed at a step from abject servitude to unlimited freedom. They were unprepared for this violent transition. Their conceptions of liberty were of the most extravagant description. What wonder that they became dizzy at their sudden elevation! What wonder that blood flowed in rivers !—that dissension and faction rent them asunder—that a fearful anarchy soon reigned triumphant—or that the confused and troubled drama closed in the iron rule of a military conqueror—the Man of Destiny! Let not this lesson be lost upon the world. Let a people who would enjoy freedom, learn to merit the boon by the study of its principles, and a preparation to exercise its privileges, under those salutary restraints which man can never throw off and be happy!

The odium excited throughout Europe by the excesses of the French Revolution, was heaped without

measure upon the American people. They were
charged with the origin of the misrule which convulsed France, and filled the eastern hemisphere with
alarm : and were tauntingly pointed to the crude theories promulgated by French democracy, and the failure of their phrenzied efforts to establish an enlightened
and permanent Republic, as conclusive evidence that
self-government, among any people, was a mere Uto-
pian dream, which could never be realized.

The establishment of a republican government in
America, had not been relished by the monarchies of
Europe. They looked upon it with distrust, as a precedent dangerous to them in the highest degree. The
succor which Louis XVI. had rendered the revolting
colonists, was not from a love of democratic institutions : it was his hope to cripple Great Britain, his
ancient enemy, and to find some opportunity, perhaps,
to win back his Canadian provinces, which had so recently been rent from his possession. When the
pent-up flames of revolution burst forth at the very
doors of the governments of the old world—when
the French throne had been robbed of its king, and
that king of his life—when a Republic had been proclaimed in their midst, and signal-notes of freedom
were ringing in their borders —they became seriously
alarmed. The growing evil must be checked immediately. Led on by England, the continental powers
combined to exterminate at a blow, if possible, every
vestige of Republicanism in France. Then commenced

the long series of bloody wars, which, with little intermission, convulsed Europe for nearly a quarter of a century, and ceased only when the rock of St. Helena received its lonely exile.

In the meantime affairs at home had attained to a critical juncture. The Constitution had been adopted. The new government had been set in operation under the supervision of Washington, as the first President of the Republic. The people, influenced by certain "elective affinities," had become sundered into two great political parties—*Conservative* and *Progressive*, or Federal and Democratic. Both were distrustful of the Constitution. The former believed it too weak to consolidate a government capable of protecting its subjects in the peaceful enjoyment of their rights, from discord within, and attacks from without. The latter apprehended that it might easily be transformed, by some ambitious Napoleon, into an instrument of oppression more fearful even than the limited monarchy from which they had but recently escaped, at an expense of so much blood and treasure. Each of these parties are entitled to the credit of equal sincerity and honesty of purpose.

Washington, with a loftiness of purpose truly characteristic of a great and good mind, refused to identify himself with either party. In forming his first cabinet, moved with a desire to heal the dissensions which distracted the country, he selected its members equally from the adverse factions. Hamilton and Knox represented the Federal party, and Jefferson and Randolph the opposite. During his entire administration, "the Father of his country" steadily aimed to keep himself clear from all party entanglements. He was emphatically the President of the whole people, and not of a faction. His magnanimous spirit would not stoop to party favoritism, nor allow him to exercise the power entrusted him, to promote the interests of any political clique. In all his measures his great object was to advance the welfare of the nation, without regard to their influence on conflicting parties. In these things he left behind him a pure and noble example, richly worthy the imitation of his successors in that high station.

The Revolution in France, and the measures adopted by the Allied Sovereigns to arrest its progress, excited the liveliest interest among the people of the United States. But their sympathies ran in different channels, and very naturally took the hue of their party predilections. The Democrats, believing the French Revolution to be the up-springing of the same principles which had triumphed here—a lawful attempt of an oppressed people to secure the exercise of inalienable rights—although shuddering at the excesses which had been perpetrated, still felt it to be our own cause, and insisted that we were in honor and duty bound to render all the assistance in our power, even to a resort to arms, if need be. The Federalists, on the other hand, were alarmed at the anarchical tendencies in

France. They were fearful that law, order, government, and society itself, would be utterly and speedily swept away, unless the revolutionary movement was arrested. Cherishing these apprehensions, they were disposed to favor the views of Great Britain and other European powers, and were anxious that the government of the United States should adopt some active measures to assist in checking what they could not but view as rapid strides to political and social anarchy. However the two parties differed as to the measures proper to be adopted in this crisis, they were united in the conviction that our government should take *some* part as a belligerant, in these European struggles; and exerted each its influence to bring about such an interference as would be in accordance with their conflicting views of duty and expediency.

There was residing, at this period, in Boston, a young and nearly briefless lawyer, whose views on these important matters differed materially from those entertained by both parties. It was John Quincy Adams. While he could not countenance the attempts of the Allied Powers to destroy the French Republic, and reestablish a monarchy, he was equally far from favoring the turn which affairs were clearly taking in that unhappy country. He evidently foresaw the French Revolution would prove a failure; and that it was engendering an influence which, unchecked, would be deeply injurious to American liberty and order. To counteract this tendency, he published in the Boston

Centinel, in 1791, a series of articles, signed "Publicola,"
in which he discussed with great ability, the wild va-
garies engendered among political writers in France,
and which had been caught up by many in our own
country. These articles attracted much attention, both
at home and abroad. They were re-published in England, as an answer to several points in Paine's "Rights
of Man." So profound was the political sagacity they
displayed, and so great the familiarity with public
affairs, that they were, by general consent, attributed to
the elder Adams. On this subject, John Adams writes
his wife as follows, from Philadelphia, on the 5th
December, 1793 :—

"The Viscount Noailles called on me. * * * * He seemed very
critical in his inquiries concerning the letters printed as mine in
England. I told him candidly that I did not write them, and as
frankly, in confidence, who did. He says they made a great impression upon the people of England ; that he heard Mr. Windham
and Mr. Fox speak of them as the best thing that had been written,
and as one of the best pieces of reasoning and style they had ever
read."

The younger Adams, in surveying the condition of the
country at this critical period, became convinced it
would be a fatal step for the new government to take
sides with either of the great parties in Europe, who
were engaged in the settlement of their difficulties by
the arbitrement of arms. However strongly our sympathies were elicited in behalf of the French Republic—however we may have been bound in gratitude
for the assistance rendered us during our Revolution-

ary struggle, to co-operate with France in her defence of popular institutions—still, self-preservation is the first law of nature. Mr. Adams saw, that to throw ourselves into the melee of European conflicts, would prostrate the interests of the country, and peril the very existence of the government.

These views he embodied in a series of articles, which he published in the Boston Centinel, in 1793, under the signature of "Marcellus." He insisted it was alike the dictate of duty and policy, that the United States should remain strictly neutral between France and her enemies. These papers attracted general attention throughout the Union, and made a marked impression on the public mind. They were read by Washington, with expressions of the highest satisfaction; and he made particular inquiries respecting the author.

The position of Mr. Adams on neutrality was new, and in opposition to the opinions of the great mass of the country. To him, it is believed, belongs the honor of first publicly advocating this line of policy, which afterwards became a settled principle of the American government. Non-interference with foreign affairs, is a principle to which the Union has rigidly adhered to the present hour. In these articles too, Mr. Adams developed the political creed which governed him through life in regard to two great principles—union at home, and independence of all foreign alliances or entanglements

—independence not only politically, but in manufactures and in commerce.

On the 25th of April, 1793, Washington issued a proclamation, announcing the neutrality of the United States between the belligerent nations of Europe. This proclamation was not issued until after Mr. Adams' articles urging this course had been before the public for some time. It is an honorable testimony to the sagacity of his views, that Washington, and the eminent men composing his cabinet, adopted a policy which coincided so perfectly with opinions he had formed purely from the strength of his own convictions. The proclamation pleased neither of the belligerent nations in Europe. It aroused the enmity of both; and laid open our commerce to the depredations of all parties, on the plea that the American government was inimical to their interests.

While in the practice of law in Boston, Mr. Adams was not well satisfied with his condition or prospects. That he was laudably ambitious to arise to distinction in some honorable line is quite certain. But, singular as it may appear at this day, in view of his early life, and his acknowledged talents, he was not looking for, nor expecting, political preferment. These facts appear in the following passages from his diary, written at that time; and which, moreover, will be found to contain certain rules of action for life, which the young men of our country should studiously seek to imitate.

" Wednesday, May 16th, 1792. I am not satisfied with the manner in which I employ my time. It is calculated to keep me forever fixed in that state of useless and disgraceful insignificancy, which has been my lot for some years past. At an age bearing close upon twenty-five, when many of the characters who were born for the benefit of their fellow-creatures have rendered themselves conspicuous among their cotemporaries, and founded a reputation upon which their memory remains, and will continue to the latest posterity—at that period, I still find myself as obscure, as unknown to the world, as the most indolent, or the most stupid of human beings. In the walks of active life I have done nothing. Fortune, indeed, who claims to herself a large proportion of the merit which exhibits to public view the talents of professional men, at an early period of their lives, has not hitherto been peculiarly indulgent to me. But if to my own mind I inquire whether I should, at this time, be qualified to receive and derive any benefit from an opportunity which it may be in her power to procure for me, my own mind would shrink from the investigation. My heart is not conscious of an unworthy ambition ; nor of a desire to establish either fame honor, or fortune upon any other foundation than that of desert But it is conscious, and the consideration is equally painful and humiliating, it is conscious that the ambition is constant and unceasing, while the exertions to acquire the talents which ought alone to secure the reward of ambition, are feeble, indolent, frequently interrupted, and never pursued with an ardor equivalent to its purposes. My future fortunes in life are, therefore, the objects of my present speculation, and it may be proper for me to reflect further upon the same subject, and if possible, to adopt some resolutions which may enable me, as uncle Toby Shandy said of his miniature sieges, to answer the great ends of my existence.

" First, then, I begin with establishing as a fundamental principle upon which all my subsequent pursuits and regulations are to be established, that the acquisition, at least, of a respectable reputation is (subject to the overruling power and wisdom of Providence,) within my own power ; and that on my part nothing is wanting, but a constant and persevering determination to tread in the steps which naturally lead to honor. And, at the same time, I am equally convinced, that I never shall attain that credit in the world, which my nature directs me to wish, without such a steady, patient, and persevering pursuit of the means adapted to the end I have in view, as has often been the subject of my speculation, but never of my practice.

> 'Labor and toil stand stern before the throne,
> And guard—so Jove commands—the sacred place.'

" The mode of life adopted almost universally by my cotemporaries and equals is by no means calculated to secure the object of my ambition. My emulation is seldom stimulated by observing the industry and application of those whom my situation in life gives me for companions. The pernicious and childish opinion that extraordinary genius cannot brook the slavery of plodding over the rubbish of antiquity (a cant so common among the heedless votaries of indolence), dulls the edge of all industry, and is one of the most powerful ingredients in the Circean potion which transforms many of the most promising young men into the beastly forms which, in sluggish idleness, feed upon the labors of others. The degenerate sentiment, I hope, will never obtain admission in my mind ; and, if my mind should be loitered away in stupid laziness, it will be under the full conviction of my conscience that I am basely bartering the greatest benefits with which human beings can be indulged, for the miserable gratifications which are hardly worthy of contributing to the enjoyments of the brute creation.

" And as I have grounded myself upon the principle, that my character is, under the smiles of heaven, to be the work of my own hands, it becomes necessary for me to determine upon what part of active or of speculative life I mean to rest my pretensions to eminence. My own situation and that of my country equally prohibit me from seeking to derive any present expectations from a public career. My disposition is not military ; and, happily, the warlike talents are not those which open the most pleasing or the most reputable avenue to fame. I have had some transient thoughts of undertaking some useful literary performance, but the pursuit would militate too much at present with that of the profession upon which I am to depend, not only for my reputation, but for my subsistence.

" I have, therefore, concluded that the most proper object of my present attention is that *profession itself.* And in acquiring the faculty to discharge the duties of it, in a manner suitable to my own wishes and the expectations of my friends, I find ample room for close and attentive application ; for frequent and considerate observation; and for such benefits of practical experience as occasional opportunities may throw in the way."

The following letter from John Adams, at this time Vice President of the United States, written to his wife at Quincy, will be interesting, as showing, among other things, his anxiety that his sons should make some start in life, which would give promise of future usefulness. He was far from believing that sons should repose in idleness on the reputation or wealth of parents.

"*Philadelphia*, 2 *March*, 1793.

" My Dear,

" Your letter from your sick chamber, if not from your sick bed, has made me so uneasy, that I must get away as soon as possible. Monday morning, at six, I am to set off in the stage; but how many days it will take to get home, will depend on the roads or the winds. I don't believe Abby [his daughter,] will go with me. Her husband [Col. William S. Smith,] is so proud of his wealth, that he would not let her go, I suppose, without a coach-and-four; and such monarchical trumpery I will in future have nothing to do with. I will never travel but by stage, nor live at the seat of government but at lodgings, while they give me so despicable an allowance. Shiver my jib and start my planks if I do!

" I will stay but one night in New York. Smith says that my books are upon the table of every member of the Committee for framing a constitution of government for France, except Tom Paine, and he is so conceited as to disdain to have anything to do with books. Although I abused Smith a little above, he is very clever and agreeable; but I have been obliged to caution him against his disposition to boasting. Tell not of your prosperity, because it will make two men *mad* to one *glad;* nor of your adversity, for it will make two men *glad* to one *sad.* He boasts too much of having made his fortune, and placed himself at ease, above all favors of government. This is a weakness, and betrays too little knowledge of the world; too little penetration; too little discretion. I wish,

however, that my boys had a little more of his activity. I must
soon treat them as the pigeons treat their squabs—push them off
the limb, and make them put out their wings or fall. Young
pigeons will never fly till this is done. Smith has acquired the confidence of the French ministry, and the better sort of the members
of the National Convention. But the Executive is too changeable
in that country to be depended on, without the utmost caution.

" Adieu, adieu, tendrement,   J. A."

One of the sons of the noble patriot, soon " put out
his wings," and soared, ultimately, to a pinnacle of
honor and renown attained by few among men. In
the winter of 1793 and 1794, the public mind had become highly excited from the inflammatory appeals in
behalf of France, by Citizen Genet, the French Minister to the United States. A large portion of the anti-
Federal party took sides with Mr. Genet, against the
neutral position of our Government, and seemed determined to plunge the Union into the European contest,
in aid of the French Republic. Some idea may be
obtained of the excitement which prevailed at this
time, and of the perilous condition of the country, by
an extract or two from letters of Vice-President John
Adams. In a letter dated Philadelphia, Dec. 5, 1793,
he writes as follows :—

" It will require all the address, all the temper, and all the firmness of Congress and the States, to keep this people out of the war ;
or rather, to avoid a declaration of war against us, from some mis-
chievous power or other. It is but little that I can do, either by the
functions which the Constitution has entrusted to me, or by my personal influence ; but that little shall be industriously employed, until it is put beyond a doubt that it will be fruitless ; and then, I shall
be as ready to meet unavoidable calamities, as any other citizen."

Under date of Jan. 9, 1794, he says :—

"The prospects of this country are gloomy, but the situation of
all Europe is calamitous beyond all former examples. At what
time, and in what manner, and by what means, the disasters which
are come, and seem to be coming on mankind, may be averted, I
know not. Our own people have been imprudent, as I think, and
are now smarting under the effects of their indiscretion ; but this,
instead of a consolation, is an aggravation of our misfortune. Mr.
Genet has been abusive on the President [Washington] and all his
ministers, beyond all measure of decency or obligations of truth,
and in other respects, not yet publicly investigated, his conduct has
been such as to make it difficult to know what to do with him.
* * * * * The news of this evening is, that the Queen of France
is no more.* When will savages be satiated with blood ? No
prospect of peace in Europe, and therefore none of internal harmony
in America. We cannot well be in a more disagreeable situation
than we are with all Europe, with all Indians, and with all Barbary
rovers. Nearly one half of the Continent is in constant opposition
to the other, and the President's situation, which is highly responsible, is very distressing."

It taxed the wisdom and skill of Mr Jefferson, then
Secretary of State, to counteract the influence of the
French Minister, and prevent citizens of the United
States from committing overt acts against the Allied
Sovereigns, and embroiling the Union in a foreign war.
In this endeavor he was greatly assisted by the pen of
Mr. J. Q. Adams. This gentleman wrote a series of
essays for the public prints, under the signature of
"Columbus," reviewing the course of Mr. Genet. In
these articles, he pointed out, with great clearness, the
principles of the law of nations applicable to the situ-

* Marie Antoinette was beheaded in Paris, on the 16th of October,
1793.

ation of the country in the neutral line of policy which had been wisely adopted.

In reference to this topic, John Adams writes his wife, as follows, under date of Dec. 19, 1793 :—

    " The President has considered the conduct of Genet very nearly in the same light with ' Columbus,' and has given him a bolt of thunder. We shall see how this is supported by the two Houses. There are who gnash their teeth with rage which they dare not own as yet. We shall soon see whether we have any government or not in this country."

The political writings of the younger Adams had now brought him prominently before the public. They attracted the especial attention of Mr. Jefferson, who saw in them a vastness of comprehension, a maturity of judgment and critical discrimination, which gave large promise of future usefulness and eminence. Before his retirement from the State Department, he commended the youthful statesman to the favorable regard of President Washington, as one pre-eminently fitted for public service.

General Washington, although a soldier by profession, was a lover of peace. His policy during his administration of the government, was pre-eminently pacific. Convinced that, in the infant state of the Union, war with a foreign nation could result only in evil and ruin, he was anxious to cultivate the most friendly relations with foreign governments, and to carry out, both in letter and spirit, the strict neutrality he had proclaimed. To declare and maintain these

principles abroad, and to form political and commercial relations with European powers, Washington looked
anxiously around for one fitted for a mission so important.   His attention soon became fixed on John
Quincy Adams.   He saw in him qualities not only of
deep political sagacity, and views of policy at unity
with his own, but a familiarity with the languages and
customs of foreign courts, which marked him as one
every way calculated to represent our government with
credit in the old world.   He accordingly, in May, 1794,
appointed Mr. Adams Minister of the United States at
the Hague.

That this prominent appointment was as flattering to
Mr. Adams as it was unexpected, is naturally true.   It
was the more to his credit in consideration of the fact,
that in those days elevation to offices of this importance
was the award of merit and talent, and not the result
of importunity, or the payment of party services.   Mr.
Adams was at this time in the twenty-seventh year of
his age—a younger man, undoubtedly, than has since
ever been selected by our Government to fulfil a trust
so important.   But the ability and discretion of the
young diplomatist, and the success which attended his
negotiations in Europe, so creditable to himself and his
country, fully justified the wisdom of Washington in
selecting him for this important duty.

Although the father of Mr. Adams was then Vice
President of the United States, yet it is well known his
appointment on a foreign mission was obtained without

the influence or even the request of his parent. It is
not strictly correct, however, as stated by several bi-
ographers, that he was selected for the mission to Holland without any previous intimation of the President's
intentions to his father. This is made evident by the
following extract of a letter from John Adams to his
wife, dated Philadelphia, 27th May, 1794, conveying
intelligence which must have made a mother's heart
swell with honest pride and satisfaction :—

"It is proper that I should apprize you, that the President has it
in contemplation to send your son to Holland, that you may recollect yourself and prepare for the event. I make this communication to you in confidence, at the desire of the President, communicated to me yesterday by the Secretary of State. You must keep
it an entire secret until it shall be announced to the public in the
journal of the Senate. But our son must hold himself in readiness
to come to Philadelphia, to converse with the President, Secretary
of State, Secretary of the Treasury, &c., and receive his commis-
sions and instructions, without loss of time. He will go to Providence in the stage, and thence to New York by water, and thence
to Philadelphia in the stage. He will not set out, however, until
he is informed of his appointment."

"Your son!" is the phrase by which the father
meant to convey his own sense of how large a part the
mother had in training that son ; and to enhance the
compliment, it is communicated to her at the desire of
President Washington.

CHAPTER III.

MR. ADAMS presented himself at the Hague, as Minister Plenipotentiary of the United States, in the summer or fall of 1794. Ten years before, he was there
with his father—a lad, attending school—at which time
the father wrote: "They give him a good character
wherever he has been, and I hope he will make a good
man." How abundantly that hope was likely to be
fulfilled, the elevated and responsible position occupied
by the son at the expiration of the first ten years after
it was expressed, gave a promising and true indication.

On his arrival in Holland, Mr. Adams found the affairs of that country in great confusion, in consequence
of the French invasion. So difficult was it to prosecute
any permanent measures for the benefit of the United
States, owing to the existing wars and the unsettled
state of things in Europe, that after a few months he
thought seriously of returning home. A report of this
nature having reached President Washington, drew
from him a letter to Vice President John Adams,

dated Aug. 20, 1795, in which the following language occurs :—

> "Your son must not think of retiring from the path he is now in. His prospects, if he pursues it, are fair ; and I shall be much mistaken if, in as short a time as can well be expected, he is not found at the head of the Diplomatic Corps, be the government administered by whomsoever the people may choose."

This approbation of his proceedings thus far, and encouragement as to future success, from so high a source, undoubtedly induced the younger Adams to forego his inclination to withdraw from the field of diplomacy. He continued in Holland until near the close of Washington's administration. That he was not an inattentive observer of the momentous events then transpiring in Europe, but was watchful and faithful in all that pertained to the welfare of his country, is abundantly proved by his official correspondence with the government at home. His communications were esteemed by Washington, as of the highest value, affording him, as they did, a luminous description of the movement of continental affairs, upon which he could place the most implicit reliance.

The following extract of a letter from John Adams, will show the interest he naturally took in the welfare of his son while abroad, and also afford a brief glance at the political movements of that day. It is dated Philadelphia, Jan. 23, 1796 :—

> "We have been very unfortunate in the delays which have attended the dispatches of our ambassadors. Very lucky, Mr. John

Quincy Adams, that you are not liable to criticism on this occasion! This demurrage would have been charged doubly, both to your account and that of your father. It would have been a scheme, a trick, a design, a contrivance, from hatred to France, attachment to England, monarchical manœuvres, and aristocratical cunning! Oh! how eloquent they would have been!

"The southern gentry are playing, at present, a very artful game, which I may develope to you in confidence hereafter, under the seal of secrecy. Both in conversation and in letters, they are representing the Vice-President [John Adams,] as a man of moderation. Although rather inclined to limited monarchy, and somewhat attached to the English, he is much less so than Jay or Hamilton. For their part, for the sake of conciliation, they should be very willing he should be continued as Vice-President, provided the northern gentlemen would consent that Jefferson should be President. I most humbly thank you for your kind condescension, Messieurs Transchesapeakes.

"Witness my hand,

" JOHN ADAMS."

Another allusion to his son while abroad, is made by the elder Adams, in a letter dated Philadelphia, March 25, 1796.

"The President told me he had that day received three or four letters from his new Minister in London, one of them as late as the 29th of December. Mr. Pickering informs me that Mr. Adams* modestly declined a presentation at court, but it was insisted on by Lord Grenville; and, accordingly, he was presented to the King, and I think the Queen, and made his harangues and received his answers. By the papers I find that Mr. Pinckney appeared at court on the 28th of January, after which, I presume, Mr. Adams had nothing to do but return to Holland."

During his residence as Minister at the Hague, Mr. Adams had occasion to visit London, to exchange the ratifications of the treaty recently formed with Great

* John Quincy Adams.

Britain, and to take measures for carrying its provisions into effect. (Alluded to in the above letter from John Adams.) It was at this time that he formed an acquaintance with Miss LOUISA CATHARINE JOHNSON, daughter of Joshua Johnson, Esq., of Maryland, Consular Agent of the United States at London, and niece of Governor Johnson of Maryland, a Judge of the Supreme Court of the United States, and a signer of the Declaration of Independence. The friendship they formed for each other, soon ripened into a mutual attachment and an engagement. They were married on the 26th of July, 1797. It was a happy union. For more than half a century they shared each other's joys and sorrows. The venerable matron who for this long period accompanied him in all the vicissitudes of his eventful life, still survives, to deplore the loss of him who had ever proved a faithful protector and the kindest of husbands.

In the meantime, the elder Adams had been elected President of the United States, in 1796. The curious reader may have a desire to know something of the views, feelings and anticipations of those elevated to places of the highest distinction, and of the amount of enjoyment they reap from the honors conferred upon them. A glance behind the scenes is furnished in the following correspondence between John Adams and his wife, which took place at his election to the Presidency.*

* Letters of John Adams, v. ii. pp. 242, 243. Mrs. Adams' Letters, p. 373.

MR. ADAMS TO HIS WIFE.

" Philadelphia, 4th of Feb., 1797.

" MY DEAREST FRIEND,

" I hope you will not communicate to anybody the hints I give you about our prospects; but they appear every day worse and worse. House rent at twenty-seven hundred dollars a year, fifteen hundred dollars for a carriage, one thousand for one pair of horses, all the glasses, ornaments, kitchen furniture, the best chairs, settees, plateaus, &c., all to purchase; all the china, delph or wedgewood, glass and crockery of every sort to purchase, and not a farthing probably will the House of Representatives allow, though the Senate have voted a small addition. All the linen besides. I shall not pretend to keep more than one pair of horses for a carriage, and one for a saddle. Secretaries, servants, wood, charities, which are demanded as rights, and the million *dittoes*, present such a prospect as is enough to disgust any one. Yet not one word must we say. We cannot go back. We must stand our ground as long as we can. Dispose of our places with the help of our friend Dr. Tufts, as well as you can. We are impatient for news, but that is always so at this season. I am tenderly your J. A."

THE SAME TO THE SAME.

" Philadelphia, 9th Feb., 1797.

" MY DEAREST FRIEND,

" The die is cast,* and you must prepare yourself for honorable trials. I must wait to know whether Congress will do anything or not to furnish my house. If they do not, I will have no house before next fall, and then a very moderate one, with very moderate furniture. The prisoners from Algiers† arrived yesterday in this city, in good health, and looking very well. Captain Stevens is among them. One woman rushed into the crowd and picked out her husband, whom she had not seen for fourteen years.

" I am, and ever shall be, yours, and no other's, J. A."

---

* Mr. Adams had, the day previous, been announced President elect of the United States.

† American citizens who had long been in captivity among the Algerines.

MRS. JOHN ADAMS TO HER HUSBAND.

" *Quincy, 8th Feb.,* 1797.

" 'The sun is dressed in brightest beams,
    To give thy honors to the day.'

" And may it prove an auspicious prelude to each ensuing season. You have this day to declare yourself head of a nation. ' And now, O Lord, my God, thou hast made thy servant ruler over the people. Give unto him an understanding heart, that he may know how to go out and come in before this great people ; that he may discern between good and bad. For who is able to judge this thy so great a people ?' were the words of a royal sovereign ; and not less applicable to him who is invested with the Chief Magistracy of a nation, though he wear not a crown, nor the robes of royalty.

" My thoughts and my meditations are with you, though personally absent ; and my petitions to Heaven are, that ' the things which make for peace may not be hidden from your eyes.' My feelings are not those of pride or ostentation, upon the occasion. They are solemnized by a sense of the obligations, the important trusts, and numerous duties connected with it. That you may be enabled to discharge them with honor to yourself, with justice and impartiality to your country, and with satisfaction to this great people, shall be the daily prayer of your   A. A."

MR. ADAMS TO HIS WIFE.

" *Philadelphia, 5th March,* 1797.

" MY DEAREST FRIEND,

" Your dearest friend never had a more trying day than yesterday.* A solemn scene it was indeed ; and it was made more affecting to me by the presence of the General, [Washington,] whose countenance was as serene and unclouded as the day. He seemed to me to enjoy a triumph over me. Methought I heard him say ' Ay! I am fairly out, and you fairly in ! See which of us will be happiest.' When the ceremony was over, he came and made me a visit, and cordially congratulated me, and wished my administration might be happy, successful, and honorable.

---

* The day of his inauguration as President.

"It is now settled that I am to go into his house. It is whispered that he intends to take French leave to-morrow. I shall write you as fast as we proceed. My chariot is finished, and I made my first appearance in it yesterday. It is simple, but elegant enough. My horses are young, but clever.

"In the chamber of the House of Representatives, was a multitude as great as the space could contain, and I believe scarcely a dry eye but Washington's. The sight of the sun setting full orbed, and another rising, though less splendid, was a novelty. Chief Justice Ellsworth administered the oath, and with great energy. Judges Cushing, Wilson, and Iredell, were present. Many ladies. I had not slept well the night before, and did not sleep well the night after. I was unwell, and did not know whether I should get through or not. I did, however. How the business was received, I know not; only I have been told that Mason, the treaty publisher, said we should lose nothing by the change, for he never heard such a speech in public in his life.

"All agree that, taken altogether, it was the sublimest thing ever exhibited in America.

"I am, my dearest friend, most affectionately and kindly yours,

"JOHN ADAMS."

On entering upon the duties of the Presidency, John Adams was greatly embarrassed in regard to the line he should adopt toward his son. True, the younger Adams had been entrusted by Washington with an important embassy abroad, and had acquitted himself with great credit in his responsible station; but the father, with a delicacy highly honorable, hesitated continuing him in office, lest he might be charged with unworthy favoritism, and a disposition to promote the interest of his family at the expense of public good. In this exigency, not daring to trust his own judgment, lest its decisions might be warped by parental solicitude, he resorted to the wisdom and experience of

Washington. Writing him for advice on this subject, he received the following reply:—

"*Monday, Feb.* 20, 1797.

'Dear Sir,

"I thank you for giving me a perusal of the enclosed. The sentiments do honor to the head and the heart of the writer; and if my wishes would be of any avail, they should go to you in a strong hope, that you will not withhold merited promotion from John Q. Adams, because he is your son. For without intending to compliment the father or the mother, or to censure any others, I give it as my decided opinion, that Mr. Adams is the most valuable public character we have abroad; and that there remains no doubt in my mind, that he will prove himself to be the ablest of all our diplomatic corps. If he was now to be brought into that line, or into any other public walk, I could not, upon the principle which has regulated my own conduct, disapprove of the caution which is hinted at in the letter. But he is already entered; the public, more and more, as he is known, are appreciating his talents and worth; and his country would sustain a loss, if these were to be checked by over delicacy on your part.

"With sincere esteem, and affectionate regard,

"I am ever yours,

"George Washington."

This letter is characteristic of the discernment and nobleness of Washington. Appreciating at a glance the perplexed position of Mr. Adams, and wisely discriminating between the bringing forward of his son for the first time into public service, and the continuing him where he had already been placed by others, and shown himself worthy of all trust and confidence, he frankly advised him to overcome his scruples, and permit his son to remain in a career so full of promise to himself and his country. President Adams, in agreement with this counsel, determined to allow his son to continue in Europe in the public capacity to which he had been promoted by Washington.

Shortly previous to the close of Washington's administration, he transferred the younger Adams from the Hague, by an appointment as Minister Plenipotentiary to Portugal, but before proceeding to Lisbon, his father, in the meantime having become President, changed his destination to Berlin. He arrived in that city in the autumn of 1797, and immediately entered upon the discharge of his duties as Minister of the United States. In 1798, while retaining his office at Berlin, he was commissioned to form a commercial treaty with Sweden.

During his residence at Berlin, Mr. Adams, while attending with unsleeping diligence to his public duties, did not forego the more congenial pursuits of literature. He cultivated the acquaintance of many eminent German scholars and poets, and manifested a friendly sympathy in their pursuits. In a letter to the late Dr. Follen, he writes of that day as follows:—

"At this time, Wieland was there the most popular of the German poets. And although there was in his genius neither the originality nor the deep pathos of Goethe, Klopstock, or Schiller, there was something in the playfulness of his imagination, in the tenderness of his sensibility, in the sunny cheerfulness of his philosophy, and in the harmony of his versification, which delighted me."

To perfect his knowledge of the German language, Mr. Adams made a metrical translation of Wieland's

Oberon into the English language. The publication
of this work, which at one time was designed, was su-
perseded by the appearance of a similar translation by
Sotheby.

In the summer of 1800, Mr. Adams made a tour
through Silesia. He was charmed with the inhabitants of that region, their condition and habits. In
many respects he found them bearing a great similarity
to the people of his own native New England. He
communicated his impressions during this excursion, in
a series of letters to a younger brother in Philadelphia.
These letters were interesting, and were considered of
great value at that time, in consequence of many important facts they contained in regard to the manufacturing establishments of Silesia. They were published,
without Mr. Adams's knowledge, in the Port Folio, a
weekly paper edited by Joseph Dennie, at Philadelphia. The series was afterwards collected and published in a volume, in London, and has been translated
into German and French, and extensively circulated on
the continent.

Among other labors while at Berlin, Mr. Adams succeeded in forming a treaty of amity and commerce
with the Prussian government. The protracted correspondence with the Prussian commissioners, which
resulted in this treaty, involving as it did the rights of
neutral commerce, was conducted with consummate
ability on the part of Mr. Adams, and received the
fullest sanction of the government at home.

Mr. Adams' missions at the Hague and at Berlin, constituted his first step in the intricate paths of diplomacy. They were accomplished amid the momentous events which convulsed all Europe, at the close of the eighteenth century. Republican France, exasperated at the machinations of the Allied Sovereigns to destroy its liberties, so recently obtained, was pushing its armies abroad, determined, in self-defence, to kindle the flames of revolution in every kingdom on the continent. Great Britain, combined with Austria and other European powers, was using every effort to crush the French democracy, and remove from before the eyes of down-trodden millions, an example so dangerous to monarchical institutions. The star of Napoleon had commenced its ascent, with a suddenness and brightness which startled the imbecile occupants of old thrones. His legions had rushed down from the Alps upon the sunny plains of Italy, and with the swoop of an eagle, had demolished towns, cities, kingdoms.

Amid this conflict of nations, the commerce and navigation of the United States, a neutral power, were made a common object of prey to all. Great Britain and France especially, did not hesitate to make depredations, at once the most injurious and irritating. Our ships were captured, our rights disregarded. In the midst of these scenes, surrounded by difficulties and embarrassments on every hand, the youthful ambassador was compelled to come into collision with the veteran and wily politicians of the old world. How well he maintained the dignity and honor of his government—how sleepless the vigilance with which he watched the movements on the vast field of political strife—how prompt to protest against all encroachments—how skilful in conducting negotiations—and how active to promote the interests of the Union, wherever his influence could be felt—the archives of our country will abundantly testify. It was a fitting and promising commencement of a long public career which has been full of usefulness and of honor.

The administration of John Adams, as President of the United States, was characterized by great prudence and moderation, considering the excited state of the times. There cannot be a doubt he was anxious to copy the worthy example of his illustrious predecessor, in administering the government on principles of strict impartiality, for the good of the whole people, without respect to conflicting parties. Immediately on his inauguration, he had an interview with Mr. Jefferson, then Vice-President, and proposed the adoption of steps that would have a tendency to quell the spirit of faction which pervaded the country. That Mr. Jefferson, on his part, cherished a profound respect for Mr. Adams, his old co-laborer in the cause of American freedom, is evident from his letters and speeches of that day. In his speech on taking the chair of the Senate, as Vice-President, he expressed himself in the following terms :—

" I might here proceed, and with the greatest truth, to declare my zealous attachment to the Constitution of the United States ; that I consider the union of these States as the first of blessings ; and as the first of duties the preservation of that Constitution which secures it ; but I suppose these declarations not pertinent to the occasion of entering into an office, whose primary business is merely to preside over the forms of this House ; and no one more sincerely prays that no accident may call me to the higher and more important functions, which the Constitution eventually devolves on this office. These have been justly confided to the eminent character which has preceded me here, whose talents and integrity have been known and revered by me, through a long course of years ; have been the foundation of a cordial and uninterrupted friendship between us ; and I devoutly pray he may be long preserved for the government, the happiness and the prosperity of our common country."

The sincere attempts of President Adams to produce harmony of political action among the American people, were unavailing. The extraordinary events transpiring in Europe, exerted an influence on domestic politics, which could not be neutralized. " The enemies of France"—" the friends of England," or *vice versa,* were cries which convulsed the nation to its centre. The entire population was sundered into contending parties.

John Adams was a true republican. His political opponents charged him with monarchical tendencies and aspirations, but charged him most falsely. His life, devoted unreservedly to the service of his country, through all its dark and perilous journey to the achievement of its independence—his public speeches and documents—his private letters, written to his bosom companion, with no expectation that the eye of any

other would ever rest upon them—all testify his ardent
devotion to the principles of republicanism. At the
breaking out of the French Revolution, he yielded it
his hearty support, and did not withdraw his countenance, until compelled, by the scenes of anarchy and
of carnage which soon ensued, to turn away with horror and raise his voice against proceedings of savage
ferocity. But while condemning the excesses of the
French revolutionists, he was no friend of Great Britain. This is made evident by a multitude of facts.
Read, for instance, the following extract from a letter,
not written for public effect, addressed to his wife,
dated Philadelphia, April 9, 1796 :—

"I have read 'the minister's' dispatches from London. The
King could not help discovering his old ill humor. The mad idiot
will never recover. Blunderer by nature, accidents are all against
him. Every measure of his reign has been wrong. It seems they
don't like Pinckney. They think he is no friend to that country,
and too much of a French Jacobin. They wanted to work up some
idea or other of introducing another in his place, but our young
politician* saw into them too deeply to be duped. At his last visit
to Court, the King passed him without speaking to him, which, you
know, will be remarked by courtiers of all nations. I am glad of
it; for I would not have my son go so far as Mr. Jay, and affirm
the friendly disposition of that country to this. I know better. I
know their jealousy, envy, hatred, and revenge, covered under pretended contempt."

While President Adams cherished no partialities for
Great Britain, and had no desire to promote her especial interest, he was compelled by the force of circum-

* J. Q. Adams.

stances, during his administration, to assume a hostile attitude towards France. The French Directory, chagrined at the failure of all attempts to induce the government of the United States to abandon its neutrality and take up arms in their behalf against the Allied Sovereigns, and deeply incensed at the treaty recently concluded between England and the United States, resorted to retaliatory measures. They adopted commercial regulations designed to cripple and destroy our foreign trade. They passed an ordinance authorizing, in certain cases, the seizure and confiscation of American vessels and cargoes. They refused to receive Mr. Pinckney, the American minister, and ordered him peremptorily to leave France.

Mr. Adams convened Congress, by proclamation, on the 15th of June, 1797, and in his message laid before that body a lucid statement of the aggressions of the French Directory. Congress made advances, with a view to a reconciliation with France. But failing in this attempt, immediate and vigorous measures were adopted to place the country in a condition for war. A small standing army was authorized. The command was tendered to Gen. Washington, who accepted of it with alacrity, sanctioning as he did these defensive measures of the government. Steps were taken for a naval armament, and the capture of French vessels authorized. These energetic demonstrations produced their desired effect. The war proceeded no farther

than a few collisions at sea. The French Directory
became alarmed, and made overtures of peace.

Washington did not survive to witness the restoration of amicable relations with France. On the 14th
of December, 1799, after a brief illness, he departed this
life, at Mount Vernon, aged sixty-eight years. On receiving this mournful intelligence, Congress, then in
session at Philadelphia, passed the following resolution :—

" Resolved, That the Speaker's chair should be shrouded in black ;
that the members should wear black during the session, and that
a joint committee, from the Senate and the House, be appointed to
devise the most suitable manner of paying honor to the memory of
the Man, first in war, first in peace, and first in the hearts of his
countrymen."

Testimonials of sorrow were exhibited, and funeral
orations and eulogies were delivered, throughout the
United States. The Father of his Country slept in
death, and an entire people mourned his departure !

On assuming the duties of the Presidency, the elder
Adams found the finances of the country in a condition of the most deplorable prostration. To sustain
the government in this department, it was deemed indispensable to establish a system of direct taxation, by
internal duties. This produced great dissatisfaction
throughout the Union. An "alien law" was passed,
which empowered the President to banish from the
United States, any foreigner whom he should consider
dangerous to the peace and safety of the country.
And a "sedition law," imposing fine and imprisonment

for "any false, scandalous, and malicious writing against the government of the United States, or either house of Congress, or the President."

These measures are not justly chargeable to John Adams. They were not recommended nor desired by him; but were brought forward and urged by Gen. Hamilton and his friends. Nevertheless upon Mr. Adams was heaped the odium they excited. The leading measures of his administration—the demonstration against France; the standing army; the direct taxation; the alien and sedition laws—all tended to injure his popularity with the mass of the people, and to destroy his prospects of a re-election to the presidency. The perplexities he was compelled to encounter during his administration, may be conceived on perusal of his language in a letter dated March 17, 1797 :—

"From the situation where I now am, I see a scene of ambition beyond all my former suspicions or imaginations; an emulation which will turn our government topsy-turvy. Jealousies and rivalries have been my theme, and checks and balances as their antidotes, till I am ashamed to repeat the words; but they never stared me in the face in such horrid forms as at present. I see how the thing is going. At the next election England will set up Jay or Hamilton, and France Jefferson, and all the corruption of Poland will be introduced; unless the American spirit should rise and say, we will have neither John Bull nor Louis Baboon."

In 1800, the seat of government was removed to Washington. In taking possession of the President's house, Mr. Adams bestowed a benediction on it, which must ever meet with a response from all American

hearts—" Before I end my letter, I pray heaven to bestow the best of blessings on this house, and on all that
shall hereafter inhabit it. May none but honest and
wise men ever rule under this roof!" A description
of the house and the city, at that time, is furnished
in a letter from Mrs. Adams to her daughter, written
in November, 1800 :—

" I arrived here on Sunday last, and without meeting any accident worth noticing, except losing ourselves when we left Baltimore,
and going eight or nine miles on the Frederick road, by which
means we were obliged to go the other eight through the woods,
where we wandered two hours without finding a guide or the path.
Fortunately, a straggling black came up with us, and we engaged
him as a guide to extricate us out of our difficulty ; but woods are
all you see, from Baltimore, until you reach *the city*, which is only
so in name. Here and there is a small cot, without a glass window,
interspersed among the forests, through which you travel miles
without seeing any human being. * * * * * * * * * The house is
made habitable, but there is not a single apartment finished, and all
withinside, except the plastering, has been done since Briesler came.
We have not the least fence, yard, or other convenience without,
and the great unfinished audience-room I make a drying-room of,
to hang up the clothes in. The principal stairs are not up, and
will not be this winter. Six chambers are made comfortable ; two
are occupied by the President and Mr. Shaw ; two lower rooms,
one for a common parlor, and one for a levee room. Up stairs there
is the oval room, which is designed for the drawing-room, and has
the crimson furniture in it. It is a very handsome room now ; but
when completed, it will be beautiful."

The presidential contest in 1800, was urged with a
warmth and bitterness, by both parties, which has not
been equalled in any election since that period. It
was the first time two candidates ever presented themselves to the people as rival aspirants for the highest

honor in their gift. Both were good men and true—both were worthy of the confidence of the country. But Mr. Adams, weighed down by the unpopularity of acts adopted during his administration, and suffering under the charge of being an enemy to revolutionary France, and a friend of monarchical England, was distanced and defeated by his competitor. Mr. Jefferson was elected the third President of the Republic, and was inaugurated on the 4th of March, 1801. One of the last acts of John Adams, before retiring from the Presidency, was to recall his son from Berlin, that Mr. Jefferson might have no embarrassment in that direction.

CHAPTER IV.

MR. ADAMS' RETURN TO THE UNITED STATES—ELECTED TO THE
MASSACHUSETTS SENATE—APPOINTED U. S. SENATOR—SUP-
PORTS MR. JEFFERSON—PROFESSOR OF RHETORIC AND
BELLES LETTRES—APPOINTED MINISTER TO RUSSIA.

JOHN QUINCY ADAMS returned to the United States
from his first foreign embassy, in 1801. During the
stormy period of his father's administration, and the
ensuing presidential canvass, he was fortunately absent
from the country. Had he been at home, his situation
would have been one of great delicacy. It can hardly
be supposed he would have opposed his father's measures, or his reëlection. Yet to have thrown his influence in their behalf, would have subjected him to
the imputation of being moved by filial attachment
rather than the convictions of duty. From this painful
dilemma, he was saved by his foreign residence. He
came home uncommitted to party measures, untram-
melled by party tactics or predilections ; and thus stood
before the people, as he could wish to stand, perfectly
unshackled, and ready to act as duty and conscience
should direct.

Arriving in the United States with distinguished
honors gained by successful foreign diplomacy, Mr.

Adams was not allowed to remain long in inactivity. In 1802, he was elected to the Senate of Massachusetts, from the Boston district. During his services in that body, he gave an indication of that independence, as a politician, which characterized him through life, by his opposition to a powerful combination of banking interests, which was effected among his immediate constituents. Although his opposition was unavailing, yet it clearly showed that the integrity of the man was superior to the policy of the mere politician. But higher honors awaited him.

In 1803, he was elected to the Senate of the United States, by the Legislature of Massachusetts. Thus at the early age of thirty-six years, he had attained to the highest legislative body of the Union. Young in years, but mature in talent and experience, he took his seat amid the conscript fathers of the country, to act a part which soon drew upon him the eyes of the nation, both in admiration and in censure.

The period of Mr. Adams' service in the United States Senate, was one in which the position and the interests of the country were surrounded by embarrassments and perils of the most threatening character. The party which had supported his father had become divided and defeated. Mr. Jefferson, elevated to the Presidency after a heated and angry contest, was an object of the dislike and suspicion of the Federalists. The conflicts of the belligerent nations in Europe, and the measures of foreign policy they severally adopted, not only affected the interests of the United States, but were added elements to inflame the party contests at home.

In 1804, Bonaparte stepped from the Consul chamber to the throne of the French Empire. All Europe was bending to his giant rule. Great Britain alone, with characteristic and inherent stubbornness, had set itself as a rock against his ambitious aspirations, and prosecuted with unabated vigor its determined hostility to all his measures of trade and of conquest. In November, 1807, the British Government issued the celebrated "Orders in Council," forbidding all trade with France and her allies. This measure was met by Napoleon, in December, with his "Milan Decree," prohibiting every description of commerce with England or her colonies. Between these checks and counterchecks of European nations, the commerce of the United States was in peril of being swept entirely from the ocean.

During most of this perplexed and trying period, Mr. J. Q. Adams retained his seat in the United States Senate. Although sent there by the suffrages of the Federal party, in the Massachusetts Legislature, yet he did not, and would not, act simply as a partisan. This in fact was a prominent characteristic in Mr. Adams throughout his entire life, and is the key which explains many of his acts otherwise inexplicable. His noble and patriotic spirit arose above the shackles of party. He loved the interests of his country, the happiness of

MAN, more than the success of a mere party. So far as the party with which he acted advocated measures which he conceived to be wise and healthful, he yielded his hearty and vigorous co-operation. But whenever it swerved from this line of integrity, his influence was thrown into the opposite scale. This was the rule of his long career. No persuasions or emoluments, no threats, no intimidations, could turn him from it, to the breadth of a hair. It was in consequence of this characteristic, that it has so frequently been said of Mr. Adams, that he was not a *reliable* party man. This was to a degree true. He was not reliable for any policy adopted simply to promote party interests, and secure party ends. But in regard to all measures which in his judgment would advance the welfare of the people, secure the rights of man, and elevate the race, no politician, no statesman the world has produced, could be more perfectly relied upon.

This disposition to act *right*, whether with or against his party, was developed by the first vote he ever gave in a legislative body. While in the Massachusetts Senate, the Federalists were the dominant party. It was the custom in that State, to choose the whole of the Governor's Council from the party which had the majority in the Legislature. In May, 1802, Mr. Adams was desirous that a rule should be adopted more regardful of the rights of the minority. He accordingly proposed that several anti-Federalists should have seats in the Council of Gov. Strong, and gave his first vote to that measure.

On a certain occasion, Mr. Adams was asked, " What are the recognized principles of politics ?" He replied, that there were no *principles* in politics—there were recognized *precepts*, but they were bad ones. But, continued the inquirer, is not this a good one—" To seek the greatest good of the greatest number ?" No, said he, that is the worst of all, for it looks specious, while it is ruinous. What shall become of the minority, in that case ? This is the only principle to seek— " the greatest good of all."*

A few months after Mr. Adams' entrance into the Senate of the United States, a law was passed by Congress, at the suggestion of Mr. Jefferson, authorizing the purchase of Louisiana. Mr. Adams deemed this measure an encroachment on the Constitution of the United States, and opposed it on the ground of its unconstitutionality. He was one of six senators who voted against it. Yet when the measure had been legally consummated, he yielded it his support. In passing laws for the government of the territory thus obtained, the right of trial by jury was granted only in capital cases. Mr. Adams labored to have it extended to all criminal offences. Before the territory had a representative in Congress, the government proposed to levy a tax on the people for purposes of revenue. This attempt met the decided opposition of Mr. Adams.

* Massachusetts Quarterly, June, 1848.

He insisted it would be an exercise of government, without the consent of the governed, which, to all intents, is a despotism.

In 1805, he labored to have Congress pass a law levying a duty on the importation of slaves. This was the first public indication of his views on the subject of slavery. It was a premonition of the bold, unflinching, noble warfare against that institution, and of the advocacy of human freedom and human rights in the widest sense, which characterized the closing scenes of his remarkable career, and which will perpetuate his fame, when other acts of his life shall have passed from the remembrance of men. Although at that early day but little was said in regard to slavery, yet the young senator saw it was fraught with danger to the Union —conferring political power and influence on slave-holders, on principles false and pernicious, and calculated ultimately to distract the harmony of the country, and endanger the permanency of our free institutions. He labored, therefore, to check the increase of slave power, by the only means which, probably, appeared feasible at that time.

But a crisis in his senatorial career at length arrived. The commerce of the United States had suffered greatly by "Orders in Council," and "Milan Decrees." Our ships were seized, conducted into foreign ports and confiscated, with their cargoes. American seamen were impressed by British cruisers, and compelled to serve in a foreign navy. The American frigate Chesapeake, while near the coast of the United States, on refusing to give up four men claimed to be British subjects, was fired into by the English man-of-war Leopard, and several of her crew killed and wounded. These events caused the greatest excitement in the United States. Petitions, memorials, remonstrances, were poured in upon Congress from every part of the Union. Mr. Jefferson endeavored by embassies, negotiations, and the exertion of every influence in his power, to arrest these destructive proceedings, and obtain a redress of grievances. But all was in vain. At length he determined on an *embargo*, as the only means of securing our commerce from the grasp of the unscrupulous mistress of the seas. An act to that effect was passed in Dec., 1807. This effectually prostrated what little foreign commerce had been left to the United States.

In these proceedings Mr. Jefferson was stoutly opposed by the Federal party. Massachusetts, then the chief commercial State in the Union, resisted with its utmost influence the Embargo Act, as pre-eminently destructive to its welfare, and looked to its Senators and Representatives in Congress to urge an opposition to the extreme. What course should Mr. Adams adopt? On the one hand, personal friendship, the party which elected him to the Senate, the immediate interests of his constituents, called upon him to oppose the measures of the administration. On the other hand, more enlarged considerations presented themselves.

The interest, the honor, the ultimate prosperity of the whole country—its reputation and influence in the eyes of the world—demanded that the Government should be supported in its efforts to check the aggressions of foreign nations, and establish the rights of American citizens. In such an alternative John Quincy Adams could not hesitate. Turning from all other considerations but a desire to promote the dignity and welfare of the Union, he threw himself, without reserve, into the ranks of the administration party, and labored zealously to second the measures of Mr. Jefferson.

This act subjected Mr. Adams to the severest censure. He was charged with basely forsaking his party —with the most corrupt venality—with the low motive of seeking to promote ambitious longings and selfish ends. But those who made these charges in sincerity labored under an entire misapprehension of his character and principles of action. At this day, aided by the instructive history of his life, and by a perfect knowledge of his patriotism and devotion to truth and principle, as developed in his long and spotless career, it is clearly seen that in the event under consideration he but acted up to the high rule he had adopted, of making party and sectional considerations secondary to the honor and interest of the nation—an example which no pure and high-minded statesman can hesitate to follow.

The Legislature of Massachusetts disapproved the course of Mr. Adams. By a small majority of Federal votes, it elected another person to take his place in the Senate at the expiration of his term, and passed resolutions instructing its Senators in Congress to oppose the measures of Mr. Jefferson. Mr. Adams could not, consistently with his views of duty, obey these instructions; and having no disposition to represent a body whose confidence he did not retain, he resigned his seat in the Senate, in March, 1808.

Although Mr. Adams gave most of his days to the service of his country, yet he was fond of literary pursuits, and acquired, during his hours of relaxation from sterner duties, a vast fund of classic lore and useful learning. At an early day, he had become distinguished as a ripe scholar, and an impressive, dignified, and eloquent public speaker. His reputation for literary and scholastic attainments quite equalled his fame as a politician and statesman.

In 1804, on the death of President Willard, Mr. Adams was urged by several influential individuals, to be a candidate for the presidency of Cambridge University. He declined the proffered honor. During the following year, however, he was appointed Professor of Rhetoric and Belles Lettres, in that institution. He accepted the office, on condition that he should be allowed to discharge its duties at such times as his services in Congress would permit. His inaugural address, on entering the professorship, was delivered on the 12th of June, 1806. His lectures on rhetoric and oratory were very popular. They were attended by large crowds from Boston and the surrounding towns, in addition to the collegiate classes—a compliment which few of the professors since his day have received.

Mr. Adams continued his connection with the University, delivering lectures and conducting exercises in declamation, until July, 1809. "It was at this time, and as a member of one of the younger classes at college, that I first saw Mr. Adams, and listened to his well-remembered voice from the chair of instruction; little anticipating, that after the lapse of forty years, my own humble voice would be heard, in the performance of this mournful office. Some who now hear me will recollect the deep interest with which these lectures were listened to, not merely by the youthful audience for which they were prepared, but by numerous voluntary hearers from the neighborhood. They formed an era in the University; and were, I believe, the first successful attempt, in this country, at this form of instruction in any department of literature. They were collected and published in two volumes, completing the theoretical part of the subject. I think it may be fairly said, that they will bear a favorable comparison with any treatise on the subject, at that time extant in our language. The standard of excellence, in every branch of critical learning, has greatly advanced in the last forty years, but these lectures may still be read with pleasure and instruction. Considered as a systematic and academical treatise upon a subject which constituted the chief part of the intellectual education of the Greeks and Romans, these lectures, rapidly composed as they were delivered, and not revised by the author before publication, are not to be regarded in the light of a standard performance. But let any statesman or jurist, even of the present day, in America or Europe—whose life, like Mr. Adams's, has been actively passed in professional and political engagements, at home and abroad—attempt, in the leisure of two or thee summers—his mind filled with all the great political topics of the day—to prepare a full course of lectures on any branch of literature, to be delivered to a difficult and scrutinizing, though in part a youthful audience, and then trust them to the ordeal of the press, and he will be prepared to estimate the task which was performed by Mr. Adams."*

Mr. Adams's devotion to literary pursuits was destined to an early termination. On the 4th of March, 1809, Mr. Madison was inducted into the office of President of the United States. It was at that time far from being an enviable position. At home the country was rent into contending factions. Our foreign affairs were in a condition of the utmost perplexity, and evidently approaching a dangerous crisis. The murky clouds of war, which had for years overshadowed Europe, seemed rolling hitherward, filling the most sanguine and hope-

* Edward Everett's Eulogy on the Life and Character of John Quincy Adams.

ful minds with deep apprehension. Russia, under its youthful Emperor Alexander, was rising to a prominent and influential position among the nations of Europe. Mr. Madison deemed it of great importance that the United States should be represented at that court by some individual eminent alike for talents, experience, and influence. John Quincy Adams was selected for the mission. In March, 1809, he was appointed Minister to Russia, and the summer following, sailed for St. Petersburgh.

In the meantime, our relations with Great Britain became every day more dubious. While striving, in every honorable manner, to come to terms of reconciliation, President Madison was making rapid preparations for war. The people of the United States, deprived by the non-intercourse act of the cheap productions of England, began to turn their attention and capital to domestic manufactures. At length the American Government demanded peremptorily, that the restrictions of Great Britain and France on our commerce should be abrogated; war being the alternative of a refusal. The French emperor gave satisfactory assurances that the Berlin decree should be withdrawn. The English government hesitated, equivocated, and showed evident disinclination to take any decided step.

" In this doubtful state of connexion between America and England, an accidental collision took place between vessels of the respective countries, tending

much to inflame and widen the existing differences. An
English sloop-of-war, the Little Belt, commanded by
Capt. Bingham, descried a ship off the American coast,
and made sail to come up with it; but finding it a
frigate, and dubious of its nation, he retired. The
other, which proved to be American, the President,
under Capt. Rogers, pursued in turn. Both captains
hailed nearly together; and both, instead of replying,
hailed again; and from words, as it were, came to
blows, without explanation. Capt. Bingham lost upwards of thirty men, and his ship suffered severely. A
Court of Inquiry was ordered on the conduct of Capt.
Rogers, which decided that it had been satisfactorily
proved to the court, that Capt. Rogers hailed the Little Belt first, that his hail was not satisfactorily answered, that the Little Belt fired the first gun, and
that it was without previous provocation or justifiable
cause."*

Several attempts were made after this, to preserve
the peace of the two countries, but in vain. England,
it is true, withdrew her obnoxious Orders in Council.
It was, however, too late. Before intelligence of this
repeal reached the shores of the United States, war
was declared by Congress, on the 18th of June, 1812.

It was a popular war. Although strenuously opposed by portions of the Eastern States, as destructive
to their commerce, yet with the mass of the people
throughout the Union, it was deemed justifiable and

* Lives of the Presidents.

indispensible. A long series of insults and injuries on the part of Great Britain—the seizure and confiscation of our ships and cargoes ; the impressing of our seamen, under circumstances of the most irritating description ; and the adoption of numerous measures to the injury of our interests—had fully prepared the public mind in the United States, with the exception of a small minority, to enter upon this war with zeal and enthusiasm.

With occasional reverses, general success attended our arms in every direction. On land and on sea, the American eagle led to victory. The combatants were worthy of each other. Of the same original stock—of the same stern, unyielding material—their contests were bloody and destructive in the extreme. But the younger nation, inspirited by a sense of wrongs endured, and of the justness of its cause, bore away the palm, and plucked from the brow of its more aged competitor many a laurel yet green from the ensanguined fields of Europe. In scores of hotly-contested battles, the British lion, unused as it was to cower before a foe, was compelled to "lick the dust" in defeat. At York, at Chippewa, at Fort Erie, at Lundy's Lane, at New Orleans, on Lake Champlain, on Lake Erie, on the broad ocean, Great Britain and the world were taught lessons of American valor, skill, and energy, which ages will not obliterate.

This war, though prosecuted at the expense of many valuable lives, and of a vast public debt, was, unquestionably, highly beneficial to the United States. It convinced all doubters that our government was abundantly able to resent aggressions, and to maintain its rights against the assaults of any nation on earth. This reputation has been of great service in protecting our commerce, and commanding respect for our flag, throughout the world. But the chief benefit of the war was the development of our internal resources, which, after all, form the great fountain of the wealth, strength, and permanence of a nation. Deprived by the embargo, the non-intercourse act, and the ensuing hostilities, of all foreign importation of goods, the American people were compelled to supply themselves by their own industry and ingenuity, with those articles for which they had always before been dependent on their transatlantic neighbors. Thus was laid the foundation of that system of domestic manufactures which is destined to make the United States the greatest productive mart among men, and to bring into its lap the wealth of the world.

CHAPTER V.

Mr. Adams arrived at St. Petersburg, as Minister
Plenipotentiary from the United States, in the autumn
of 1809. Twenty-eight years before, while a lad of
fourteen, he was at the same place, as private secretary to Mr. Dana, the American Minister. The promising boy returned to the northern capital a mature
man, ripe in experience, wisdom, patriotism, and prepared to serve his country in the highest walks of
diplomacy. So truly had the far-seeing Washington
prophesied in 1795 :—" I shall be much mistaken, if,
in as short a time as can well be expected, he is not
found at the head of the diplomatic corps, be the
government administered by whomsoever the people
may choose !"

The United States, though but little known in
Russia at that period, was still looked upon with
favor, as a nation destined, in due time, to exert a

great influence upon the affairs of the world. Mr.
Adams was received with marked respect at the Court
of St. Petersburg. His familiarity with the French
and German languages—the former the diplomatic
language of Europe—his literary acquirements, his
perfect knowledge of the political relations of the
civilized world, his plain appearance, and republican
simplicity of manners, in the midst of the gorgeous
embassies of other nations, enabled him to make a
striking and favorable impression on the Emperor
Alexander and his Court. The Emperor, charmed
by his varied qualities, admitted him to terms of personal intimacy seldom granted to the most favored
individuals.

During his residence in Russia, the death of Judge
Cushing caused a vacancy on the bench of the Supreme Court of the United States. President Madison
nominated Mr. Adams to the distinguished office.
The nomination was confirmed by the Senate, but he
declined its acceptance.

A circumstance occurred at this time, which attracted the attention of Mr. Adams. The Russian Minister
of the Interior, then advanced in years, having received
many valuable presents while in office, became troubled
with scruples of conscience, in regard to the disposal
he should make of them. He at length calculated the
value of all his gifts, and paid the sum into the imperial treasury. This transaction made a deep impression on Mr. Adams, and probably led him to the

resolution of never accepting gifts. In order to act with that freedom of bias which he deemed indispensable to the faithful discharge of public duty, he endeavored to avoid, as far as possible, laying himself under obligations to any man. When a certain bookseller once sent him an elegant copy of the Scriptures, he kept the book, but returned its full equivalent in money.

While sojourning at St. Petersburg, Mr. Adams wrote a series of letters to a son at school in Massachusetts, on the value of the Bible, and the importance of its daily perusal. Since his decease they have been published in a volume, entitled "Letters of John Quincy Adams to his son, on the Bible and its teachings." "Their purpose is the inculcation of a love and reverence for the Holy Scriptures, and a delight in their perusal and study. Throughout his long life, Mr. Adams was himself a daily and devout reader of the Scriptures, and delighted in comparing and considering them in the various languages with which he was familiar, hoping thereby to acquire a nicer and clearer appreciation of their meaning. The Bible was emphatically his counsel and monitor through life, and the fruits of its guidance are seen in the unsullied character which he bore, through the turbid waters of political contention, to his final earthly rest. Though long and fiercely opposed and contemned in life, he left no man behind him who would wish to fix a stain on the name he has inscribed so high on the roll of his

country's most gifted and illustrious sons. The intrin-
sic value of these letters, their familiar and lucid style,
their profound and comprehensive views, their candid
and reverent spirit, must win for them a large measure
of the public attention and esteem. But, apart from
even this, the testimony so unconsciously borne by
their pure-minded' and profoundly learned author, to
the truth and excellence of the Christian faith and
records, will not be lightly regarded. It is no slight
testimonial to the verity and worth of Christianity,
that in all ages since its promulgation, the great mass
of those who have risen to eminence by their profound
wisdom, integrity, and philanthropy, have recognized
and reverenced, in Jesus of Nazareth, the Son of the
living God. To the names of Augustine, Xavier,
Fenelon, Milton, Newton, Locke, Lavater, Howard,
Chateaubriand, and their thousands of compeers in
Christian faith, among the world's wisest and noblest, it
is not without pride that the American may add, from
among his countrymen, those of such men as WASHING-
TON, JAY, PATRICK HENRY, and JOHN QUINCY ADAMS."*

Mr. Adams was a practical Christian. This is
proved by his spotless life, his strict honesty and integrity, his devotion to duty, his faithful obedience to the
dictates of conscience, at whatever sacrifice, his reverence of God, of Christ, his respect for religion and its
institutions, and recognition of its claims and responsi-

* Preface to "Letters of John Quincy Adams to his Son, on the
Bible and its Teachings."

bilities. Although a Unitarian* in his belief of doc-
trines, yet he was no sectarian. In religion, as in
politics, he was independent of parties. He would
become linked to no sect in such manner as to prevent
him from granting his countenance and assistance
wherever he thought proper. He was a frequent
attendant at Presbyterian and Episcopalian churches,
and was liberal in his contributions to these and other
denominations; it being his great desire to aid in
building up Christianity, and not a sect.

The influence which Mr. Adams had obtained at
St. Petersburg, with the Emperor and his Court, was
turned to the best account. It laid the foundation of
those amicable relations which have ever character-
ized the intercourse of that government with the
United States. To this source, also, is unquestionably
to be attributed the offer, by the Emperor Alexander,
of mediation between Great Britain and the United
States. This offer was accepted by the American
Government, and Mr. Adams, in connection with
Messrs. Gallatin and Bayard, was appointed by the
President to take charge of the negotiation. The lat-
ter gentlemen joined Mr. Adams at St. Petersburg, in
July, 1813. Conferences were held by the Commis-
sioners with Count Romanzoff, the Chancellor of the
Russian Empire, with a view to open negotiations.
The British Government, however, refused to treat

* Mr. Adams was a member of the Unitarian Church, in Quincy,
Mass., at his death.

under the mediation of Russia ; but proposed at the same time to meet American Commissioners either at London or Gottenburg. Messrs. Gallatin and Bayard withdrew from St. Petersburg in January, 1814, leaving Mr. Adams in the discharge of his duties as resident Minister.

The proposition of the British Ministry to negotiate for peace, at London or Gottenburg, was accepted by the United States. Mr. Adams and Messrs. Bayard, Clay, Russell, and Gallatin, were appointed Commissioners, and directed to proceed to Gottenburg for that purpose. Mr. Adams received his instructions in April, 1814 ; and as soon as preparations for departure could be made, took passage for Stockholm. After repeated delays, on account of the difficulties of navigation at that early season in the northern seas, he arrived at that city on the 25th of May. Learning there that the place for the meeting of the Commissioners had been changed to Ghent, in Belgium, Mr. Adams proceeded to Gottenburg. From thence he embarked on board an American sloop-of-war, which had conveyed Messrs. Clay and Russell from the United States, and landing at Texel, proceeded immediately to Ghent, where he arrived on the 24th of June.

In the ensuing negotiation, Mr. Adams was placed at the head of the American Commissioners. They were men of unsurpassed talents and skill, in whose hands neither the welfare nor the honor of the United States could suffer. In conducting this negotiation, they exhibited an ability, a tact, an understanding of international law, and a knowledge of the best interests of their country, which attracted the favorable attention both of Europe and America. Their "Notes" with the British Commissioners, exhibited a dignified firmness and manly moderation, with a power of argument, and force of reasoning, which highly elevated their reputation, and that of their country, in the estimation of European statesmen. The Marquis of Wellesley declared in the British House of Lords, that, "in his opinion the American Commissioners had shown the most astonishing superiority over the British, during the whole of the correspondence." Their despatches to the Government at home, describing and explaining the progress of the negotiation in its several stages, gave the highest satisfaction to the people of the United States. It was declared in the public prints, that they sustained the honor of the Union as ably at Ghent as the patriotism and bravery of its defenders had been established by its seamen on the ocean, and its troops in their battles with "Wellington's Invincibles." A good share of these encomiums of right belongs to Mr. Adams, who, from his knowledge of foreign affairs, and experience in diplomacy, as well as acknowledged talents, took a leading part in the negotiations.

The American commissioners were treated with marks of highest respect, by the citizens of Ghent, and the public authorities of that town. On the anniversary of the Academy of Sciences and Fine Arts, at Ghent, they were unanimously elected members of the institution, and were invited to attend and unite in the exercises of the occasion.   An oration on the objects of the institution was delivered.   In the evening, a sumptuous banquet was served up to a numerous company.   After the removal of the cloth, among the toasts given, was the following, by the Intendant of Ghent :—

"Our distinguished guests and fellow-members, the American Ministers : May they succeed in making an honorable peace, to secure the liberty and independence of their country."

This sentiment was received with immense applause. The band struck up "Hail Columbia," and the company was filled with enthusiasm.   It was some minutes before the tumult sufficiently subsided to admit of a response.   Mr. Adams then arose, and, in behalf of the American Legation, returned thanks for the very flattering manner in which they had been treated by the municipality of Ghent, and particularly for the unexpected honor conferred upon them by the Academy. After making some pertinent remarks on the importance and usefulness of the Fine Arts, he concluded by offering as a toast—" The Intendant of the city of Ghent."

The British Commissioners were Lord Gambier, Henry Goulburn, and Wm. Adams.   The negotiations opened dubiously.   The demands of the British Ministers were at first of such a character, that it was impossible to comply with them, with any regard to the honor or welfare of the United States.   They insisted that the line separating the United States from the

Canadas, should run on the southern borders of all the lakes from Ontario to Superior—that the American Government should keep no armed force on these lakes, nor maintain any military posts on their borders, while the British should have the privilege of establishing such posts wherever they thought proper, on the southern shores of the lakes and connecting rivers, and maintaining a navy on their waters—that a large part of the district of Maine should be relinquished and ceded to England, to permit a direct route of communication between Halifax and Quebec—that the right of search should be granted to British ships-of-war—together with many other terms equally unacceptable.

The letters of the American Commissioners to the Government at home, in the early stages of the proceedings, were couched in desponding tones. They gave it as their opinion that no terms of peace could be agreed upon. But the demands of the English Plenipotentiaries were met in a manner so decided, and reasons were offered for non-compliance so cogent and incontrovertible, that they were compelled to recede, and come to terms of a more reasonable description. Moreover the British nation was heartily sick of foreign wars, which plunged the Government into debt, sacrificed the lives of its subjects, crippled their manufactories, and secured them, in fact, nothing! At length, after a protracted negotiation of six months, articles of peace were signed by the British and American Commissioners, on the 24th of December, 1814.

The announcement of this event, at Ghent, was in a manner somewhat peculiar. Mr. Todd, one of the Secretaries of the American Commissioners, and son-in-law of President Madison, had invited several gentlemen, Americans and others, to take refreshments with him on the 24th of December. At noon, after having spent some time in pleasant conversation, the refreshments entered, and Mr. Todd said,—"It is 12 o'clock. Well, gentlemen, I announce to you that peace has been made and signed between America and England." In a few moments, Messrs. Gallatin, Clay, Carroll and Hughes entered, and confirmed the annunciation. This intelligence was received with a burst of joy by all present. The news soon spread through the town, and gave general satisfaction to the citizens.

At Paris, the intelligence was hailed with acclamations. In the evening the theatres resounded with cries of "God save the Americans."

In the United States the news of peace spread with the speed of the wind. Everywhere it excited the most lively emotions of joy. Processions, orations, bonfires, illuminations, attested the gratification of the people, and showed that, notwithstanding the general success which had attended our arms, they viewed peace as one of the highest blessings a nation can enjoy.

Recognizing in this important event the hand of a wise and gracious overruling Providence, the hearts of a great Christian nation turned in gratitude toward

God. President Madison issued the following proclamation for a day of thanksgiving :—

"The Senate and House of Representatives of the
United States have, by a joint resolution, signified
their desire that a day may be recommended, to be observed by the people of the United States with religious solemnity, as a day of thanksgiving and of devout acknowledgments to Almighty God, for his great
goodness, manifested in restoring to them the blessings
of peace.

"No people ought to feel greater obligations to celebrate the goodness of the Great Disposer of events,
and of the destiny of nations, than the people of the
United States. His kind providence originally conducted them to one of the best portions of the dwelling-
place allowed for the great family of the human race.
He protected and cherished them under all the difficulties and trials to which they were exposed in their
early days. Under his fostering care, their habits,
their sentiments and their pursuits prepared them for a
transition in due time to a state of independence and
self-government. In the arduous struggle by which it
was attained, they were distinguished by multiplied
tokens of his benign interposition During the interval
which succeeded, he reared them into the strength,
and endowed them with the resources, which have enabled them to assert their national rights, and to enhance their national character, in another arduous conflict, which is now happily terminated by a peace and

reconciliation with those who have been our enemies And to the same Divine Author of every good and perfect gift we are indebted for all those privileges and advantages, religious as well as civil, which are so richly enjoyed in this favored land.

"It is for blessings such as these, and more especially for the restoration of the blessings of peace, that I now recommend that the second Thursday in April next, be set apart as a day on which the people of every religious denomination may in their solemn assemblies unite their hearts and their voices, in a free-will offer-,ng, to their Heavenly Benefactor, of their homage of thanksgiving and their songs of praise."

Before leaving Ghent, the American Commissioners gave a public dinner to the British Ambassadors, at which the Intendant of Ghent, and numerous staff officers of the Hanoverian service, were present. Everything indicated that the most perfect reconciliation had taken place between the two nations. Lord Gambier had arisen to give, as the first toast, "The United States of North America," but he was prevented by the courtesy of Mr. Adams, who gave "His Majesty, the King of England"—on which the music struck up "God save the King." Lord Gambier gave as the second toast, "The United States of North America," and the music played "Hail Columbia." Count H. Von Sheinhuyer presented as a toast—"The Pacificators of the States—May their union contribute to the nappiness of the Department which is confided to my government; and may their Excellencies communicate to their Governments the lively interest which those under me take in their reconciliation." Mr. Adams and Lord Gambier both begged the Intendant to certify to the city of Ghent the gratitude of the Ministers, for the attention which the inhabitants had shown them during their residence in their midst.

Having concluded their labors at Ghent by signing the treaty of peace, Mr. Adams, together with Messrs. Albert Gallatin and Henry Clay, was directed to proceed to London, for the purpose of entering into negotiations for a treaty of commerce with Great Britain. Before leaving the continent, Mr. Adams visited Paris, where he witnessed the return of Napoleon from Elbe, and his meteoric career during the Hundred Days. Here he was joined in March, 1815, by his family, after a long and perilous journey from St. Petersburg.

On the 25th of May, Mr. Adams arrived in London and joined Messrs. Gallatin and Clay, who had already entered upon the preliminaries of the proposed commercial convention with Great Britain. In the mean time, Mr. Adams had received official notice of his appointment as Minister to the Court of St. James. On the 3d of July, 1815, the convention for regulating the commercial intercourse between the United States and Great Britain was concluded, and duly signed. It was afterwards ratified by both Governments, and has formed the basis of commerce and trade between the two countries, to the present time. At the conclusion of these negotiations, Messrs. Gallatin and Clay returned to the United States, and Mr. Adams remained in London, in his capacity as resident Minister.

Thus had the prediction of Washington been fulfilled. In "as short a time as could well be expected," John Quincy Adams, as the well-merited reward of faithful services, had attained to the head of the Diplomatic Corps of the United States. His career had been singularly successful; and his elevation to the highest foreign stations received the general approbation of his countrymen. His simple habits, his plain appearance, his untiring industry, his richly stored mind, his unbending integrity, his general intercourse and correspondence with foreign courts and diplomatists of the greatest distinction, all tended to elevate, in a high degree, the American character, in the estimation of European nations.

The impression he made in the most eminent circles during his residence in London, as a statesman of unsurpassed general information, and critical knowledge of the politics of the world, was retained for years afterwards. Mr. Rush, who was subsequently Minister to Great Britain, in an account of a dinner party at Lord Castlereagh's, notes a corroborating incident: "At table, I had on my left the Saxon Minister, Baron Just. * * * * * * He inquired of me for Mr. Adams, whom he had known well, and of whom he spoke highly.   He said that he knew the politics of all Europe."*

" It was while Mr. Adams was Minister of the United States in London, that it was my personal good fortune to be admitted to his intimacy and friendship.   Being then in London on private business, and having some previous acquaintance with Mr. Adams, I found in his house an ever kind welcome, and in his intercourse and conversation unfailing attraction and improvement.   Accustomed as he had been from earliest youth to the society of the most eminent persons in Europe, alike in station and in ability, Mr. Adams never lost the entire simplicity of his own habits and character.   Under an exterior of, at times, almost repulsive coldness, dwelt a heart as warm, sympathies as quick, and affections as overflowing, as ever animated any bosom.   His tastes, too, were all refined. Literature and art were familiar and dear to him, and hence it was that his society was at once so agreeable and so improving.   At his hospitable board, I have listened to disquisitions from his lips on poetry, especially the dramas of Shakspeare, music, painting, sculpture—of rare excellence, and untiring interest.   The extent of his knowledge, indeed, and its accuracy, in all branches, were not less remarkable than the complete command which he appeared to possess over all his varied stores of learning and information.   A critical scholar, alike in the dead languages, in French,

* Rush's Residence at the Court of London.

in German, in Italian, not less than in English—he could draw at will from the wealth of all these tongues to illustrate any particular topic, or to explain any apparent difficulty. There was no literary work of merit in any of these languages, of which he could not render a satisfactory account; there was no fine painting or statue, of which he did not know the details and the history; there was not even an opera, or a celebrated musical composer, of which or of whom he could not point out the distinguishing merits and the chief compositions. Yet he was a hard-working, assiduous man of business, in his particular vocation, and a more regular, punctual, comprehensive, voluminous diplomatic correspondence than his no country can probably boast of; and it is thought the more necessary to note this fact, because sometimes an opinion prevails that graver pursuits must necessarily exclude attention to what used to be called the "humanities" of education—those ornamental and graceful acquirements, which, as Mr. Adams well proved, not only are not inconsistent with, but greatly adorn, the weightier matters of the law and of diplomacy. I could dwell with much satisfaction upon the memory and incidents of the days to which I am now adverting, but am admonished, by the length to which these remarks have already extended, that I may not loiter."*

* Eulogy on John Quincy Adams, by Charles King.

CHAPTER VI.

JAMES MADISON, after serving his country eight
years as President, in a most perilous period of its
history, retired to private life, followed by the respect
and gratitude of the people of the United States. He
was succeeded by James Monroe, who was inaugurated
on the 4th of March, 1817.

Mr. Monroe was a politician of great moderation.
It was his desire, on entering the presidency, to heal
the unhappy dissensions which had distracted the
country from the commencement of its government,
and conciliate and unite the conflicting political parties.
In forming his cabinet, he consulted eminent individuals of different parties, in various sections of the
Union, expressing these views. Among others, he addressed Gen. Jackson, who, on account of his successful military career, was then rising rapidly into public
notice. In his reply the general remarked:—

" Everything depends on the selection of your ministry.   In every
selection, party and party feeling should be avoided.   Now is the
time to exterminate that *monster*, called party spirit.   By selecting
characters most conspicuous for their probity, virtue, capacity, and
firmness, without any regard to party, you will go far, if not entirely, to eradicate those feelings, which on former occasions, threw
so many obstacles in the way of government, and, perhaps, have the
pleasure and honor of uniting a people heretofore politically divided.
The Chief Magistrate of a great and powerful nation, should never
indulge in party feelings."

Admirable advice !   Sentiments worthy an exalted
American statesman !   The President of a vast
Republic, should indeed know nothing of the interest
of party in contradistinction to the interest of the
whole people ; and should exercise his power, his
patronage, and his influence, not to strengthen factions, and promote the designs of political demagogues,
but to develop and nourish internal resources, the
only sinews of national prosperity, and diffuse abroad
sentiments of true patriotism, liberality, and philanthropy.   No suggestions more admirable could have
been made by Gen. Jackson, and none could have
been more worthy the consideration of Mr. Monroe
and his successors in the presidential chair.

In carrying out his plans of conciliation, President
Monroe selected John Quincy Adams for the responsible post of Secretary of State.   Mr. Adams had
never been an active partizan.   In his career as Senator, both in Massachusetts and in Washington, during
Mr. Jefferson's administration, he had satisfactorily
demonstrated his ability to rise above party considera-

tions, in the discharge of great and important duties. And his long absence from the country had kept him free from personal, party, and sectional bias, and peculiarly fitted him to take the first station in the cabinet of a President aiming to unite his countrymen in fraternal bonds of political amity.

Referring to this appointment, Mr. Monroe wrote Gen. Jackson as follows, under date of March 1, 1817:—"I shall take a person for the Department of State from the eastward; and Mr. Adams, by long service in our diplomatic concerns appearing to be entitled to the preference, supported by his acknowledged abilities and integrity, his nomination will go to the Senate." Gen. Jackson, in his reply, remarks:—"I have no hesitation in saying you have made the best selection to fill the Department of State that could be made. Mr. Adams, in the hour of difficulty, will be an able helpmate, and I am convinced his appointment will afford general satisfaction." This prediction was well founded. The consummate ability exhibited by Mr. Adams in foreign negotiations had elevated him to a high position in the estimation of his countrymen. His selection for the State Department was received with very general satisfaction throughout the Union.

On receiving notice of his appointment to this responsible office, Mr. Adams, with his family, embarked for the United States, on board the packet-ship

Washington, and landed in New York on the 6th of August, 1817.

A few days after his arrival, a public dinner was given Mr. Adams, in Tammany Hall, New York. The room was elegantly decorated.   In the centre was a handsome circle of oak leaves, roses, and flags— the whole representing, with much effect,.our happy Union—and from the centre of which, as from her native woods, appeared our eagle, bearing in her beak this impressive scroll :—

> " Columbia, great Republic, thou art blest,
>   While Empires droop, and Monarchs sink to rest."

Gov. De Witt Clinton, the Mayor of New York, and about two hundred citizens of the highest respect-ability, sat down to the table.   Among other speeches made on the occasion, was the following from an English gentleman, a Mr. Fearon, of London :—

" As several gentlemen have volunteered songs, I would beg leave to offer a sentiment, which I am sure will meet the hearty concurrence of all present.   But, previous to which, I desire to express the high satisfac-tion which this day's entertainment has afforded me. Though a native of Great Britain, and but a few days in the United States, I am for the first time in my life in a free country, surrounded by free men ; and when I look at the inscription which decorates your eagle, I rejoice that I have been destined to see this day.   A great number of the enlightened portion of my coun-

trymen advocate your cause—admire your principles.
And though we have, unfortunately, been engaged in
a war, I trust the result has taught wisdom to both
parties. In your political institutions you have set a
noble example, which, if followed throughout the
world, will rescue mankind from the dominion of those
tyrants who jeer at the destruction which they produce—

> ' Like the moonbeams on the blasted heath,
>   Mocking its desolation.'

"Gentlemen, in conclusion, I beg to express the
delight which I feel, and propose to you as a toast—
May the United States be an example to the world ;
and may civil and religious liberty cover the earth, as
the waters do the channels of the deep."

A public dinner was also given Mr. Adams on his
arrival in Boston. Mr. Gray presided, and Messrs.
Otis, Blake, and Mason, acted as Vice Presidents.
His father, the venerable ex-President John Adams,
was present as a guest. Among other toasts given on
the occasion, were the following :—

"The United States.—May our public officers, abroad and at home,
continue to be distinguished for integrity, talents, and patriotism."

"The Commissioners at Ghent.—The negotiations for peace
have been declared, in the British House of Lords, to wear the
stamp of American superiority."

"American Manufactures.—A sure and necessary object for the
security of American independence."

This occasion must have been one of great interest

to the patriarch John Adams, then more than four-score years of age. Nearly forty years before, he had said of his son :—" He behaves like a man !" That son, in the prime of his days, had recently been called from foreign service, where he had obtained accumulated honors, to fill the highest station in the gift of the Executive of his country. The people of two continents would now unite with the venerable sage, in repeating the declaration—" He behaves like a man !" The patriarch stood upon the verge of the grave. But as the sun of his existence was gently and calmly sinking beneath the horizon, lo ! its beams were reflected in their pristine brightness by another orb, born from its bosom, which was steadily ascending to the zenith of earthly fame !

John Quincy Adams took up his residence at Washington, and entered upon his duties as Secretary of State, in September, 1817.

During the eight years of President Monroe's administration, Mr. Adams discharged the duties of the state department, with a fidelity and success which received not only the unqualified approbation of the President, but of the whole country. To him that office was no *sinecure.* His labors were incessant. He spared no pains to qualify himself to discuss, with consummate skill, whatever topics legitimately claimed his attention. The President, the cabinet, the people, reposed implicit trust in his ability to promote the interests of the nation in all matters of diplomacy, and confided unreservedly in his pure American feelings and love of country. Perfectly familiar as he was with the political condition of the world, Mr. Monroe entrusted him, without hesitation, with the management of the foreign policy of the Government, during his administration.

In the autumn of 1817, the Seminole and a portion of the Creek Indians commenced depredations on the frontiers of Georgia and Alabama. Troops were sent to reduce them, under Gen. Gaines. His force being too weak to bring them to subjection, Gen. Jackson was ordered to take the field with a more numerous army, with which he overran the Indian country. Believing it necessary to enter Florida, then a Spanish territory, for the more effectual subjugation of the Indians, he did not hesitate to pursue them thither. The Spanish authorities protested against the invasion of their domains, and offered some opposition. Gen. Jackson persisted, and in the result, took possession of St. Marks and Pensacola, and sent the Spanish authorities and troops to Havana.

Among the prisoners taken in this expedition, were a Scotchman and an Englishman, named Arbuthnot and Ambrister. They were British subjects, but were charged with supplying the Indians with arms and munitions of war ; stirring them up against the whites, and acting as spies. On these charges they were tried by a court martial, of which Gen. Gaines was President—found guilty—condemned to death, and executed on the 27th of April, 1818.

These transactions of Gen. Jackson caused great excitement throughout the United States, and subjected him to no little blame. The subject excited much debate in Congress. A resolution censuring him for his summary proceedings was introduced, but voted down by a large majority. In Mr. Monroe's cabinet, there was a strong feeling against Gen. Jackson. The President, and all the members, with a single exception, were disposed to hold him responsible for having transcended his orders. Hon. Wm. H. Crawford, who was in Mr. Monroe's cabinet at that time, in a letter to Mr. Forsyth, says:—"Mr. Calhoun's proposition in the cabinet was, that Gen. Jackson should be punished in some form, or reprimanded in some form."

Mr. Adams alone vindicated Gen. Jackson. He insisted that inasmuch as the Government had ordered him to pursue the enemy into Florida, if necessary, they were responsible for the acts of the American general, in the exercise of the discretionary power with which he had been clothed. Several cabinet meetings were held on the subject, in July, 1818, in which the whole matter was thoroughly discussed. Mr. Adams succeeded at length in bringing the President into the adoption of his views, which Mr. Monroe substantially embodied in his next annual message to Congress.

The intelligence of the execution of Arbuthnot and Ambrister, excited the highest indignation in England. The people viewed it as a violation of the rights of British subjects, and an insult to their nation, and were ready to rush to war. Lord Castlereagh declared to Mr. Rush, the American Minister, that had the English cabinet but held up a finger, war would have been declared against the United States. But so able and convincing were the arguments which Mr. Adams directed Mr. Rush to lay before the British Ministers, in defence of the proceedings of Gen. Jackson, that they became convinced there was no just cause of war between the two countries, and exerted their influence against any movement in that direction.

On the 22nd of February, 1819, a treaty was concluded at Washington, between the United States and Spain, by which East and West Florida, with the adjacent islands, were ceded to the Union. The negotiations which resulted in the consummation of the treaty, were conducted by Mr. Adams and Luis de Onis the Spanish Ambassador. This treaty was very advantageous to the United States. It brought to a close a controversy with Spain, of many years' standing, which had defied all the exertions of former administrations to adjust, and placed our relations with that country on the most amicable footing. In effecting this reconciliation, Mr. Adams deserved and received a high share of credit.

The recognition of the independence of the Spanish South American Provinces, by the Government of the United States, took place during Mr. Adams's administration of the State Department. The honor of first proposing this recognition, in the Congress of the

United States, and of advocating it with unsurpassed
eloquence and zeal, belongs to the patriotic Henry
Clay. Mainly by his influence, the House of Representatives, in 1820, passed the following resolutions :—

"Resolved, That the House of Representatives participate with
the people of the United States, in the deep interest which they feel
for the success of the Spanish Provinces of South America, which
are struggling to establish their liberty and independence.

"Resolved, That this House will give its constitutional support
to the President of the United States, whenever he may deem it expedient to recognize the sovereignty and independence of any of
said Provinces."

Mr. Adams at first hesitated on this subject. Not
that he was opposed to the diffusion of the blessings of
freedom to the oppressed. No man was a more ardent
lover of liberty, or was more anxious that its institutions should be established throughout the earth, at the
earliest practicable moment. But he had many and serious doubts whether the people of the South American
Provinces were capable of originating and maintaining
an enlightened self-government. There was a lack of
general intelligence among the people—a want of an
enlarged and enlightened understanding of the principles of rational freedom—which led him to apprehend
that their attempts at self-government would for a long
season, at least, result in the reign of faction and
anarchy, rather than true republican principles. The
subsequent history of these countries—the divisions
and contentions, the revolutions and counter-revolu-
tions, which have rent them asunder, and deluged

them in blood—clearly show that Mr. Adams but exercised a far-seeing intelligence in entertaining these doubts. Nevertheless, as they had succeeded in throwing off the Spanish yoke, and had, in fact, achieved their independence, Mr. Adams would not throw any impediment in their way. Trusting that his fears as to their ability for self-government might be groundless, he gave his influence to the recognizing of their independence by the United States.

In 1821 the Greek revolution broke out. The people of that classic land, after enduring ages of the most brutal and humiliating oppression from the Turks, nobly resolved to break the chains of the Ottoman power, or perish in the attempt. The war was long, and sanguinary, but finally resulted in the emancipation of Greece, and the establishment of its independence as a nation.

The inhabitants of the United States could not witness such a struggle with indifference. A spirit of sympathy ran like electricity throughout the land. Public meetings were held in nearly every populous town in the Union, in which resolutions, encouraging the Greeks in their struggle, were passed, and contributions taken up to aid them. Money, clothing, provisions, arms, were collected in immense quantities and shipped to Greece. In churches, colleges, academies and schools—at the theatres, museums, and other places of amusement and public resort—aid was freely and generously given in behalf of the struggling patriots. Many citizens of the United States, when the first blast of the trumpet of liberty rang along the Ionian seas, and through the Peloponnesus, sped across the ocean, and, throwing themselves into the midst of the Grecian hosts, contended heroically for their emancipation. Among these volunteers, was Col. J. P. Miller, of Vermont, who not only gallantly fought in the battles of Greece, but was greatly serviceable in conveying supplies from the United States to that struggling people.

The deep sympathy which prevailed in every section of the Union, was soon felt in Congress. Many public men were anxious that the Government should take some important and decisive step, even to hostilities, in behalf of Greece. Eloquent speeches were delivered in the House of Representatives on the exciting topic. Mr. Clay electrified the country with his stirring appeals in behalf of the land in which was established the first republic on earth. Mr. Webster submitted the following resolution to the House of Representatives :—

" Resolved, That provision ought to be made by law, for defraying the expense incident to the appointment of an Agent, or Commissioner, to Greece, whenever the President shall deem it expedient to make such appointment."

In support of this resolution, Mr. Webster made a most eloquent speech, of which the following is the conclusion :—

" Mr. Chairman—There are some things which, to be well done, must be promptly done. If we even determine to do the thing that is now proposed, we may do it too late. Sir, I am not of those who are for withholding aid when it is most urgently needed, and when the stress is past, and the aid no longer necessary, overwhelming the sufferers with caresses. I will not stand by and see my fellow-man drowning, without stretching out a hand to help him, till he has, by his own efforts and presence of mind, reached the shore in safety, and then encumber him with aid. With suffering Greece, now is the crisis of her fate—her great, it may be her last struggle. Sir, while we sit here deliberating, her destiny may be decided. The Greeks, contending with ruthless oppressors, turn their eyes to us, and invoke us, by their ancestors, by their slaughtered wives and children, by their own blood poured out like water, by the hecatombs of dead they have heaped up, as it were, to heaven; they invoke, they implore from us some cheering sound, some look of sympathy, some token of compassionate regard. They look to us as the great Republic of the earth—and they ask us, by our common faith, whether we can forget that they are struggling, as we once struggled, for what we now so happily enjoy ? I cannot say, sir, they will succeed ; that rests with heaven. But, for myself, sir, if I should to-morrow hear that they have failed—that their last phalanx had sunk beneath the Turkish cimetar, that the flames of their last city had sunk in its ashes, and that nought remained but the wide, melancholy waste where Greece once was—I should still eflect, with the most heartfelt satisfaction, that I have asked you, in the name of seven millions of freemen, that you would give them, at least, the cheering of one friendly voice."

The committee having in charge the raising of a fund for the assistance of the Greeks, in New York, addressed a circular to the venerable ex-President John Adams, to which they received the following reply :—

" *Quincy, Dec.* 29, 1823.

" GENTLEMEN :—I have received your circular of the 12th inst., and I thank you for the honor you have done me in addressing it to me. Be assured my heart beats in unison with yours, and with those of your constituents, and I presume with all the really civilized part of mankind, in sympathy with the Greeks, suffering, as they are, in the great cause of liberty and humanity. The gentlemen of Boston have taken measures to procure a general subscription in their favor, through the State, and I shall contribute my mite with great pleasure. In the meantime I wish you, and all other gentlemen engaged in the virtuous work, all the success you or they can wish ; for I believe no effort in favor of virtue will be ultimately lost.

" I have the honor to be, Gentlemen, your very humble Servant,

" JOHN ADAMS."

The sympathies of John Quincy Adams were ardently enlisted in behalf of the Greek Revolution. But with a prudence and wisdom which characterized all his acts, he threw his influence against any direct interference on the part of the Government of the United States. It would have been a departure from that neutral policy, in regard to European conflicts, on which the country had acted from the commencement of our national existence, alike injurious and dangerous.

He knew if we once entered into these wars, on any pretext whatever, a door would be opened for foreign entanglements and endless conflicts, which would result in standing armies, immense national debts, and the long trail of evils of which they are the prolific source.

When an application was made to Mr. Adams, as Secretary of State, through Mr. Rush, our Minister at London, by an Agent of Greece, for aid from the United States, he was compelled, on principles above stated, to withhold the required assistance. The correspondence which grew out of this application is sufficiently interesting to find a place in these pages :—

"*Andreas Luriottis, Envoy of the Provisional Government of Greece, to the Hon. John Quincy Adams, Secretary of State to the United States of America.*

SIR :—I feel no slight emotion, while, in behalf of Greece, my country, struggling for independence and liberty, I address myself to the United States of America.

" The independence for which we combat, you have achieved. The liberty to which we look, with anxious solicitude, you have obtained, and consolidated in peace and in glory.

" Yet Greece, old Greece, the seat of early civilization and freedom, stretches out her hands, imploringly, to a land which sprung into being, as it were, ages after her own lustre had been extinguished ! and ventures to hope that the youngest and most vigorous sons of liberty, will regard, with no common sympathy, the efforts of the descendants of the heir and the elder born, whose precepts and whose example have served—though insufficient, hitherto, for our complete regeneration—to regenerate half a world.

" I know, Sir, that the sympathies of the generous people of the United States have been extensively directed towards us ; and since I have reached this country, an interview with their Minister, Mr. Rush, has served to convince me more strongly, how great their claim is on our gratitude and our affection. May I hope that some means may be found to communicate these our feelings, of which I am so proud to be the organ ? We will still venture to rely on their friendship. We would look to their individual, if not to their national, co-operation. Every, the slightest, assistance under present circumstances, will aid the progress of the great work of liberty ; and if, standing, as we have stood, alone and unsupported, with everything opposed to us, and nothing to encourage us but patriotism, enthusiasm, and sometimes even despair : if thus we have gone forward, liberating our provinces, one after another, and subduing every force which has been directed against us, what may we not do with the assistance for which we venture to appeal to the generous and the free ?

"Precipitated by circumstances into that struggle for independence, which, ever since the domination of our cruel and reckless tyrants, had never ceased to be the object of our vows and prayers, we have, by the blessing of God, freed a considerable part of Greece from the ruthless invaders. The Peloponnesus, Etolia, Carmania, Attica, Phocida, Boetia, and the Islands of the Archipelago and Candia, are nearly free. The armies and the fleets which have been sent against us, have been subdued by the valor of our troops and our marine. Meanwhile we have organized a government, founded upon popular suffrages : and you will probably have seen how closely our organic law assimilates to that constitution under which your nation so happily and so securely lives.

"I have been sent hither by the government of Greece, to obtain assistance in our determined enterprize, on which we, like you, have staked our lives, our fortunes, and our sacred honor : and I believe my journey has not been wholly without success. I should have been wanting to my duty had I not addressed you, supplicating the earliest display of your amiable purposes; entreating that diplomatic relations may be established between us ; communicating the most earnest desire of my government that we may be allowed to call you allies as well as friends ; and stating that we shall rejoice to enter upon discussions which may lead to immediate and advantageous treaties, and to receive diplomatic agents without delay. Both at Madrid and at Lisbon, I have been received with great kindness by the American Representative, and am pleased to record the expression of my gratitude.

" Though, fortunately, you are so far removed, and raised so much above the narrow politics of Europe as to be little influenced by their vicissitudes, I venture to believe that Mr. Rush will explain to you the changes which have taken place, and are still in action around us, in our favor. And I conclude, rejoicing in the hope that North America and Greece may be united in the bonds of long-enduring, and unbroken concord : and have the honor to be, with every sentiment of respect, your obedient humble servant.

" AND. LURIOTTIS.

' *London, February* 20, 1823."

MR. ADAMS TO MR. RUSH.

" *Department of State,*
Washington, 18*th August,* 1823.

" SIR :—I have the honor of inclosing, herewith, an answer to the letter from Mr. Luriottis, the Agent of the Greeks addressed to me, and a copy of which was transmitted with your dispatch No. 295.

" If, upon the receipt of this letter, Mr. Luriottis should still be in London, it will be desirable that you should deliver it to him in person, accompanied with such remarks and explanations as may satisfy him, and those whom he represents, that, in declining the proposal of giving active aid to the cause of Grecian emancipation, the Executive Government of the United States has been governed not by its inclinations, or a sentiment of indifference to the cause, but by its constitutional duties, clear and unequivocal.

" The United States could give assistance to the Greeks, only by the application of some portion of their public forces or of their public revenue in their favor, which would constitute them in a state of war with the Ottoman Porte, and perhaps with all the Barbary powers. To make this disposal either of force or of treasure, you are aware is, by our constitution, not within the competency of the Executive. It could be determined only by an act of Congress, which would assuredly not be adopted, should it even be recommended by the Executive.

" The policy of the United States, with reference to foreign nations, has always been founded upon the moral principle of natural law—*Peace* with all mankind. From whatever cause war between other nations, whether foreign or domestic, has arisen, the unvarying law of the United States has been *peace* with both belligerents. From the first war of the French Revolution, to the recent invasion of Spain, there has been a succession of wars, national and civil, in almost every one of which one of the parties was contending for liberty or independence. In the first French revolutionary war, a strong impulse of feeling urged the people of the United States to take side with the party which, at its commencement, was *contending*, apparently, at least, for both. Had the policy of the United States not been essentially pacific, a stronger case to claim their interference could scarcely have been presented. They nevertheless declared themselves neutral, and the principle, then deliberately settled, has been invariably adhered to ever since.

" With regard to the recognition of sovereign States, and the establishment with them of a diplomatic intercourse, the experience of the last thirty years has served also to ascertain the limits proper for the application of principles in which every nation must exercise some latitude of discretion. Precluded by their neutral position from interfering in the question of right, the United States have recognized the *fact* of foreign sovereignty only when it was undisputed, or disputed without any rational prospect of success. In this manner the successive changes of government in many of the European states, and the revolutionary governments of South America, have been acknowledged. The condition of the Greeks is not yet such as will admit of their recognition, upon these principles.

" Yet, as we cherish the most friendly feelings towards them, and are sincerely disposed to render them any service which may be compatible with our neutrality, it will give us pleasure to learn, from time to time, the actual state of their cause, political and military. Should Mr. Luriottis be enabled and disposed to furnish this information, it may always be communicated through you, and will be received with satisfaction here. The public accounts from that quarter have been of late very scanty, and we shall be glad to obtain any authentic particulars, which may come to your knowledge from this, or through any other channel.

" I am with great respect, Sir, your very humble and obedient servant,   JOHN QUINCY ADAMS."

MR. ADAMS TO MR. LURIOTTIS.

} " *Department of State,*
} *Washington,* 18*th August,* 1823.

"Sir: A copy of the letter which you did me the honor of addressing to me, on the 20th of February last, has been transmitted to me by the Minister of the United States at London, and has received the deliberate consideration of the President of the United States.

"The sentiments with which he has witnessed the struggles of your countrymen for their national emancipation and independence, had been made manifest to the world in a public message to the Congress of the United States. They are cordially felt by the people of this Union; who, sympathizing with the cause of freedom and independence wherever its standard is unfurled, behold with peculiar interest the display of Grecian energy in defence of Grecian liberties, and the association of heroic exertions, at the present time, with the proudest glories of former ages, in the land of Epaminondas and Philopoemon.

"But while cheering with their best wishes the cause of the Greeks, the United States are forbidden, by the duties of their situation, from taking part in the war, to which their relation is that of neutrality. At peace themselves with all the world, their established policy, and the obligations of the laws of nations, preclude them from becoming voluntary auxiliaries to a cause which would involve them in war.

"If in the progress of events the Greeks should be enabled to establish and organize themselves as an independent nation, the United States will be among the first to welcome them, in that capacity, into the general family; to establish diplomatic and commercial relations with them, suited to the mutual interests of the two countries; and to recognize, with special satisfaction, their constituted state in the character of a sister Republic.

"I have the honor to be, with distinguished consideration, Sir, your very humble and obedient servant,

"JOHN QUINCY ADAMS."

The sentiments, in regard to the foreign policy of

our Government, which Mr. Adams embodies in this correspondence, he had previously expressed in an oration delivered in the city of Washington, on the 4th of July, 1821, of which the following is an extract:—

"America, in the assembly of nations, since her admission among them, has invariably, though often fruitlessly, held forth to them the hand of honest friendship, of equal freedom, of generous reciprocity; she has uniformly spoken among them, though often to heedless, and often to disdainful ears, the language of equal liberty, of equal justice, and equal rights; she has, in the lapse of nearly half a century, without a single exception, respected the independence of other nations while asserting and maintaining her own; she has abstained from interference in the concerns of others, even when the conflict has been for principles to which she clings as to the last vital drop that visits the heart. She has seen that probably for centuries to come all the contests of that Aceldama, the European world, will be contests of inveterate power and emerging right. Wherever the standard of freedom and independence has been or shall be unfurled, there will her heart, her benedictions, and her prayers be. But she goes not abroad in search of monsters to destroy. She is the well-wisher to the freedom and independence of all—she is the champion and vindicator only of her own. She will recommend the general cause, by the countenance of her voice, and the benignant sympathy of her example:—she well knows that by once enlisting under other banners than her own, were they even the banners of foreign independence, she would involve herself beyond the power of extrication, in all the wars of interest and intrigue, of individual avarice, envy and ambition, which assume the colors, and usurp the standard of freedom.   The fundamental maxims of her policy would insensibly change from *liberty* to *force;* the frontlet on her brow would no longer beam with the ineffable splendor of freedom and independence; but in its stead would soon be substituted an imperial diadem, flashing in false and tarnished lustre, the murky radiance of dominion and power.   She might become the dictatress of the world : she would be no longer the ruler of her own spirit."

During Mr. Adams's occupancy of the state department, efforts were made by the American Government to abolish the African slave trade, and procure its denunciation as piracy, by the civilized world.   On the 28th of Feb., 1823, the following resolution was adopted by the House of Representatives, at Washington, by a vote of 131 to 9 :—

" Resolved, That the President of the United States be requested to enter upon and to prosecute, from time to time, such negotiations with the several maratime powers of Europe and America, as he may deem expedient for the effectual abolition of the African slave trade, and its ultimate denunciation as piracy, under the law of nations, by the consent of the civilized world."

In compliance with this resolution, Mr. Adams, as Secretary of State, issued directions to the American

Ministers in Spain, Russia, the Netherlands, Colombia, and Buenos Ayres, to enter into negotiations with the Governments of these countries on this subject.   Mr. Adams also maintained an able correspondence with the Hon. Stratford Canning, the British Minister at Washington, in relation to the basis on which a treaty should be formed with Great Britain for the suppression of the foreign slave trade.

Mr. Rush, the American Minister at the Court of St. James, was directed to enter upon negotiations in London, to this end. His instructions were written by Mr. Adams, with his usual sound judgment and enlarged views of national policy, and the claims of humanity. The convention was in due time completed, and signed by the Plenipotentiaries of both nations, on the 13th of March, 1824, and was sent by Mr. Rush to Washington for ratification. Mr. Monroe and Mr. Adams were ready to give it their sanction; but the Senate insisted on striking out a provision in the first article. The article commenced as follows :—

"The commanders and commissioned officers of each of the two high contracting parties, duly authorized, under the regulations and instructions of their respective Governments, to cruise on the coasts of Africa, of America, and of the West Indies, for the suppression of the slave trade, shall be empowered, under the conditions, limitations, and restrictions hereinafter specified," &c.

The Senate struck out the words "*of America.*" This amendment the British Government would not assent to. Thus the negotiation on the slave trade, so near a consummation, fell to the ground.

Mr. Monroe's administration closed on the 3rd of March, 1825. It was a period of uninterrupted prosperity to the country. Our foreign commerce, recovering from the paralysis caused by the embargo, the non-intercourse act, and the war, spread forth its wings and whitened every sea and ocean on the globe. The domestic condition of the Union was thriving beyond the precedent of many former years. Improvements in agriculture were developed; domestic manufactures received a fair protection and encouragement; internal improvements, gaining more and more the attention and confidence of the people, had been prosecuted to the evident benefit of all branches of business and enterprize.

Another characteristic of the administration of Mr. Monroe is worthy of note. So judiciously and patriotically had he exercised the powers entrusted to him, that he disarmed opposition. Divisions, jealousies and contentions were destroyed, and a thorough fusion of all political parties took place. At his re-election for the second term of the presidency, there was no opposing candidate. There was but one party, and that was the great party of the American people. His election was unanimous.

In all these measures, Mr. Adams was the coadjutor and confidential adviser of Mr. Monroe. It is no derogation from the well-merited reputation of the latter

to say, that many of the most striking and praiseworthy
features of his administration were enstamped upon
it by the labor and influence of the former. His success in maturing and carrying into execution his most
popular measures must be attributed, in no small extent, to the ability and faithfulness of his eminent
Secretary of State.   And the historian may truly record that to John Quincy Adams, in an eminent degree,
belongs a portion of the honor and credit which have
been so generally accorded to the administration of
James Monroe.

CHAPTER VII.

MR. ADAMS' NOMINATION TO THE PRESIDENCY — SPIRITED
PRESIDENTIAL CAMPAIGN—NO CHOICE BY THE PEOPLE—
ELECTION GOES TO THE HOUSE OF REPRESENTATIVES—MR.
ADAMS ELECTED PRESIDENT—HIS INAUGURATION—FORMS
HIS CABINET.

James Monroe was the last of the illustrious line of
Presidents whose claims to that eminent station dated
back to the revolution. A grateful people had conferred the highest honors in their gift upon the most
conspicuous of those patriots who had faithfully served
them in that perilous struggle, and aided in construct-
ing and consolidating the union of these States. This
debt punctually and honorably discharged, they looked
to another generation, possessing claims of a different
description, for servants to elevate to the dignity of
the presidential chair.

In the midst of a large class of public men who had
in the mean time become conspicuous for talents and
services of various descriptions, it is no matter of surprise that the people of the United States should
entertain a diversity of opinions in regard to the most
suitable individual to fill a station which had hitherto
been occupied by men whose virtues and whose patriot-

ism had shed the brightest lustre on the American name and character throughout the world. Candidates for the presidency were nominated in various sections of the Union. The eastern States turned their eyes instinctively towards JOHN QUINCY ADAMS, as one, among all the eminent competitors, the most fitted, by character and services, for the office of President of the United States. The members of the Legislature of Maine resolved—

" That the splendid talents and incorruptible integrity of JOHN QUINCY ADAMS, his republican habits and principles, distinguished public services, and extensive knowledge of, and devoted attachment to, the vital interests of the country, justly entitle him to the first honors in the gift of an enlightened and grateful people."

The republican members of the Massachusetts Legislature adopted the following resolutions :—

" Resolved, That the ability, experience, integrity and patriotism of JOHN QUINCY ADAMS; his manly efforts to defend the principles of that government under which, in God's providence, we hope to die ; his unshaken fortitude and resolution in all political exigencies ; his long, faithful, and valuable services, under the patronage of all the Presidents of the United States, present him to the people of this nation, as a man eminently qualified to subserve the best interests of his country, and as a statesman without reproach.

" Resolved, That a man who has given such continued and indubitable pledges of his patriotism and capacity, may be safely placed at the head of this nation. Every impulse of his heart, and every dictate of his mind, must unite promptly in the support of the interests, the honor, and the liberty of his country.

" Resolved, That JOHN QUINCY ADAMS is hereby recommended by us to the people of the United States, as the most suitable candidate for the office of President, at the approaching election."

A meeting of the citizens of Rhode Island passed the following among other resolutions :—

" Resolved, That, although we duly acknowledge the talents and public services of all the candidates for the presidency, we have the fullest confidence in the acknowledged ability, integrity and experience of JOHN QUINCY ADAMS, the accomplished scholar, the true republican, the enlightened statesman, and the honest man ; and we are desirous that his merits should be rewarded with the first office in the gift of the people of the United States—that his future services may continue unto us those blessings which, under the present administration of the General Government, we have so abundantly enjoyed."

These were high encomiums. But who among the American people, now that the patriot has departed from earth, can survey his life, his character, and his services, and not acknowledge they were justly and richly deserved ? Similar resolutions were passed in all the eastern and many of the northern States.

The west brought forward HENRY CLAY, one of the most popular orators and eminent statesman of the day. Gen. JACKSON, who had earned a splendid military reputation, was nominated in the southwest, and WM. H. CRAWFORD was selected as the candidate representing the southern portion of the confederacy. These were all men of eminence and of acknowledged talents. They were worthy competitors for the highest honors of the Republic.

The friends of Mr. Adams rested his claims for the presidency on no factitious qualities. They urged that his characteristics were such as to commend him

to the confidence of every true republican and well-
wisher of his country. While his attainments were
not of the showy and popular cast possessed by many
public men, they yet were of that solid, practical and
valuable desc. iption which must ever receive the sanction of intelligent and reflecting minds.

The qualifications on which his supporters depended,
and to which they called the attention of the American
people, as reasons for elevating him to the head of the
General Government, may be summarily enumerated
as follows :—1. The purity of his private character—
the simplicity of his personal habits—his unbending integrity and uprightness, even beyond suspicion. 2. His
commanding talents, and his acquirements both as a
scholar and a statesman. 3. His love of country—his
truly American feelings, in all that concerned the welfare and honor of the United States. 4. His long
experience in public affairs, especially his familiarity
with our foreign relations, and his perfect knowledge of
the institutions, the internal condition and policy of
European nations. 5. His advocacy of protection to
domestic manufactures, and of a judicious system of
internal improvements.

In regard to internal improvements by the General
Government, there was a difference of opinion between
Mr. Adams and President Monroe. The latter was
strongly impressed with the beneficial tendency of a
well-digested system of internal improvements; but he
believed the constitution conferred no power on Con-

gress to make appropriations for such a purpose. It was in this view of the subject that he vetoed a bill which assumed the right to adopt and execute such a system, passed by Congress during the session of 1820–21. But anxious that internal improvements, confined to great national purposes, and with proper limitations, should be prosecuted, he suggested that an amendment of the constitution to that effect should be recommended to the several States.

Mr. Adams, however, had no doubts that Congress already possessed a constitutional power to prosecute such internal improvements as were of a national character, and calculated to benefit the Union, and to levy duties for the protection of domestic manufactures. During his entire political career he had deemed these to be two great points toward which the American Government and people should turn their especial attention; and he ever gave them his faithful advocacy and support. With consummate wisdom, he foresaw that the more completely our internal resources were developed, and the less dependent we were on foreign powers, the greater would be our public and private prosperity. He insisted that by an adequate protection of domestic manufactures, there would be an increased demand for our raw materials at home, and thus the several productive and manufacturing sections of the Republic would realize the benefits of a dependence on each other, and the Union would be consolidated and perpetuated for ages to come.

While a candidate for the presidency, Mr. Adams received a letter inquiring his views on the subject of internal improvement. The following is an extract from his reply :—

"On the 23rd of Feb., 1807, I offered, in the Senate of the United States, of which I was then a member, the first resolution, as I believe, that ever was presented to Congress, contemplating a *general system* of internal improvement. I thought that Congress possessed the power of appropriating money to such improvement, and of authorizing the works necessary for making it—subject always to the territorial rights of the several States in or through which the improvement is to be made, to be secured by the consent of their Legislatures, and to proprietary rights of individuals, to be purchased or indemnified. I still hold the same opinions ; and, although highly respecting the purity of intention of those who object, on constitutional grounds, to the exercise of this power, it is with heartfelt satisfaction that I perceive those objections gradually yielding to the paramount influence of the *general welfare*. Already have appropriations of money to great objects of internal improvement been freely made ; and I hope we shall both live to see the day, when the only question of our statesmen and patriots, concerning the authority of Congress to improve, by public works essentially beneficent, and beyond the means of less than national resources, the condition of our common country, will be how it ever could have been doubted."

On another occasion, Mr. Adams expressed himself on the subject of internal improvements in the following manner :—

"The question of the power of Congress to authorize the making of internal improvements, is, in other words, a question whether the people of this Union, in forming their common social compact, as avowedly for the purpose of promoting their general welfare, have performed their work in a manner so ineffably stupid as to deny themselves the means of bettering their own condition. I have too much respect for the intellect of my country to believe it. The first object of human association is the improvement of the condition of the associated. Roads and canals are among the most essential means of improving the condition of nations. And a people which should deliberately, by the organization of its authorized power, deprive itself of the faculty of multiplying its own blessings, would be as wise as a creator who should undertake to constitute a human being without a heart."

In addition to other claims, the friends of Mr. Adams urged his elevation to the presidency on the ground of *locality*. During the thirty-six years which had passed since the adoption of the constitution, the General Government had been administered but four years by a northern President. It was insisted with much force that the southern portion of the Republic had thus far exerted a disproportionate influence in the executive department of the nation. While the north, although far the most populous, and contributing much the largest portion of the means for defraying the national expenditures, would not claim to monopolize an undue degree of power in controlling the measures of administration, yet it could justly insist that its demands for an equitable share of influence should be heeded. These suggestions unquestionably possessed a weight in the minds of the people, favorable to the prospects of Mr. Adams.

The Presidential campaign of 1824, was more spirited and exciting than any that had taken place since the first election of Mr. Jefferson. It was novel in the number of candidates presented for the suffrages of the people, and was conducted with great zeal and vigor by the friends of the different aspirants. Strictly speaking, it could not be called a party contest. Mr. Monroe's wise and prudent administration had obliterated party lines, and left a very general unanimity of sentiment on political principles and measures, throughout the Union. The various candidates—Adams, Jackson, Clay, Crawford—all subscribed, substantially, to the same political creed, and entertained similar views as to the principles on which the General Government should be administered. The struggle was a personal and sectional one, more than of a party nature.

It had long been foreseen that a choice of President would not be effected by the people. The result verified this prediction. Of two hundred and sixty-one electoral votes, Gen. Jackson received ninety-nine, Mr. Adams eighty-four, Mr. Crawford forty-one, and Mr. Clay thirty-seven. Neither of the candidates having received a majority in the electoral colleges, the election devolved on the House of Representatives. This took place on the 9th of Feb., 1825.

On the morning of that day, the House met at an earlier hour than usual. The galleries, the lobbies, and the adjacent apartments, were filled to overflowing with spectators from every part of the Union to witness the momentous event. It was a scene the most sublime that could be witnessed on earth. The Representatives of the People, in the exercise of the highest right of freemen, were about to select a citizen to administer the Government of a great Republic.

All the members of the House were present, with the exception of one, who was confined by indisposition. The Speaker (Henry Clay) took his chair, and the ordinary business of the morning was attended to in the usual manner. At 12 o'clock, precisely, the members of the Senate entered the hall, preceded by their Sergeant-at-arms, and having the President of the Senate at their head, who was invited to a seat on the right hand of the Speaker. The Senators were assigned seats in front of the Speaker's chair.

The President of the Senate (Mr. Gaillard) then rose, and stated that the certificates forwarded by the electors from each State would be delivered to the Tellers. Mr. Tazewell of the Senate, and Messrs. John W. Taylor and Philip P. Barbour on the part of the House, took their places, as Tellers, at the Clerk's table. The President of the Senate then opened two packets, one received by messenger and the other by mail, containing the certificates of the votes of the State of New Hampshire. One of these certificates was then read by Mr. Tazewell, while the other was compared with it by Messrs. Taylor and Barbour. The whole having been read, and the votes of New Hampshire declared, they were set down by the Clerks of the Senate and of the House of Representatives, seated at different tables. Thus the certificates from all the States were gone through with. At the conclusion, the Tellers left the Clerk's tables, and, presenting themselves in front of the Speaker, Mr. Tazewell delivered their report of the votes given.

The President of the Senate then rose, and declared that no person had received a majority of the votes given for President of the United States: that Andrew Jackson, John Quincy Adams, and William H. Crawford, were the three persons who had received the highest number of votes; and that the remaining duties in the choice of a President now devolved on the House of Representatives. He further declared, that John C. Calhoun of South Carolina, having received 182 votes, was duly elected Vice President of the United States, to serve four years from the 4th of March next. The members of the Senate then retired.

The Speaker directed the roll of the House to be called by States, and the members of the respective delegations to take their seats in the order in which the States should be called, beginning at the right hand of the Speaker. The delegations took their seats accordingly. Ballot-boxes were distributed to each delegation, by the Sergeant-at-arms, and the Speaker directed that the balloting should proceed. The ballots having all been deposited in the boxes, Tellers were named by the respective delegations, being one from each State, who took their seats at two tables.

Mr. Webster of Massachusetts was appointed by those Tellers who sat at one table, and Mr. Randolph of Virginia by those at the other, to announce the result. After the ballots were counted out, Mr. Webster rose, and said :—

" Mr. Speaker : The Tellers of the votes at this table have proceeded to count the ballots contained in the boxes set before them. The result they find to be, that there are for John Quincy Adams, of Massachusetts, thirteen votes ; for Andrew Jackson, of Tennessee, seven votes; for William H. Crawford, of Georgia, four votes."

Mr. Randolph, from the other table, made a statement corresponding with that of Mr. Webster.

The Speaker then stated this result to the House, and announced that JOHN QUINCY ADAMS, having a majority of the votes of these United States, was duly elected President of the same, for four years, commencing on the 4th day of March, 1825.

A committee was appointed to wait upon Mr. Adams, and announce to him the result of the election, of which Mr. Webster was chairman. On performing this duty, they received from Mr. Adams the following reply :—

GENTLEMEN :—In receiving this testimonial from the Representatives of the People and States of this Union, I am deeply sensible of the circumstances under which it has been given. All my predecessors have been honored with majorities of the electoral voices, in the primary colleges. It has been my fortune to be placed, by the divisions of sentiment prevailing among our countrymen on this occasion, in competition, friendly and honorable, with three of my fellow-citizens, all justly enjoying, in eminent degrees, the public favor ; and of whose worth, talents and services no one entertains a higher and more respectful sense than myself. The names of two of them were, in the fulfilment of the provisions of the constitution, presented to the selection of the House of Representatives in concurrence with my own,—names closely associated with the glory of the nation, and one of them farther recommended by a larger majority of the primary electoral suffrages than mine.

In this state of things, could my refusal to accept the trust thus delegated to me give an opportunity to the people to form, and to express, with a nearer approach to unanimity, the object of their preference, I should not hesitate to decline the acceptance of this eminent charge, and to submit the decision of this momentous question again to their determination. But the constitution itself has not so disposed of the contingency which would arise in the event of my refusal. I shall, therefore, repair to the post assigned me by the call of my country, signified through her constitutional organs; oppressed with the magnitude of the task before me, but cheered with the hope of that generous support from my fellow-citizens, which, in the vicissitudes of a life devoted to their service, has never failed to sustain me —confident in the trust, that the wisdom of the legislative councils will guide and direct me in the path of my official duty ; and relying, above all, upon the superintending providence of that Being " in whose hands our breath is, and whose are all our ways."

" Gentlemen, I pray you to make acceptable to the House, the assurance of my profound gratitude for their confidence, and to accept yourselves my thanks for the friendly terms in which you have communicated to me their decision."

The diffidence manifested by Mr. Adams in accepting the office of President, under the peculiar circumstances of his election, and his wish, if it were possible, to submit his claims again to the people, were unquestionably uttered with great sincerity of heart. He was the choice of but a minority, as expressed in the electoral vote ; and in accordance with his republican principles and feelings, he would have preferred another

expression of public opinion. But the constitution
made no provision for such an arbitrament. He must
either serve or resign. In the latter case, the Vice
President would have discharged the duties of President during the term. Mr. Adams had no alternative,
therefore, but to accept the office, agreeably to the
terms of the constitution. Had either of his competitors been elected by the House of Representatives, they
would have been, as he was, a minority President.
Notwithstanding Gen. Jackson received fifteen more
electoral votes than Mr. Adams, yet it is believed that
in the primary assemblies the latter obtained a greater
number of the actual votes of the people than the
former.

"Although Gen. Jackson had a plurality in the nom-
inal returns from the electoral colleges, the question is,
whether he had a plurality in the popular votes of the
States. In North Carolina, the Crawford men had a
great plurality over either of the Jackson and Adams
sections ; but the two latter joining their forces, gave
the electoral vote of the State, it being fifteen, to Gen.
Jackson. Deduct this from Gen. Jackson's plurality—
as it should be, if the principle of plurality is to govern—and it leaves him *eighty-four*, the same as the
vote of Mr. Adams. But Mr. Adams had a great
plurality of the popular vote of New York, and on
this principle should be credited the entire *thirty-six*
votes of that State, whereas, he received only *twenty-
six*. This adjustment would carry Mr. Adams up to

ninety-four, and leave Gen. Jackson with *eighty-four*. Besides, the popular majorities for Mr. Adams in the six New England States were greatly in excess of the Jackson majorities in the eight States which gave their vote for him; which largely augments Mr. Adams' aggregate plurality in the Union over Gen. Jackson's. Then deduct the constitutional allowance for the *slave* vote in the slave States, as given by their masters. It will not be pretended that this is a *popular* vote, though constitutional. Gen. Jackson obtained *fifty-five* electoral votes, more than half his entire vote, and Mr. Adams only *six* from slave States. It will therefore be seen, that on the principle of a popular plurality, carried out, and carried through, (it ought not to stop for the advantage of one party,) Mr. Adams, in the election of 1824, was FAR AHEAD of Gen. Jackson."*

On the the 4th of March, 1825, John Quincy Adams was inaugurated as President of the United States, and took the executive chair, which had been entered twenty-eight years before by his venerated father. The declaration of that father in reference to the son, when a lad—"He behaves like a man!"—had gathered strength and meaning in the lapse of years. The people of the American republic, taught by a long series of faithful and eminent services, in the fulfilment of the

---

* Colton's Life and Times of Henry Clay.

prophetic words, placed him in a position the most elevated and honorable, the most worthy the aim of a pure and patriotic ambition, that earth can afford !

The scene at the inauguration was splendid and imposing. At an early hour of the day the avenues leading to the capitol presented an animated spectacle. Crowds of citizens on foot, in carriages, and on horseback, were hastening to the great centre of attraction. Strains of martial music, and the movements of the various military corps, heightened the excitement.

At 12 o'clock, the military escort, consisting of general and staff officers, and several volunteer companies, received the President elect at his residence, together with President Monroe, and several officers of government. The procession, led by the cavalry, and accompanied by an immense concourse of citizens, proceeded to the capitol, where it was received, with military honors, by the U. S. Marine Corps under Col. Henderson.

Meanwhile the hall of the House of Representatives presented a brilliant spectacle. The galleries and the lobbies were crowded with spectators. The sofas between the columns, the bar, the promenade in the rear of the Speaker's chair, and the three outer rows of the members' seats, were occupied by a splendid array of beauty and fashion. On the left, the Diplomatic Corps, in the costume of their respective Courts, occupied the place assigned them, immediately before the steps which lead to the chair. The officers of the army and navy were scattered in groups throughout the hall.   In front of the Clerk's table chairs were placed for the Judges of the Supreme Court.

At twenty minutes past 12 o'clock, the marshals, in blue scarfs, made their appearance in the hall, at the head of the august procession.   First came the officers of both Houses of Congress.   Then appeared the President elect, followed by the venerable ex-president Monroe, with his family.   To these succeeded the Judges of the Supreme Court, in their robes of office, the members of the Senate, preceded by the Vice-President, with a number of the members of the House of Representatives.

Mr. Adams, in a plain suit of black, made entirely of American manufactures, ascended to the Speaker's chair, and took his seat.   The Chief Justice was placed in front of the Clerk's table, having before him another table on the floor of the hall, on the opposite side of which sat the remaining Judges, with their faces towards the chair.   The doors having been closed, and silence proclaimed, Mr. Adams arose, and, in a distinct and firm tone of voice, read his inaugural address.

At the conclusion of the address, a general plaudit burst forth from the vast assemblage, which continued some minutes.   Mr. Adams then descended from the chair, and, proceeding to the Judges' table, received from the Chief Justice a volume of the Laws of the United States, from which he read, with a loud voice, the oath of office.   The plaudits and cheers of the multitude were at this juncture repeated, accompanied by salutes of artillery from without.

The congratulations which then poured in from every side occupied the hands, and could not but reach the heart, of President Adams. The meeting between him and his venerated predecessor, had in it something peculiarly affecting. General Jackson was among the earliest of those who took the hand of the President; and their looks and deportment towards each other were a rebuke to that littleness of party spirit which can see no merit in a rival, and feel no joy in the honor of a competitor.

Shortly ofter 1 o'clock, the procession commenced leaving the hall. The President was escorted back as he came. On his arrival at his residence, he received the compliments and respects of a great number of ladies and gentlemen, who called on him to tender their congratulations. The proceedings of the day were closed by an "inaugural ball" in the evening. Among the guests present, were the President and Vice-President, Ex-President Monroe, a number of foreign ministers, with many civil, military, and naval officers.*

Mr. Adams's Inaugural Address is as follows:—

"In compliance with an usage coeval with the existence of our federal constitution, and sanctioned by the example of my predecessors in the career upon which I am about to enter, I appear, my

* National Intelligencer.

fellow-citizens, in your presence, and in that of heaven, to bind
myself, by the solemnities of a religious obligation, to the faithful
performance of the duties allotted to me, in the station to which I
have been called.

" In unfolding to my countrymen the principles by which I shall
be governed, in the fulfilment of those duties, my first resort will
be to that constitution which I shall swear, to the best of my ability, to preserve, protect, and defend. That revered instrument enu-
merates the powers and prescribes the duties of the Executive
Magistrate, and in its first words, declares the purposes to which
these, and the whole action of the Government instituted by it,
should be invariably and sacredly devoted—to form a more perfect
union, establish justice, ensure domestic tranquillity, provide for the
common defence, promote the general welfare, and secure the blessings of liberty to the people of this Union, in their successive
generations. Since the adoption of this social compact, one of
these generations has passed away. It is the work of our forefathers. Administered by some of the most eminent men, who
contributed to its formation, through a most eventful period in the
annals of the world, and through all the vicissitudes of peace and
war, incidental to the condition of associated man, it has not disappointed the hopes and aspirations of those illustrious benefactors of
their age and nation. It has promoted the lasting welfare of that
country so dear to us all; it has, to an extent far beyond the ordinary lot of humanity, secured the freedom and happiness of this
people. We now receive it as a precious inheritance from those to
whom we are indebted for its establishment, doubly bound by the
examples which they have left us, and by the blessings which we
have enjoyed, as the fruits of their labors, to transmit the same, unimpaired, to the succeeding generation.

" In the compass of thirty-six years, since this great national
covenant was instituted, a body of laws enacted under its authority, and in conformity with its provisions, has unfolded its powers,
and carried into practical operation its effective energies. Subordinate departments have distributed the executive functions in
their various relations to foreign affairs, to the revenue and expenditures, and to the military force of the Union, by land and
sea. A co-ordinate department of the judiciary has expounded
the constitution and the laws; settling, in harmonious coincidence

with the legislative will, numerous weighty questions of construction, which the imperfection of human language had rendered unavoidable. The year of jubilee since the first formation of our Union, has just elapsed; that of the Declaration of our Independence is at hand. The consummation of both was effected by this constitution. Since that period, a population of four millions has multiplied to twelve. A territory bounded by the Mississippi has been extended from sea to sea. New States have been admitted to the Union, in numbers nearly equal to those of the first confederation. Treaties of peace, amity, and commerce, have been concluded with the principal dominions of the earth. The people of other nations, inhabitants of regions acquired, not by conquests, but by compact, have been united with us in the participation of our rights and duties, of our burdens and blessings. The forest has fallen by the axe of our woodsmen—the soil has been made to teem by the tillage of our farmers; our commerce has whitened every ocean. The dominion of man over physical nature has been extended by the invention of our artists. Liberty and law have marched hand in hand. All the purposes of human association have been accomplished as effectually as under any other Government on the globe, and at a cost little exceeding, in a whole generation, the expenditures of other nations in a single year.

" Such is the unexaggerated picture of our condition under a constitution founded upon the republican principle of equal rights. To admit that this picture has its shades, is but to say, that it is still the condition of men upon earth. From evil—physical, moral, and political—it is not our claim to be exempt. We have suffered, sometimes by the visitation of Heaven through disease, often by the wrongs and injustice of other nations, even to the extremities of war; and lastly, by dissentions among ourselves—dissentions, perhaps, inseparable from the enjoyment of freedom, but which have more than once appeared to threaten the dissolution of the Union, and, with it, the overthrow of all the enjoyments of our present lot, and all our earthly hopes of the future. The causes of these dissensions have been various, founded upon differences of speculation in the theory of republican government, upon conflicting views of policy in our relations with foreign nations; upon jealousies of partial and sectional interests, aggravated by prejudices and prepossessions, which strangers to each other are ever apt to entertain.

"It is a source of gratification and of encouragement to me, to observe that the great result of this experiment upon the theory of human rights, has, at the close of that generation by which it was formed, been crowned with success equal to the most sanguine expectations of its founders. Union, justice, tranquillity, the common defence, the general welfare, and the blessings of liberty—all have been promoted by the Government under which we have lived. Standing at this point of time, looking back to that generation which has gone by, and forward to that which is advancing, we may at once indulge in grateful exultation and in cheering hope. From the experience of the past, we derive instructive lessons for the future.

"Of the two great political parties which have divided the opinions and feelings of our country, the candid and the just will now admit, that both have contributed splendid talents, spotless integrity, ardent patriotism, and disinterested sacrifices, to the formation and administration of the Government, and that both have required a liberal indulgence for a portion of human infirmity and error. The revolutionary wars of Europe, commencing precisely at the moment when the Government of the United States first went into operation under the constitution, excited collisions of sentiments and of sympathies, which kindled all the passions and embittered the conflict of parties, till the nation was involved in war, and the Union was shaken to its centre. This time of trial embraced a period of five-and-twenty years, during which the policy of the Union in its relations with Europe constituted the principal basis of our own political divisions, and the most arduous part of the action of the Federal Government. With the catastrophe in which the wars of the French Revolution terminated, and our own subsequent peace with Great Britain, this baneful weed of party strife was uprooted. From that time no difference of principle, connected with the theory of government, or with our intercourse with foreign nations, has existed or been called forth in force sufficient to sustain a continued combination of parties, or given more than wholesome animation to public sentiment or legislative debate. Our political creed, without a dissenting voice that can be heard, is, that the will of the people is the source, and the happiness of the people is the end, of all legitimate government upon earth: that the best security for the beneficence, and the best guaranty against the abuse of power, consists in the freedom, the purity, and the frequency of popular elections : that the General Government of the Union, and the separate Governments of the States, are all sovereignties of legitimate powers, fellow-servants of the same masters—uncontrolled within their respective spheres, uncontrollable by encroachments on each other. If there have been those who doubted whether a confederated representative democracy was a Government competent to the wise and orderly management of the common concerns of a mighty nation, those doubts have been dispelled. If there have been projects of partial confederacies to be erected upon the ruins of the Union, they have been scattered to the winds. If there have been dangerous attachments to one foreign nation, and antipathies against another, they have been extinguished. Ten years of peace at home and abroad have assuaged the animosities of political contention, and blended into harmony the most discordant elements of public opinion. There still remains one effort of magnanimity, one sacrifice of prejudice and passion, to be made by the individuals throughout the nation who have heretofore followed the standards of political party. It is that of discarding every remnant of rancor against each other, of embracing, as countrymen and friends, and of yielding to talents and virtue alone that confidence which, in times of contention for principle, was bestowed only upon those who bore the badge of party communion.

"The collisions of party spirit, which originate in speculative opinions, or in different views of administrative policy, are in their nature transitory. Those which are founded on geographical divisions, adverse interests of soil, climate, and modes of domestic life, are more permanent, and therefore, perhaps, more dangerous. It is this which gives inestimable value to the character of our Government, at once federal and national. It holds out to us a perpetual admonition to preserve, alike, and with equal anxiety, the rights of each individual State in its own Government, and the rights of the whole nation in that of the Union. Whatever is of domestic concernment, unconnected with the other members of the Union, or with foreign lands, belongs exclusively to the administration of the State Governments. Whatsoever directly involves the rights and interests of the federative fraternity, or of foreign powers, is, of the resort of this General Government. The duties of both are obvious in the general principle, though sometimes perplexed with

difficulties in the detail.   To respect the rights of the State Governments is the inviolable duty of that of the Union : the Government
of every State will feel its own obligation to respect and preserve
the rights of the whole.   The prejudices everywhere too commonly
entertained against distant strangers are worn away, and the jealousies of jarring interests are allayed, by the composition and functions of the great national councils, annually assembled, from all
quarters of the Union, at this place.   Here the distinguished men
from every section of our country, while meeting to deliberate upon
the great interests of those by whom they are deputed, learn to estimate the talents, and do justice to the virtues, of each other.   The
harmony of the nation is promoted, and the whole Union is knit
together by the sentiments of mutual respect, the habits of social
intercourse, and the ties of personal friendship, formed between the
representatives of its several parts in the performance of their service at this metropolis.

"Passing from this general review of the purposes and injunc-
tions of the Federal constitution and their results, as indicating
the first traces of the path of duty in the discharge of my public
trust, I turn to the administration of my immediate predecessor, as
the second.   It has passed away in a period of profound peace :
how much to the satisfaction of our country, and to the honor of
our country's name, is known to you all.   The great features of its
policy, in general concurrence with the will of the Legislature,
have been—To cherish peace while preparing for defensive war—
to yield exact justice to other nations, and maintain the rights of
our own—to cherish the principles of freedom and equal rights,
wherever they were proclaimed—to discharge, with all possible
promptitude, the national debt—to reduce within the narrowest limits of efficiency the military force—to improve the organization
and discipline of the army—to provide and sustain a school of military science—to extend equal protection to all the great interests of
the nation—to promote the civilization of the Indian tribes ; and—
to proceed to the great system of internal improvements, within the
limits of the constitutional power of the Union.   Under the pledge
of these promises, made by that eminent citizen at the time of his
first induction to this office, in his career of eight years the internal
taxes have been repealed ; sixty millions of the public debt have
been discharged ; provision has been made for the comfort and

relief of the aged and indigent among the surviving warriors of
the Revolution; the regular armed force has been reduced, and its
constitution revised and perfected; the accountability for the expenditures of public monies has been more effective; the Floridas have
been peaceably acquired, and our boundary has been extended to
the Pacific Ocean; the independence of the southern nations of this
hemisphere has been recognized, and recommended by example and
by counsel to the potentates of Europe; progress has been made
in the defence of the country, by fortifications and the increase of
the navy—towards the effectual suppression of the African traffic in
slaves—in alluring the aboriginal hunters of our land to the cultivation of the soil and of the mind—in exploring the interior regions
of the Union, and in preparing, by scientific researches and surveys,
for the further application of our national resources to the internal
improvement of our country.

" In this brief outline of the promise and performance of my immediate predecessor, the line of duty, for his successor, is clearly
delineated. To pursue to their consummation those purposes of
improvement in our common condition instituted or recommended
by him, will embrace the whole sphere of my obligation. To the
topic of internal improvement, emphatically urged by him at his inauguration, I recur with peculiar satisfaction. It is that from
which I am convinced that the unborn millions of our posterity, who
are in future ages to people this continent, will derive their most
fervent gratitude to the founders of the Union—that in which the
beneficent action of its Government will be most deeply felt and acknowledged. The magnificence and splendor of their public works
are among the imperishable glories of the ancient republics. The
roads and aqueducts of Rome have been the admiration of all after
ages, and have survived thousands of years after all her conquests
have been swallowed up in despotism, or become the spoil of bar-
barians. Some diversity of opinion has prevailed with regard to
the powers of Congress for legislation upon objects of this nature.
The most respectful deference is due to doubts, originating in pure
patriotism, and sustained by venerated authority. But nearly twenty
years have passed since the construction of the first national road
was commenced. The authority for its construction was then unquestioned. To how many thousands of our countrymen has it
proved a benefit? To what single individual has it ever proved an

injury ?   Repeated, liberal and candid discussions in the Legislature have conciliated the sentiments, and approximated the opinions of enlightened minds, upon the question of constitutional power.   I cannot but hope that, by the same process of friendly, patient, and persevering deliberation, all constitutional objections will ultimately be removed.   The extent and limitation of the powers of the General Government, in relation to this transcendently important interest, will be settled and acknowledged to the common satisfaction of all ; and every speculative scruple will be solved by a practical public blessing.

" Fellow-citizens, you are acquainted with the peculiar circumstances of the recent election, which have resulted in affording me the opportunity of addressing you at this time.   You have heard the exposition of the principles which will direct me in the fulfilment of the high and solemn trust imposed upon me in this station. Less possessed of your confidence, in advance, than any of my predecessors, I am deeply conscious of the prospect that I shall stand more and oftener in need of your indulgence.   Intentions upright and pure, a heart devoted to the welfare of our country, and the unceasing application of the faculties allotted to me to her service, are all the pledges that I can give for the faithful performance of the arduous duties I am to undertake.   To the guidance of the legislative councils ; to the assistance of the executive and subordinate departments ; to the friendly co-operation of the respective State Governments ; to the candid and liberal support of the people, so far as it may be deserved by honest industry and zeal ; I shall look for whatever success may attend my public service : and knowing that ' except the Lord keep the city, the watchman waketh but in vain,' with fervent supplications for His favor, to His overruling providence I commit, with humble but fearless confidence, my own fate, and the future destinies of my country."

In entering upon the discharge of his duties as President, Mr. Adams proceeded to form his cabinet by nominating Henry Clay, of Kentucky, Secretary of State ; Richard Rush, of Pennsylvania, Secretary of the Treasury ; James Barbour, of Virginia, Secretary of War ; Samuel L. Southard, Secretary of the Navy, and Wm. Wirt, Attorney General. These were all men of superior talents, of tried integrity and faithfulness, and well worthy the elevated positions to which they were called.

CHAPTER VIII.

The election of Mr. Adams to the presidency, was
a severe disappointment to the friends of Gen. Jackson. As the latter had received a majority of fifteen
electoral votes over Mr. Adams, it was confidently anticipated, nay, virtually demanded, that he should be
elected by the House of Representatives. This claim,
it was insisted, was in accordance with the will of the
people, as expressed in the electoral colleges, and to
resist it would be to violate the spirit of the constitution, and to set at nought the fundamental principles of
our republican Government. A sufficient reply to
these positions is found in the fact, that Gen. Jackson
did not receive a *majority* of the electoral votes, and
hence a majority of the people could not be considered
as desiring his election. The absolute truth, subsequently obtained on this point, was, that Mr. Adams
had received more of the primary votes of the people
than Gen. Jackson ; and thus, according to all repub-

lican principles, was entitled to be considered the first choice of the citizens of the United States.

The position of Mr. Clay, in this contest for the presidency, was one of great delicacy and difficulty. He was precisely in that critical posture, that, whatever course he might pursue, he would be subject to misrepresentation and censure, and could not but raise up a host of enemies. Originally one of the four candidates for the presidency, he failed, by five electoral votes, in having a sufficient number to be one of the three candidates returned to the House of Representatives, of which he was then Speaker. In this posture of affairs, it was evident that upon the course which should be pursued by Mr. Clay, and his friends in the House, depended the question who should be elected President. As Mr. Crawford, on account of the critical state of his health, was considered out of the question, Mr. Clay was left to choose between Mr. Adams and Gen. Jackson.

In this posture of affairs, Mr. Clay saw, that however patriotic the principles on which he acted, and however pure the motives by which he might be governed in making his selection, he must inevitably expose himself to the severest animadversions from the defeated party. But he did not hesitate, in the discharge of what he believed to be a solemn duty he owed his country, to throw his influence in behalf of the man whom he believed the best fitted to serve that country in the responsible office of the presidency. Long before it had been foreseen such a contingency would occur, he had expressed his want of confidence in the ability and fitness of Gen. Jackson for the executive chair. But in Mr. Adams he saw a man of the utmost purity and integrity of private character—a scholar of the ripest abilities—a statesman, a diplomatist, a patriot of unquestioned talents and of long experience,—one who had been entrusted with most important public interests by Washington, Adams, Jefferson, Madison and Monroe, and also had received from these illustrious men every mark of confidence—whose familiarity with the internal condition and foreign relations of the Union was unequalled by any public man ! Between men so dissimilar in their qualifications, how could Mr. Clay, with the slightest regard to the welfare of the nation, the claims of patriotism, or the dictates of his conscience, hesitate to choose ? He did not hesitate. With an intrepid determination to meet all consequences, he threw his influence in behalf of Mr. Adams, and secured his election.

This decisive step, as had been clearly foreseen, drew upon the head of Mr. Clay the severest censures of the supporters of Gen. Jackson. Motives of the deepest political corruption were attributed to him. They charged him with making a deliberate stipulation or "bargain" with Mr. Adams, to give his influence, on the understanding that he was to receive, in payment, the appointment to the state department. The undoubted object of this charge was to ruin Mr. Clay's future prospects, and make capital to the advantage of Gen. Jackson in the next presidential campaign. It implicated Mr. Adams equally with Mr. Clay. If the latter had been so corrupt as to offer his support on the promise of office, the former was quite as guilty in accepting of terms so venal. There never was a more base charge against American statesmen—there never was one more entirely destitute of foundation, or even shadow of proof! It was at no time considered entitled to the slightest particle of belief by those who were at Washington during these transactions and had an opportunity of knowing the true state of things at that time. But there were many, throughout the country, too ready to receive such reports in regard to public men. Both Mr. Adams and Mr. Clay were greatly prejudiced by this alleged collusion—a prejudice which years did not efface.

This charge first appeared in a tangible form shortly previous to the election by the House of Representatives, in an anonymous letter in the "Columbian Observer," at Philadelphia. It was soon ascertained to have been written by Mr. Kremer, a member of the House of Representatives from Pennsylvania. Mr. Clay immediately published a card in the National Intelligencer, denying, in unequivocal terms, the allegation, and pronouncing the author "an infamous calumniator, a dastard, and a liar!"

A few days after this, Mr. Kremer acknowledged himself the author of the letter in the "Columbian.

Observer," and professed himself ready to prove the corruptions alleged: whereupon Mr. Clay demanded that the House raise a committee to investigate the case. The committee was appointed; but Mr. Kremer, on grounds of the most frivolous description, refused to appear before the committee, or to furnish a particle of proof of the truth of the grave assertions he had uttered—thus virtually acknowledging their slanderous character.

Mr. Clay being in this manner denied the privilege of vindicating his innocence, and showing the depravity of his accusers, the matter continued in an unsettled state until the next presidential campaign, when it was revived in a more tangible form, and brought to bear adversely to Mr. Adams's·administration and re-election. In 1827, Gen. Jackson, in a letter to Mr. Carter Beverly, which soon appeared in public print, made the following statement:—

" Early in January, 1825, a member of Congress of high respectability visited me one morning, and observed that he had a communication he was desirous to make to me; that he was informed there was a great intrigue going on, and that it was right I should be informed of it. * * * * * * * He said he had been informed by the friends of Mr. Clay, that the friends of Mr. Adams had made overtures to them, saying, if Mr. Clay and his friends would unite in aid of Mr. Adams's election, Mr. Clay should be Secretary of State; that the friends of Mr. Adams were urging, as a reason to induce the friends of Mr. Clay to accede to their proposition, that if I were elected President, Mr. Adams would be continued Secretary of State; that the friends of Mr. Clay stated the West did not wish to separate from the West, and if I would say, or permit any of my confidential friends to say, that in case I were elected President

Mr. Adams should not be continued Secretary of State, by a complete union of Mr. Clay and his friends, they would put an end to the presidential contest in one hour. And he was of opinion it was right to fight such intriguers with their own weapons."

On a subsequent statement, Gen. Jackson asserted that the gentleman who called upon him with these propositions was James Buchanan, of Pennsylvania.

This was the Kremer charge made definite in circumstances and application ; and if well grounded, was susceptible of plain proof. On the appearance of this statement by Gen. Jackson, Mr. Clay came out with a positive denial. He said :—

" I neither made, nor authorized, nor knew of any proposition whatever, to either of the three candidates who were returned to the House of Representatives, at the last presidential election, or to the friends of either of them, for the purpose of influencing the result of the election, or for any other purpose. And all allegations, intimations, and inuendoes, that my vote on that occasion was offered to be given, or was in fact given, in consideration of any stipulation or understanding, express or implied, direct or indirect, written or verbal,—that I was, or that any other person was not, to be appointed Secretary of State ; or that I was, or in any other manner to be, personally benefitted,—are devoid of all truth, and destitute of any foundation whatever."

Here was a direct collision between Gen. Jackson and Mr. Clay. All now rested with Mr. Buchanan. His testimony would either prostrate Mr. Clay, or place him, in regard to this matter, beyond the reach of the foulest tongue of calumny. In due time Mr. Buchanan made his statement, in which he denied, in

unequivocal language, having made any such proposition to Gen. Jackson.   In his explanation he says :—

"I called upon General Jackson solely as his friend, upon my individual responsibility, and not as the agent of Mr. Clay, or any other
person. I never have been the political friend of Mr. Clay, since
he became a candidate for the office of President. Until I saw
General Jackson's letter to Mr. Beverly, of the 6th ult., and at the
same time was informed, by a letter from the editor of the United
States Telegraph, that I was the person to whom he alluded, the
conception never once entered my head, that he believed me to be
the agent of Mr. Clay, or of his friends, or that I had intended to
propose to him terms of any kind from them, or that he could have
supposed me to be capable of expressing the opinion that ' it was
right to fight such intriguers with their own weapons.'   Such a
supposition, had I entertained it, would have rendered me exceedingly unhappy, as there is no man on earth whose good opinion I
more valued than that of General Jackson. * * * * * * * * * I owe
it to my character to make another observation. Had I ever known,
or even suspected, that General Jackson believed I had been sent to
him by Mr. Clay or his friends, I should immediately have corrected
his erroneous impression, and thus prevented the necessity for this
most unpleasant explanation. * * * * * * * I had no authority from
Mr. Clay, or his friends, to propose any terms to General Jackson in
relation to their votes, nor did I ever make any such proposition."

This statement fully and triumphantly exonerated
Mr. Clay, Mr. Adams, and their friends, from the
charge of "bargain" and "corruption," which had
been so boldly made and widely disseminated.   The
only witness ever brought upon the stand to support such an allegation, asserted, in a manner the
most positive and decisive, the entire innocence of the
parties implicated.

That Mr. Clay, in throwing his influence in behalf

of Mr. Adams, was but following out a resolution formed long before he had any opportunity of communication with Mr. Adams or his friends, on the subject, is proved by the following extract of a letter from a gentleman in Lexington, Ky., to the editors of the National Intelligencer, dated March 21, 1825 :—

" At different times, before Mr. Clay left this place for Washington, last fall, I had conversations with him on the subject of the choice of a President by the House of Representatives. In all of them, he expressed himself as having long before decided in favor of Mr. Adams, in case the contest should lie between that gentleman and General Jackson. My last interview with him was, I think, the day before his departure, when he was still more explicit, as it was then certain that the election would be transferred to that tribunal, and highly probable that _he_ would not be among the number returned. In the course of this conversation, I took occasion to express my sentiments with respect to the delicate and difficult circumstances under which he would be placed. He remarked that I could not more fully apprehend them than he did himself ; but that nothing should deter him from the duty of giving his vote ; and that no state of things could arise that would justify him in preferring General Jackson to Mr. Adams, or induce him to support the former. So decisive, indeed, were his declarations on this subject, that had he voted otherwise than he did, I should have been compelled to regard him as deserving that species of censure which has been cast upon him for constantly adhering to an early and deliberate resolution."

It was thought, by some of Mr. Clay's friends, that he erred in judgment in accepting the office of Secretary of State, as it would tend to strengthen his enemies in their efforts to fix upon him the charge of corruption. Among those entertaining this opinion was Mr. Crawford, himself one of the three presidential candidates returned to the House of Representatives. In a letter to Mr. Clay he says :—

"I hope you know me too well to suppose that I have countenanced the charge of corruption which has been reiterated against you. The truth is, I approved of your vote when it was given, and should have voted as you did between Jackson and Adams. But candor compells me to say, that I disapproved of your accepting an office under him."

In replying to this letter Mr. Clay remarked :—

"I do, my dear sir, know you too well to suppose that you ever countenanced the charge of corruption against me. No man of sense and candor—at least none that know me—ever could or did countenance it. Your frank admission that you would have voted as I did, between Mr. Adams and Gen. Jackson, accords with the estimate I have ever made of your intelligence, your independence, and your patriotism. Nor am I at all surprised, or dissatisfied, with the expression of your opinion, that I erred in accepting the place which I now hold. * * * * * * * The truth is, as I have often said, my condition was one full of embarrassments, whatever way I might act. My own judgment was rather opposed to my acceptance of the department of state. But my friends—and let me add, two of your best friends, Mr. McLane of Delaware and Mr. Forsyth—urged me strongly not to decline it. It was represented by my friends, that I should get no credit for the forbearance, but that, on the contrary, it would be said that my forbearance was evidence of my having made a bargain, though unwilling to execute it. * * * * * * * * These and other similar arguments were pressed upon me ; and after a week's deliberation, I yielded to their force. It is quite possible that I may have erred * * * * * * I shall, at least, have no cause of self-reproach."

In 1829, after Mr. Adams had retired from the Presidential chair, in reply to a letter from a committee of gentlemen in New Jersey, who had addressed him, he spoke of Mr. Clay as follows: "Upon him the foulest slanders have been showered. Long known and appreciated, as successively a member of both Houses of your national Legislature, as the unrivalled Speaker, and at the same time most efficient leader of debates in one of them; as an able and successful negotiator of your interests, in war and peace, with foreign powers, and as a powerful candidate for the highest of your trusts, the department of state itself was a station which by its bestowal could confer neither profit nor honor upon him, but upon which he has shed unfading honor, by the manner in which he has discharged its duties. Prejudice and passion have charged him with obtaining that office by bargain and corruption. Before you, my fellow-citizens, in the presence of our country and heaven, I pronounce that charge totally unfounded. This tribute of justice is due from me to him, and I seize with pleasure the opportunity afforded me by your letter, of discharging the obligation. As to my motives for tendering to him the department of state when I did, let that man who questions them come forward; let him look around among statesmen and legislators, of this nation, and of that day; let him then select and name the man whom, by his pre-eminent talents, by his splendid services, by his ardent patriotism, by his all-embracing public spirit, by his fervid eloquence in behalf of the rights and liberties of mankind, and by his long experience in the affairs of the Union, foreign and domestic, a President of the United States, intent only upon the welfare and honor of his country, ought to have preferred to HENRY CLAY. Let him name the man, and then judge you, my fellow-citizens, of my motives."

When Mr. Adams was on a tour in the western States, in the fall of 1843, in addressing the chairman of the committee of his reception, at Maysville, Kentucky, he said: "I thank you, sir, for the opportunity you have given me of speaking of the great statesman who was associated with me in the administration of the General Government, at my earnest solicitation; who belongs not to Kentucky alone, but to the whole Union; and who is not only an honor to this State, and this nation, but to mankind. The charges to which you refer, after my term of service had expired, and it was proper for me to speak, I denied before the whole country. And I here reiterate and re-affirm that denial; and as I expect shortly to appear before my God, to answer for the conduct of my whole life, should these charges have found their way to the throne of eternal justice, I WILL in the presence of OMNIPOTENCE pronounce them FALSE."

Before the world Mr. Clay and Mr. Adams stand acquitted of the calumny which their enemies endeavored, with an industry worthy a better cause, to heap upon them. The history of their country will do them ample justice. Their names shall stand upon its pages, illuminated by a well-earned fame for patriotism and faithful devotion to public interests.

when those of their accusers will be lost in a merited oblivion.

Mr. Adams, having entered upon his duties as President of the United States, prosecuted them with all that diligence and industrious application which was one of the leading characteristics of his life. Unawed by the opposition and the misrepresentations of his political enemies, and uncorrupted by the power and influence at his control, he pursued the even tenor of his way, having a single object in view, the promotion of the welfare of the people over whom he had been called to preside.

In the meantime, the heart of the nation was being stirred by old and valued reminiscences. LA FAYETTE, —a hero of the revolution—the companion of Washington—whose blood had enriched American soil in defence of American, freedom—had expressed a wish to re-visit once more, before departing life, the scenes of his early struggles and well-earned glories. This intimation was first given in the following letter to Col. Willet, an old friend and fellow-soldier of La Fayette, who was then still living in New-York.

"*Paris, July* 15, 1822.

"MY DEAR SIR :—I avail myself of a good opportunity to remind you of your old friend and fellow-soldier, in whose heart no time nor distance can abate the patriotic remembrance and personal affections of our revolutionary times. We remain but too few survivors of that glorious epoch, in which the fate of two hemispheres has been decided. It is an additional monitor to think more of the ties of brotherly friendship which united us. May it be in my power, before I join our departed companions, to visit such of them as are still inhabitants of the United States, and to tell you personally, my dear Willet, how affectionately

"I am your sincere friend,   LA FAYETTE."

Intelligence of this desire to visit America having reached Congress, resolutions were passed placing a Government ship at his disposal :—

"Whereas that distinguished champion of freedom, and hero of our Revolution, the friend and associate of Washington, the Marquis de La Fayette, a volunteer General Officer in our Revolutionary War, has expressed an anxious desire to visit this country, the independence of which his valor, blood, and treasure, were so instrumental in achieving : Therefore—

"Be it Resolved, by the Senate and House of Representatives of the United States of America, in Congress assembled, That the President of the United States be requested to communicate to the Marquis de La Fayette the expression of those sentiments of profound respect, gratitude, and affectionate attachment, which are cherished towards him by the Government and people of this country; and to assure him that the execution of his wish and intention to visit this country, will be hailed by the people and Government with patriotic pride and joy.

"And be it further Resolved, That the President of the United States be requested to ascertain from the Marquis de La Fayette, the time when it will be most agreeable for him to perform his visit; and that he offer to the Marquis a conveyance to this country in one of our national ships."

La Fayette modestly declined this offer of a public ship. He sailed from Havre in the packet-ship Cadmus, accompanied by his son, George Washington La Fayette, and arrived in New York on the 15th of August, 1824.

His reception at New York was sublime and brilliant
in the extreme. The meeting between La Fayette,
Col. Willet, Gen. Van Cortland, Gen. Clarkson, and
other revolutionary worthies, was highly affecting.
He knew them all. After the ceremony of embracing
and congratulations were over, La Fayette sat down
by the side of Col. Willet. "Do you remember," said
the colonel, "at the battle of Monmouth, I was a volunteer aid to Gen. Scott? I saw you in the heat of battle, you were but a boy, but you were a serious and
sedate lad." "Aye, aye," returned La Fayette, "I remember well. And on the Mohawk I sent you fifty
Indians, and you wrote me that they set up such a yell
that they frightened the British horse, and they ran one
way, and the Indians another." Thus these veteran
soldiers "fought their battles o'er again."

From New York La Fayette proceeded on a tour
throughout the United States. Everywhere he was
received and honored, as "THE NATION'S GUEST." For
more than a year, his journey was a complete ovation
—a perpetual and splendid pageant. The people appeared delirious with joy and with anxiety to hail him,
grasp him by the hand, and shower attentions and
honors upon him. The gratitude and love of all persons, of every age, sex, and condition, seemed hardly to
be restrained within bounds of propriety. As he passed
through the country, every city, village, and hamlet,
poured out its inhabitants *en masse*, to meet him.
Celebrations, processions, dinners, illuminations, bon-

fires, parties, balls, serenades, and rejoicings of every description, attended his way, from the moment he set foot on the American soil, until his embarkation to return to his native France.

The hearts of the people in the most distant parts of the Western Hemisphere were warmed and touched with the honors paid him in the United States. A letter written at that time from Buenos Ayres, says— "I have just received newspapers from the United States, informing me of the magnificent reception of Gen. La Fayette. I have never read newspapers with such exquisite delight as these; and I firmly believe there never was so interesting and glorious an event in the civilized world, in which all classes of people participated in the general joy, as on this occasion. There is an association of ideas connected with this event, that produces in my soul emotions I cannot express, and fills my heart with such grateful recollections as I cannot forget but with my existence. That ten millions of souls, actuated by pure sentiments of gratitude and friendship, should with one voice pronounce this individual the 'Guest of the Nation,' and pay him the highest honors the citizens of a free nation can offer, is an event which must excite the astonishment of Europe, and show the inestimable value of liberty."

In June, 1825, La Fayette visited Boston, and on the 17th day of that month, it being the anniversary of the battle of Bunker Hill, he participated in the ceremony of laying the corner stone of the monument in commemoration of that event, on Bunker Hill. During his tour at the east, he visited the venerable ex-President John Adams, at Quincy.

But the time for his departure drew near. His journey had extended as far south as New Orleans, west to St. Louis, north and east to Massachusetts. He had passed through, or touched, New York, New Jersey, Pennsylvania, Delaware, Maryland, Virginia, North and South Carolina, Georgia, Alabama, Louisiana, Mississippi, Missouri, Tennessee, Kentucky, Illinois, Indiana, Ohio, Connecticut, Rhode Island, and Massachusetts.

A new frigate, the Brandywine, named in honor of the gallant exploits of Gen. La Fayette at the battle of Brandywine, was provided by Congress to convey him to France. It was deemed appropriate that he should take final leave of the nation at the seat of government in Washington. President Adams invited him to pass a few weeks in the presidential mansion. Mr. Adams had been on intimate terms with La Fayette in his youth, with whom, it is said, he was a marked favorite. During his sojourn at the capitol, he visited ex-Presidents Jefferson, Madison, and Monroe, at their several places of residence.

Having paid his respects to these venerated sages, " the Nation's Guest" prepared to take his final departure from the midst of a grateful people. The 7th of September, 1825, was the day appointed for taking leave. About 12 o'clock, the officers of the General

Government, civil, military, and naval, together with
the authorities of Washington, Georgetown, and Alexandria, with multitudes of citizens and strangers,
assembled in the President's house. La Fayette entered the great hall in silence, leaning on the Marshal
of the District, and one of the sons of the President.
Mr. Adams then with evident emotion, but with much
dignity and firmness, addressed him in the following
terms :—

" GENERAL LA FAYETTE : It has been the good fortune of many
of my fellow-citizens, during the course of the year now elapsed,
upon your arrival at their respective places of abode to greet you
with the welcome of the nation. The less pleasing task now devolves upon me, of bidding you, in the name of the nation, ADIEU !

" It were no longer seasonable, and would be superfluous, to re-
capitulate the remarkable incidents of your early life—incidents
which associated your name, fortunes, and reputation, in imperishable connection with the independence and history of the North
American Union.

" The part which you performed at that important juncture was
marked with characters so peculiar, that, realizing the fairest fable of
antiquity, its parallel could scarcely be found in the authentic records
of human history.

" You deliberately and perseveringly preferred toil, danger, the
endurance of every hardship, and privation of every comfort, in defence of a holy cause, to inglorious ease, and the allurements of
rank, affluence, and unrestrained youth, at the most splendid and
fascinating court of Europe.

" That this choice was not less wise than magnanimous, the sanction of half a century, and the gratulations of unnumbered voices,
all unable to express the gratitude of the heart, with which your
visit to this hemisphere has been welcomed, afford ample demonstration.

" When the contest of freedom, to which you had repaired as a
voluntary champion, had closed, by the complete triumph of her

cause in this country of your adoption, you returned to fulfil the duties of the philanthropist and patriot, in the land of your nativity. There, in a consistent and undeviating career of forty years, you have maintained, through every vicissitude of alternate success and disappointment, the same glorious cause to which the first years of your active life had been devoted, the improvement of the moral and political condition of man.

"Throughout that long succession of time, the people of the United States, for whom and with whom you have fought the battles of liberty, have been living in the full possession of its fruits; one of the happiest among the family of nations. Spreading in population; enlarging in territory; acting and suffering according to the condition of their nature; and laying the foundations of the greatest, and, we humbly hope, the most beneficient power, that ever regulated the concerns of man upon earth.

"In that lapse of forty years, the generation of men with whom you co-operated in the conflict of arms, has nearly passed away. Of the general officers of the American army in that war, you alone survive. Of the sages who guided our councils; of the warriors who met the foe in the field, or upon the wave, with the exception of a few to whom unusual length of days has been allotted by Heaven, all now sleep with their fathers. A succeeding, and even a third generation, have arisen to take their places; and their children's children, while rising up to call them blessed, have been taught by them, as well as admonished by their own constant enjoyment of freedom, to include in every benison upon their fathers, the name of him, who came from afar, with them and in their cause to conquer or to fall.

"The universal prevalence of these sentiments was signally manifested by a resolution of Congress, representing the whole people, and all the States of this Union, requesting the President of the United States to communicate to you the assurances of the grateful and affectionate attachment of this government and people, and desiring that a national ship might be employed, at your convenience, for your passage to the borders of our country.

"The invitation was transmitted to you by my venerable predecessor, himself bound to you by the strongest ties of personal friendship; himself one of those whom the highest honors of his country had rewarded for blood early shed in her cause, and for a long life of devotion to her welfare. By him the services of a national ship were placed at your disposal. Your delicacy preferred a more private conveyance, and a full year has elapsed since you landed upon our shores. It were scarcely an exaggeration to say that it has been to the people of the Union a year of uninterrupted festivity and enjoyment, inspired by your presence. You have traversed the twenty-four States of this great confederacy—you have been received with rapture by the survivors of your earliest companions in arms—you have been hailed, as a long-absent parent, by their children, the men and women of the present age; and a rising generation, the hope of future time, in numbers surpassing the whole population of that day when you fought at the head and by the side of their forefathers, have vied with the scanty remnants of that hour of trial, in acclamations of joy, at beholding the face of him whom they feel to be the common benefactor of all. You have heard the mingled voices of the past, the present, and the future age, joining in one universal chorus of delight at your approach; and the shouts of unbidden thousands, which greeted your landing on the soil of freedom, have followed every step of your way, and still resound like the rushing of many waters, from every corner of our land.

"You are now about to return to the country of your birth—of your ancestors—of your posterity. The executive Government of the Union, stimulated by the same feeling which had prompted the Congress to the designation of a national ship for your accommodation in coming hither, has destined the first service of a frigate, recently launched at this metropolis, to the less welcome, but equally distinguished trust, of conveying you home. The name of the ship has added one more memorial to distant regions and to future ages, of a stream already memorable at once in the story of your sufferings and of our independence.

"The ship is now prepared for your reception, and equipped for sea. From the moment of her departure, the prayers of millions will ascend to heaven, that her passage may be prosperous, and your return to the bosom of your family as propitious to your happiness as your visit to this scene of your youthful glory has been to that of the American people.

"Go then, our beloved friend: return to the land of brilliant genius, of generous sentiments, of heroic valor; to that beautiful France, the nursing mother of the twelfth Louis, and the fourth

Henry; to the native soil of Bayard and Coligne, of Turenne and Catinat, of Fenelon and D'Aguesseau! In that illustrious catalogue of names, which she claims as of her children, and with honest pride holds up to the admiration of other nations, the name of LA FAYETTE has already for centuries been enrolled. And it shall henceforth burnish into brighter fame: for, if in after days, a Frenchman shall be called to indicate the character of his nation by that of one individual, during the age in which we live, the blood of lofty patriotism shall mantle in his cheek, the fire of conscious virtue shall sparkle in his eye, and he shall pronounce the name of LA FAYETTE. Yet we, too, and our children in life, and after death, shall claim you for our own. You are ours, by that more than patriotic self-devotion with which you flew to the aid of our fathers at the crisis of their fate: ours by that long series of years in which you have cherished us in your regard: ours by that unshaken sentiment of gratitude for your services, which is a precious portion of our inheritance: ours by that tie of love, stronger then death, which has linked your name, for the endless ages of time, with the name of WASHINGTON.

"At the painful moment of parting from you, we take comfort in the thought, that wherever you may be, to the last pulsation of your heart, our country will ever be present to your affections; and a cheering consolation assures us that we are not called to sorrow, most of all, that we shall see your face no more. We shall indulge the pleasing anticipation of beholding our friend again. In the mean time, speaking in the name of the whole people of the United States, and at a loss only for language to give utterance to that feeling of attachment with which the heart of the nation beats, as beats the heart of one man—I bid you a reluctant and affectionate FAREWELL!!

At the conclusion of this address, Gen. La Fayette replied as follows:—

"Amidst all my obligations to the General Government, and particularly to you, sir, its respected Chief Magistrate, I have most thankfully to acknowledge the opportunity given me, at this solemn and painful moment, to present the people of the United States with a parting tribute of profound, inexpressible gratitude.

" To have been in the infant and critical days of these States adopted by them as a favorite son; to have participated in the trials and perils of our unspotted struggle for independence, freedom, and equal rights, and in the foundation of the American era of a new social order, which has already pervaded this, and must, for the dignity and happiness of mankind, successively pervade every part of the other hemisphere; to have received, at every stage of the revolution, and during forty years after that period, from the people of the United States and their Representatives at home and abroad, continual marks of their confidence and kindness,—has been the pride, the encouragement, the support of a long and eventful life.

" But how could I find words to acknowledge that series of welcomes, those unbounded and universal displays of public affection, which have marked each step, each hour, of a twelvemonth's progress through the twenty-four States, and which, while they overwhelm my heart with grateful delight, have most satisfactorily evinced the concurrence of the people in the kind testimonies, in the immense favors bestowed on me by the several branches of their Representatives, in every part and at the central seat of the confederacy?

" Yet gratifications still higher awaited me.   In the wonders of creation and improvement that have met my enchanted eye, in the unparalleled and self-felt happiness of the people, in their rapid prosperity and insured security, public and private, in a practice of good order, the appendage of true freedom, and a national good sense, the final arbiter of all difficulties, I have had proudly to recognize a result of the republican principles for which we have fought, and a glorious demonstration to the most timid and prejudiced minds, of the superiority, over degrading aristocracy or despotism, of popular institutions, founded on the plain rights of man, and where the local rights of every section are preserved under a constitutional bond of union.   The cherishing of that union between the States, as it has been the farewell entreaty of our great paternal Washington, and will ever have the dying prayer of every American patriot, so it has become the sacred pledge of the emancipation of the world; an object in which I am happy to observe that the American people, while they give the animating example of successful free institutions, in return for an evil entailed upon them by

Europe, and of which a liberal and enlightened sense is every-where more and more generally felt, show themselves every day more anxiously interested.

" And now, sir, how can I do justice to my deep and lively feel-ings for the assurances, most peculiarly valued, of your esteem and friendship; for your so very kind references to old times—to my beloved associates—to the vicissitudes of my life ; for your affecting picture of the blessings poured, by the several generations of the American people, on the remaining days of a delighted veteran ; for your affectionate remarks on this sad hour of separation—on the country of my birth, full, I can say, of American sympathies—on the hope, so necessary to me, of my seeing again the country that has deigned, near a half a century ago, to call me hers ? I shall content myself, refraining from superfluous repetitions, at once, be-fore you, sir, and this respected circle, to proclaim my cordial con-firmation of every one of the sentiments which I have had daily opportunities publicly to utter, from the time when your venerable predecessor, my old brother in arms and friend, transmitted to me the honorable invitation of Congress, to this day, when you, my dear sir, whose friendly connection with me dates from your earliest youth, are going to consign me to the protection, across the Atlan-tic, of the heroic national flag, on board the splendid ship, the name of which has been not the least flattering and kind among the num-berless favors conferred upon me.

" God bless you, sir, and all who surround us. God bless the American people, each of their States, and the Federal Government. Accept this patriotic farewell of an overflowing heart. Such will be its last throb when it ceases to beat."

As the last sentence of the farewell was pronounced, La Fayette advanced and took President Adams in his arms, while tears poured down his venerable cheeks. Retiring a few paces, he was overcome by his feelings, and again returned, and falling on the neck of Mr. Adams, exclaimed in broken accents, " God bless you !" It was a scene at once solemn and moving, as the

sighs and tears of many who witnessed it bore testimony.   Having recovered his self-possession, the General stretched out his hands, and was in a moment
surrounded by the greetings of the whole assembly,
who pressed upon him, each eager to seize, perhaps
for the last time, that beloved hand which was opened
so freely for our aid when aid was so precious, and
which grasped with firm and undeviating hold the
steel which so bravely helped to achieve our deliverance.   The expression which now beamed from the
face of this exalted man was of the finest and most
touching kind.   The hero was lost in the father and
the friend.   Dignity melted into subdued affection,
and the friend of Washington seemed to linger with
a mournful delight among the sons of his adopted
country.

A considerable period was then occupied in con-
versing with various individuals, while refreshments
were presented to the company.   The moment of
departure at length arrived; and having once more
pressed the hand of Mr. Adams, he entered the ba-
rouche, accompanied by the Secretaries of State, of
the Treasury, and of the Navy, and passed from the
capital of the Union.   An immense procession accompanied him to the banks of the Potomac, where the
steamboat Mount Vernon awaited to convey him down
the river to the frigate Brandywine.   The whole scene
—the peals of artillery, the sounds of numerous military
bands, the presence of the vast concourse of people,

and the occasion that assembled them, produced emotions not easily described, but which every American heart can readily conceive. As the steamboat moved off, the deepest silence was observed by the whole multitude that lined the shore. The feelings that pervaded them was that of children bidding farewell to a venerated parent.

When the boat came opposite the tomb of Washington, at Mount Vernon, it paused in its progress. La Fayette arose. The wonders which he had performed, for a man of his age, in successfully accomplishing labors enough to have tested his meridian vigor, whose animation rather resembled the spring than the winter of life, now seemed unequal to the task he was about to perform—to take a last look at " The tomb of Washington !" He advanced to the effort. A silence the most impressive reigned around, till the strains of sweet and plaintive music completed the grandeur and sacred solemnity of the scene. All hearts beat in unison with the throbbings of the veteran's bosom, as he looked, *for the last time,* on the sepulchre which contained the ashes of the first of men! He spoke not, but appeared absorbed in the mighty recollections which the place and the occasion inspired.

After this scene, the boat resumed its course, and the next morning anchored in safety near the Brandywine. Here La Fayette took leave of the Secretaries of State, the Treasury, and the Navy, and the guests who had accompanied him from Washington, together with many military and naval officers and eminent citizens who had assembled in various crafts near the frigate to bid him farewell. The weather had been boisterous and rainy, but just as the affecting scene had closed, the sun burst forth to cheer a spectacle which will long be remembered, and formed a magnificent arch, reaching from shore to shore—the barque which was to bear the venerable chief being immediately in the centre. Propitious omen! Heaven smiles on the good deeds of men! And if ever there was a sublime and virtuous action to be blessed by heaven and admired by men, it is when a free and grateful people unite to do honor to their friend and benefactor !*

* National Intelligencer.

CHAPTER IX.

THE patriarchs John Adams and Thomas Jefferson still lingered on the shores of time. The former had attained the good old age of 90 years, and the latter 82. Mrs. Adams, the venerable companion of the ex-President, died in Quincy, on the 28th of Oct., 1818, aged 74 years. Although, amid the various political strifes through which they had passed during the half century they had taken prominent parts in the affairs of their country, Adams and Jefferson had frequently been arrayed in opposite parties, and cherished many views quite dissimilar, yet their private friendship and deep attachment had been unbroken. It continued to be cherished with generous warmth to the end of their days. This pleasing fact, together with the wonderful vigor of their minds in extreme old age, is proved by the following interesting correspondence between them, which took place four years before their decease :—

MR. JEFFERSON TO MR. ADAMS.

"*Monticello, June* 1, 1822.

"It is very long, my dear sir, since I have written to you. My dislocated wrist is now become so stiff, that I write slowly, and with pain; and therefore write as little as I can. Yet it is due to mutual friendship, to ask once in a while how we do? The papers tell us that General Starke is off, at the age of ninety-three. ***** still lives at about the same age, cheerful, slender as a grasshopper, and so much without memory, that he scarcely recognizes the members of his household. An intimate friend of his called on him, not long since. It was difficult to make him recollect who he was, and sitting one hour, he told him the same story four times over. Is this life?—with laboring step

> 'To tread our former footsteps? pace the round
> Eternal?—to beat and beat
> The beaten track—to see what we have seen—
> To taste the tasted—o'er our palates to decant
> Another vintage?'

"It is, at most, but the life of a cabbage, surely not worth a wish. When all our faculties have left, or are leaving us, one by one, sight, hearing, memory, every avenue of pleasing sensation is closed, and athumy, debility, and mal-aise left in their places, when the friends of our youth are all gone, and a generation is risen around us whom we know not, is death an evil?

> 'When one by one our ties are torn,
> And friend from friend is snatch'd forlorn;
> When man is left alone to mourn,
>   Oh, then, how sweet it is to die!

> 'When trembling limbs refuse their weight,
> And films slow gathering dim the sight;
> When clouds obscure the mental light,
> 'Tis nature's kindest boon to die!'

"I really think so. I have ever dreaded a doting old age; and my health has been generally so good, and is now so good, that I dread it still. The rapid decline of my strength during the last winter, has made me hope sometimes, that I see land. During summer, I enjoy its temperature, but I shudder at the approach of winter, and wish I could sleep through it, with the dormouse, and only wake with him in spring, if ever. They say that Starke could walk about his room. I am told you walk well and firmly. I can only reach my garden, and that with sensible fatigue. I ride, however, daily; but reading is my delight. I should wish never to put pen to paper; and the more because of the treacherous practice some people have, of publishing one's letters without leave. Lord Mansfield declared it a breach of trust, and punishable at law. I think it should be a penitentiary felony; yet you will have seen that they have drawn me out into the arena of the newspapers. Although I know it is too late for me to buckle on the armor of youth, yet my indignation would not permit me passively to receive the kick of an ass.

" To return to the news of the day, it seems that the cannibals of Europe are going to eat one another again. A war between Russia and Turkey is like the battle of the kite and snake; whichever destroys the other, leaves a destroyer the less for the world. This pugnacious humor of mankind seems to be the law of his nature; one of the obstacles to too great multiplication, provided in the mechanism of the universe. The cocks of the hen-yard kill one another; bears, bulls, rams, do the same, and the horse in his wild state kills all the young males, until, worn down with age and war, some vigorous youth kills him. * * * * * * I hope we shall prove how much happier for man the Quaker policy is, and that the life of the *feeder* is better than that of the *fighter*. And it is some consolation that the desolation by these maniacs of one part of the earth is the means of improving it in other parts. Let the latter be our office; and let us milk the cow while the Russian holds her by the horns, and the Turk by the tail. God bless you, and give you health, strength, good spirits, and as much of life as you think worth having. THOMAS JEFFERSON."

MR. ADAMS' REPLY.

" *Quincy, June* 11, 1822.

" DEAR SIR :—Half an hour ago I received, and this moment have heard read, for the third or fourth time, the best letter that ever was written by an octogenarian, dated June 1st.

* * * * * * * * * *

" I have not sprained my wrist; but both my arms and hands are so overstrained that I cannot write a line. Poor Starke remembered nothing, and could talk of nothing but the battle of Bennington ! ******** is not quite so reduced. I cannot mount my horse, but I can walk three miles over a rugged, rocky mountain, and have done it within a month ; yet I feel, when sitting in my chair, as if I could not rise out of it ; and when risen, as if I could not walk across the room. My sight is very dim, hearing pretty good, memory poor enough.

"I answer your question,—Is death an evil ? It is not an evil. It is a blessing to the individual and to the world ; yet we ought not to wish for it, till life becomes insupportable. We must wait the pleasure and convenience of the ' Great Teacher.' Winter is as terrible to me as to you. I am almost reduced in it to the life of a bear or a torpid swallow. I cannot read, but my delight is to hear others read ; and I tax all my friends most unmercifully and tyrannically against their consent.

" The ass has kicked in vain ; all men say the dull animal has missed the mark.

" This globe is a theatre of war ; its inhabitants are all heroes. The little eels in vinegar, and the animalcules in pepper-water, I believe, are quarrelsome. The bees are as warlike as the Romans, Russians, Britons, or Frenchmen. Ants, caterpillars, and cankerworms are the only tribes among whom I have not seen battles ; and Heaven itself, if we believe Hindoos, Jews, Christians, and Mahometans, has not always been at peace. We need not trouble ourselves about these things, nor fret ourselves because of evil doers ; but safely trust the ' Ruler with his skies.' Nor need we dread the approach of dotage ; let it come if it must. ******, it seems, still delights in his four stories ; and Starke remembered to the last his Bennington, and exulted in his glory ; the worst of the evil is, that our friends will suffer more by our imbecility than we ourselves.

*   *   *   *   *   *   *   *   *

" In wishing for your health and happiness, I am very selfish ; for I hope for more letters. This is worth more than five hundred dollars to me ; for it has already given me, and will continue to give me, more pleasure than a thousand. Mr. Jay, who is about your age, I am told, experiences more decay than you do.

"I am your old friend,

"JOHN ADAMS."

This correspondence excited attention in Europe. The editor of the London Morning Chronicle prefaces it with the following remarks :—

" What a contrast the following correspondence of the two rival Presidents of the greatest Republic of the world, reflecting an old age dedicated to virtue, temperance, and philosophy, presents to the heart-sickening details, occasionally disclosed to us, of the miserable beings who fill the thrones of the continent. There is not, perhaps, one sovereign of the continent, who in any sense of the word can be said to honor our nature, while many make us almost ashamed of it. The curtain is seldom drawn aside without exhibiting to us beings worn out with vicious indulgence, diseased in mind, if not in body, the creatures of caprice and insensibility. On the other hand, since the foundation of the American Republic, the chair has never been filled by a man, for whose life (to say the least,) any American need once to blush. It must, therefore, be some compensation to the Americans for the absence of pure monarchy, that when they look upwards their eyes are not always met by vice, and meannesss, and often idiocy."

John Adams joined his fellow-citizens of Quincy, Mass., in celebrating the 4th of July, 1823, at the age of 88 years. Being called upon for a toast, he gave the following :—

" The excellent President, Governor, Ambassador, and Chief Justice, JOHN JAY, whose name, by accident, was not subscribed on the DECLARATION OF INDEPENDENCE, as it ought to have been, for he was one of its ablest and faithfullest supporters.—A splendid star just setting below the horizon."

It would be difficult (said the Boston Patriot,) fully to describe the delicate manner in which this toast was received and noticed by the company. Instead of loud acclamations, which succeeded the other toasts,

it was followed by soft and interrupted interjections
and aspirations, as if each individual was casting up an
ejaculatory prayer, that the two illustrious sages might
pass the remainder of their days in tranquillity and ease,
and finally be landed on the blissful shores of a happy
eternity.

In September, 1825, President Adams, with his family, left Washington, on a visit to his venerable father,
at Quincy. He travelled without ostentation, and especially requested that no public display might be manifested. At Philadelphia, Mrs. Adams was taken ill, and
the President was compelled to proceed without her.
This visit was of short duration. Called back to
Washington by public affairs, he left Quincy on the
14th of October. It was his last interview on earth
with his venerated parent. The aged patriarch had
lived to see his country emancipated from foreign thraldom, its independence acknowledged, its union consummated, its prosperity and perpetuity resting on an
immovable foundation, and his son elevated to the
highest office in its gift. It was enough! His work
accomplished—the book of his eventful life written and
sealed for immortality—he was ready to depart and be
at peace.

The 4th of July, 1826, will long be memorable for
one of the most remarkable coincidences that has
ever taken place in the history of nations. It was the
fiftieth anniversary—the "JUBILEE"—of American independence! Preparations had been made throughout

the Union, to celebrate the day with unusual pomp and display. John Adams and Thomas Jefferson had both been invited to participate in the festivities of the occasion, at their several places of abode. But a higher summons awaited them! they were bidden to a "jubilee" above, which shall have no end! On that half-century anniversary of American Independence, at nearly the same hour of the day, the spirits of Adams and Jefferson took their departure from earth!! Amid the rejoicings of the people, the peals of artillery, the strains of music, the exultations of a great nation in the enjoyment of freedom, peace, and happiness, they were released from the toils of life, and allowed to enter on their rest.

The one virtually the mover, the other the framer, of the immortal Declaration of Independence—they had together shared the dangers and the honors of the revolution—had served their country in various important and responsible capacities—had both received the highest honors in the gift of their fellow-citizens—had lived to see the nation to which they assisted in giving birth assume a proud stand among the nations of the earth—her free institutions framed, consolidated, tried, and matured—her commerce hovering over all seas—respected abroad, united, prosperous, happy at home—what more had earth in store for them? Together they had counselled—together they had dared the power of a proud and powerful Government—together they had toiled to build up a great and prosperous people—together they rejoiced in the success with which a wise and good Providence had crowned their labors —and together, on their country's natal day, amid the loud-swelling acclamations of the "national jubilee," their freed spirits soared to light and glory above!

The venerable ex-President Adams had been failing for several days before the 4th of July. In reply to an invitation from a committee of the citizens of Quincy, to unite with them in celebrating the fiftieth anniversary of American independence, he had written a note, from which the following is an extract :—

" The present feeble state of my health will not permit me to indulge the hope of participating with more than my best wishes, in the joys, and festivities, and the solemn services of that day on which will be completed the fiftieth year from its birth, of the independence of the United States : a memorable epoch in the annals of the human race, destined in future history to form the *brightest* or the *blackest* page, according to the use or the abuse of those political institutions by which they shall, in time to come, be shaped by the human mind."

Being solicited for a toast, to accompany the letter, he gave—" INDEPENDENCE FOREVER !!" He was asked if anything should be added to it. Immediately he replied—"*Not a word !*" This toast was drank at the celebration in Quincy, about fifty minutes before the departure of the venerated statesman from earth.

On the morning of the 4th, which was ushered in by the ringing of bells and firing of cannon, he was asked if he knew what day it was ?—" O yes," he replied, " it is the glorious fourth of July—God bless it !—

God bless you all!!" In the course of the day he said, "It is a great and glorious day." The last words he uttered were, "Jefferson survives!" But the spirit of Jefferson had already left the body, and was hovering over the earth, to accompany his to higher and brighter scenes of existence!!

Mr. Jefferson had been sensible for some days, that his last hour was at hand. He conversed with his family and friends, with the utmost composure, of his departure, and gave directions concerning his coffin and his funeral. He was desirous that the latter should take place at Monticello, and that it should be without any display or parade. On Monday he inquired the day of the month? Being told it was the 3d of July, he expressed an earnest desire that he might be allowed to behold the light of the next day— the fiftieth anniversary of American independence. His prayer was heard and answered. He beheld the rising of that sun on the morning of the 4th, which was to set on a nation mourning the loss of two of its noblest benefactors, and its brightest ornaments. He was cheerful to the last. A day or two previous, being in great pain, he said to his physician—"Well, doctor, a few hours more, and the struggle will be over."

On the morning of the last day, as the physician entered his apartment, he said, "You see, doctor, I am here yet." On a member of his family expressing an opinion that he was better, he replied, with evident impatience—"Do not imagine for a moment that I feel the smallest solicitude as to the result." Some individual present uttering a hope that he might recover, he asked with a smile—"Do you think I fear to die?" Thus departed Thomas Jefferson. His last words were—" I resign my soul to my God, and my daughter to my country !"

President J. Q. Adams receiving intelligence at Washington of the illness of his father, started immediately for Quincy. Shortly before arriving at Baltimore, tidings reached him that the patriarch had gone to his rest. Mr. Adams pursued his journey, but did not arrive at Quincy in season to be present at the funeral. This took place on the 7th of July. It was attended by a large body of citizens, assembled from the surrounding region. The funeral services took place at the Unitarian church in Quincy, on which occasion an impressive discourse was delivered by the Pastor, Rev. Mr. Whitney. The pall-bearers were Judge Davis, President Kirkland, Gov. Lincoln, Hon. Mr. Greenleaf, Judge Story, and Lieut. Gov. Winthrop. During the exercises and the moving of the procession, minute guns were fired from Mount Wallaston, and from various eminences in the adjoining towns, and every mark of respect was paid to the remains of one who filled so high a place in the history of his country and the regard of his fellow-citizens.

On the 2d of August, Mr. Webster delivered a eulogy on the death of Adams and Jefferson, before

the city authorities of Boston, and a vast body of
people, in Faneuil Hall.   President Adams was present.   It was one of Mr. Webster's most eloquent and
successful attempts.   He commenced as follows :—

"This is an unaccustomed spectacle. For the first time, fellow-
citizens, badges of mourning shroud the columns and overhang the
arches of this hall.   These walls, which were consecrated, so long
ago, to the cause of American liberty, which witnessed her infant
struggles and rung with the shouts of her earliest victories, proclaim
now, that distinguished friends and champions of that great cause
have fallen.   It is right that it should be thus.   The tears which
flow, and the honors that are paid, when the Founders of the Republic die, give hope that the Republic itself may be immortal.   It is
fit, that by public assembly and solemn observance, by anthem and
by eulogy, we commemorate the services of national benefactors, ex-
tol their virtues, and render thanks to God for eminent blessings,
early given and long continued to our favored country.

"ADAMS and JEFFERSON are no more ; and we are assembled,
fellow-citizens, the aged, the middle-aged and the young, by the
spontaneous impulse of all, under the authority of the municipal
government, with the presence of the chief magistrate of the commonwealth, and others of its official representatives, the university,
and the learned societies, to bear our part in these manifestations of
respect and gratitude, which universally pervade the land.   ADAMS
and JEFFERSON are no more.   On our fiftieth anniversary, the great
national jubilee, in the very hour of public rejoicing, in the midst of
echoing and re-echoing voices of thanksgiving, while their own
names were on all tongues, they took their flight together to the
world of spirits."

The conclusion of Mr. Webster's eulogy was equally
impressive :

"Fellow-citizens: I will detain you no longer by this faint and
feeble tribute to the illustrious dead.   Even in other hands, adequate
justice could not be performed, within the limits of this occasion.
Their highest, their best praise, is your deep conviction of their

merits, your affectionate gratitude for their labors and services. It is not my voice, it is this cessation of ordinary pursuits, this arresting of all attention, those solemn ceremonies, and this crowded house, which speak their eulogy. Their fame, indeed, is safe. That is now treasured up, beyond the reach of accident. Although no sculptured marble should rise to their memory, nor engraved stone bear record to their deeds, yet will their remembrance be as lasting as the land they honored. Marble columns may, indeed, moulder into dust, time may erase all impress from the crumbling stone, but their fame remains; for with American liberty it rose, and with American liberty only can it perish. It was the last swelling peal of yonder choir—'THEIR BODIES ARE BURIED IN PEACE, BUT THEIR NAME LIVETH EVERMORE!' I catch that solemn song, I echo that lofty strain of funeral triumph! '*Their name liveth evermore.*'

*   *   *   *   *   *   *   *

"It cannot be denied, but by those who would dispute against the sun, that with America, and in America, a new era commences in human affairs. This era is distinguished by free representative governments, by entire religious liberty, by improved systems of national intercourse, by a newly-awakened and an unconquerable spirit of free inquiry, and by a diffusion of knowledge through the community, such as has been before altogether unknown and unheard of. America, America, our country, fellow-citizens, our own dear and native land, is inseparably connected, fast bound up, in fortune and by fate, with these great interests. If they fall, we fall with them; if they stand, it will be because we have upholden them. Let us contemplate, then, this connection, which binds the prosperity of others to our own; and let us manfully discharge all the duties which it imposes. If we cherish the virtues and the principles of our fathers, heaven will assist us to carry on the work of human liberty, and human happiness. Auspicious omens cheer us: great examples are before us: our own firmament now shines brightly upon our path: WASHINGTON is in the clear upper sky. These other stars have now joined the American constellation; they circle around their centre, and the heavens beam with a new light. Beneath this illumination, let us walk the course of life, and at its close devoutly commend our beloved country, the common parent of us all, to the Divine Benignity."

During this visit at the East, at this time, President J. Q. Adams attended the annual examination of the public schools in Boston, and was present at the public dinner given in Faneuil Hall, to the school committee, teachers, and most meritorious scholars. In reply to a complimentary toast from the Mayor, Mr. Adams responded as follows :—

"MR. MAYOR, AND MY FELLOW-CITIZENS OF BOSTON :—A few days since, we were assembled in this Hall, as the house of mourning— in commemoration of the two last survivors of that day which had proclaimed at once our independence and our existence as a nation. We are now assembled within the same walls, at the house of feasting—at the festival of fathers rejoicing in the progressive improvement of their children.

"We have been told by the wisest man of antiquity, that it is better to go to the house of mourning, than to the house of feasting. How emphatically true would that sentence be, if the house of mourning were always such as this hall but so recently exhibited! —a mourning of gratitude—a mourning of faithful affection—a mourning full of consolation and joy. And yet, could the wisest of men now look down upon this happy meeting—of parents partaking together of the bounties of Providence, in mutual gratulation with each other at the advances of their offspring in moral and intellectual cultivation—would he, could he, my friends, have said that it is better to go to the house of mourning than to such a house of feasting ?

"For is not the spirit of that solemnity, and of this, effectively the same ? If that was the commemoration of the good deeds of your forefathers, may not this be called the commemoration of the future achievements of your sons ? If that day was dedicated to the blessed memory of the past, is not this devoted to the no less blessed hope of the future ? It was from schools of public instruction, instituted by our forefathers, that the light burst forth. It was in the primary schools; it was by the midnight lamps of Harvard hall, that were conceived and matured, as it was within these hallowed walls that were first resounded the accents of that independence which is now canonized in the memory of those by whom it was proclaimed.

" Was it not there that were formed, to say nothing of him ' fit for the praise of any tongue but mine,'—but was it not there that were formed, and prepared for the conflicts of the mind, for the intellectual warfare which distinguishes your Revolution from all the brutal butcheries of vulgar war, your James Otis, your John Hancock, your Samuel Adams, your Robert Treat Paine, your Elbridge Gerry, your James and your Joseph Warren, and last, not least, your Josiah Quincy, so worthily represented by your Chief Magistrate here at my side ?

" Indulge me, fellow-citizens, with the remark, that I have been called to answer to myself these questions, before I could enjoy the happiness, at the very kind invitation of your Mayor and Aldermen, of presenting myself among you this day.

" In conformity to my own inclinations, and to the usages of society, I have deemed it proper, on the recent bereavement I have sustained, to withdraw for a time from the festive intercourse of the world, and in retirement, so far as may be consistent with the discharge of public trusts, to prepare for and perform the additional duties devolving upon me, as a son, and as a parent, from this visitation of heaven.   To that retirement I have hitherto been confined ; and in departing from it for a single day, I have needed an apology to myself, as I trust I shall need one to you.   Seek for it, my fellow-citizens in your own paternal hearts.   I have been unable to resist the invitation of the authorities of this my own almost native city, to mingle with her inhabitants in the joyous festivities of this occasion—and, after witnessing, in the visitation of the schools, hundreds and thousands of the rising generation training ' up in the way they should go ;' to come here and behold the distinguished proficients of the schools sharing at the social board the pleasures of their fathers, and to congratulate the fathers on the growing virtues and brightening talents of their children.

" But, fellow-citizens, I will no longer trespass upon your indulgence.   I thank you for the sentiment with which you have honored me.   I thank you for the many affecting testimonials of kindness and sympathy which I have so often received at your hands; and will give you as a token of my good wishes, not your-selves, but objects dearer to your hearts.   Mr. Mayor, I propose to you for a toast—

"The blooming youth of Boston—May the maturity of the fruit be equal to the promise of the blossom."

CHAPTER X.

In administering the Government of the United
States, Mr. Adams adhered with rigid fidelity to the
principles embodied in his inaugural speech. Believing that "the will of the people is the source, and the
happiness of the people the end, of all legitimate government on earth," it was his constant aim to act up to
this patriotic principle in the discharge of his duties
as chief magistrate. He was emphatically the President of the entire people, and not of a section, or a
party. His administration was truly national in its
scope, its objects, and its results. His views of the
sacred nature of the trust imposed upon him by his
fellow-citizens were too exalted to allow him to desecrate the power with which it clothed him to the promotion of party or personal interests. Although not
unmindful of the party which elevated him to the

presidency, nor forgetful of the claims of those who yielded sympathy and support to the measures of his administration, yet in all his doings in this respect, his primary aim was the general good. Simply a friendship for him, or his measures, without other and requisite qualifications, would not ensure from Mr. Adams an appointment to office. Neither did an opposition to his administration alone, except there was a marked practical unfitness for office, ever induce him to remove an individual from a public station.

Looking back to the administration of Mr. Adams from the present day, and comparing it with those which have succeeded it, or even those which preceded it, the acknowledgment must be made by all candid minds, that it will lose nothing in purity, patriotism, and fidelity, in the discharge of all its trusts. He was utterly incapable of proscription for opinion's sake. With a stern integrity worthy the highest admiration, and which the people at that period were far too slow to acknowledge and appreciate, he would not displace his most active political opponents from public stations he found them occupying, provided they were competent to their duty and faithful in the discharge of the same. "It was in my hearing that, to a representation that a certain important and influential functionary of the General Government in New York was using the power of his office adversely to Mr. Adams's re-election, and that he ought to desist or be removed, Mr. Adams made this reply:—' That gentleman is one of the best officers in the public service. I have had occasion to know his diligence, exactness, and punctuality. On public grounds, therefore, there is no cause of complaint against him, and upon no other will I remove him. *If I cannot administer the Government on these principles, I am content to go back to Quincy !*"* Being in Baltimore on a certain occasion, among those introduced to him was a gentleman who accosted him thus—"Mr. President, though I differ from you in opinion, I am glad to find you in good health." The President gave him a hearty shake of the hand, and replied,—" Sir, in our happy and free country, we can differ in opinion without being enemies."

These anecdotes illustrate the character and principles of Mr. Adams. He knew nothing of the jealousy and bitterness which are gendered, in little minds and hearts, by disparities of sentiment. Freedom of opinion he considered the birthright of every American citizen, and he would in no instance be the instrument of inflicting punishment upon the head of any man on account of its exercise. High and pure in all his aims, he sought to reach them by means of a corresponding character. If he could not succeed in the use of such instruments, he was content to meet defeat. The rule by which he was governed in the discharge of his official duties, is beautifully expressed by the dramatic bard :—

* King's Eulogy on John Quincy Adams.

"Be just and fear not.
Let all the ends thou aim'st at, be thy COUNTRY's,
Thy GOD's, and TRUTH's. Then if thou fall'st, O Cromwell,
Thou fall'st a blessed martyr!"

In the truly republican position which Mr. Adams took in regard to appointments to office, and which, it is humiliating to believe, was one means of his subsequent defeat, he but faithfully imitated the example of "the Father of his country." When Gen. Washington occupied the presidential chair, application was made for the appointment of one of his old and intimate friends to a lucrative office. At the same time a petition was received asking the same station for a most determined political opponent. The latter received the appointment. The friend was greatly disappointed and hurt in his feelings at his defeat. Let the explanation of Washington be noted and ever remembered :—" My friend," said he, " I receive with cordial welcome. He is welcome to my house, and welcome to my heart; but with all his good qualities he is not a man of business. His opponent, with all his politics so hostile to me, *is* a man of business. My private feelings have nothing to do in the case. I am not George Washington, but President of the United States. As George Washington, I would do this man any kindness in my power—as President of the United States, I can do nothing."

The period of Mr. Adams's administration, was not

one which admitted of acts calculated to rivet the attention, or excite the admiration and applause of the multitude. No crisis occurred in national affairs—no imminent peril from without, or danger within, threatened the well-being of the country! Quietness reigned throughout the world, and the nations were allowed once more to cultivate the arts of peace, to enlarge the operations of commerce, and to fix their attention on domestic interests—the only true fountain of national prosperity. But though lacking in some of the more striking elements of popularity, the administration of Mr. Adams was pre-eminently useful in all its measures and influences. During no Presidential term since the organization of the Government, has more been done to consolidate the Union, and develop its resources, and lay the foundations of national strength and prosperity.

The two great interests which, perhaps, received the largest share of attention from Mr. Adams' administration, were internal improvements and domestic manufactures. A special attention to these subjects was recommended in his messages to Congress. And throughout his term, he failed not to urge these vital matters upon the attention of the people, and their representatives. He recommended the opening of national roads and canals—the improvement of the navigation of rivers, and the safety of harbors—the survey of our coasts, the erection of light houses, piers, and breakwaters. Whatever tended to facilitate communication and transportation between extreme portions of the Union—to bring the people of distant sections into a more direct intercourse with each other, and bind them together by ties of a business, social and friendly nature —to promote enterprize, industry, and enlarged views of national and individual prosperity—obtained his earnest sanction and recommendation. To encourage home labor—to protect our infant manufactories from a fatal competition with foreign pauper wages—to foster and build up in the bosom of the country a system of domestic production, which should not only supply home consumption, and afford a home market for raw materials and provisions, the produce of our own soil, but enable us in due time to compete with other nations in sending our manufactures to foreign markets—he yielded all his influence to the levying of protective duties on foreign articles, especially such as could be produced in our own country. The wisdom of this policy, its direct tendency to promote national wealth and strength, and to render the Union truly independent of the fluctuations and vicissitudes of foreign countries, cannot be doubted, it would seem, by those possessing clear minds and sound judgment, of all parties.

Under the faithful supervision of one so vigilant as Mr. Adams, the foreign relations of the Government could not have been neglected. The intimate knowledge of the condition of foreign nations, their resources and their wants, which was possessed by himself and by Mr. Clay, the Secretary of State, afforded facilities in this department, from which the country reaped the richest benefit.   During the four years of his administration, more treaties were negotiated at Washington than during the entire thirty-six years through which the preceding administrations had extended.   New treaties of amity, navigation and commerce, were concluded with Austria, Sweden, Denmark, the Hanseatic League, Prussia, Colombia, and Central America Commercial difficulties and various arrangements of a satisfactory character, were settled with the Netherlands, and other European Governments.   The claims of our citizens against Sweden, Denmark and Brazil, for spoilations of commerce, were satisfactorily consummated.

" As time advances, the evidences are accumulating on all sides, that the administration of John Quincy Adams was one of the most wise, patriotic, pacific, just, and wealth-producing, in the history of the country; and no small part of that benefit may justly be ascribed to the aid he received from his Secretary of State. Mr. Adams himself was a great statesman, bred in the school of statesmen, and all his life exercised in the business of state, with recognized skill, and approved fidelity.   The seven years immediately preceding the administration of Mr. Adams, was a period of great commercial embarrassment and distress ; and the seven years subsequent to his entrance on the duties of chief executive, was a period of great public and private prosperity."*

While Mr. Adams was thus seeking to foster and encourage the industrial and monetary interests of the country, he was not forgetful of the important claims of literature and science. President Washington, during his administration, had repeatedly urged on Congress the importance of establishing a national university at the capital; and he had located and bequeathed a site for that purpose. But his appeals on this subject had been in vain. In Mr. Adams's first message, he earnestly called on Congress to carry into execution this recommendation of the Father of his Country—insisting that "among the first, perhaps the very first instrument for the improvement of the condition of men, is knowledge; and to the acquisition of much of the knowledge adapted to the wants, the comforts, and the enjoyments of human life, public institutions and seminaries of learning are essential."

In the same message Mr. Adams recommended the establishment of a national observatory. "Connected with the establishment of an university," he said "or, separate from it, might be undertaken the erection of an astronomical observatory, with provision for the support of an astronomer, to be in constant attendance of observation upon the phenomena of the heavens, and for the periodical publication of his observations. It is with no feeling of pride, as an American, that the re-

* Cotton's Life of Clay.

mark may be made, that, on the comparatively small
territorial surface of Europe, there are existing upwards
of one hundred and thirty of these light-houses in the
skies; while, throughout the whole American hemisphere, there is not one.   If we reflect a moment upon
the discoveries which, in the last four centuries, have
been made in the physical constitution of the universe,
by the means of these buildings, and of observers stationed in them, shall we doubt of their usefulness to
every nation ?   And while scarcely a year passes over
our heads without bringing some new astronomical
discovery to light, which we must fain receive at second
hand from Europe, are we not cutting ourselves off from
the means of returning light for light, while we have
neither observatory nor observer upon our half of the
globe, and the earth revolves in perpetual darkness to
our unsearching eyes ?"

It is humiliating to reflect that neither of these rec-
ommendations received an encouraging response from
Congress.   The latter suggestion, indeed, excited the
ridicule of many of the opposers of Mr. Adams, and
"a light-house in the skies," became a term of reproach
in their midst.   In this, however, it must be confessed,
their ridicule was greatly at the expense of their intelligence, their public spirit, and their devotion to the
highest interests of man.   There are few reflections
more mortifying to an American citizen, than that
while so large a portion of the resources of the national Government have been exhausted in prosecuting

party measures, rewarding partisan services, and promoting sectional and personal schemes, little or nothing has been devoted to the encouragement of the arts and sciences, and the cultivation of those higher walks of human attainment which exalt and refine a people, and fit them for the purest and sweetest enjoyments of life.

It was during the first year of his administration, that the attention of Mr. Adams was called to a proposed Congress of all the Republics on the American Continent, to meet at Panama. The objects designed to be accomplished by such a Congress have been variously stated. It has been believed by some to have been called for the purpose of opposing a supposed project, entertained by the Allied Powers of Europe, of combining for the purpose of reducing the American Republics to their former condition of European vassalage. Be this as it may, the Panama Congress, among its objects, aimed at the cementing of the friendly relations of all the independent States of America, and the forming of a kind of mutual council, to act as an umpire to settle the differences which might arise between them.

The United States was invited to send representatives to Panama. Mr. Adams, as President, in view of the beneficial influences which in various ways might flow from such a meeting, accepted the invitation, with the understanding that the Government of the United States would take no part that could conflict with its neutral position, in the wars which might then be in existence between any of the South American Republics and other powers. The acceptance of this invitation was announced by Mr. Adams in his first message to Congress. This was immediately followed by the nomination of Messrs. Richard C. Anderson and John Sargeant, as commissioners to the Congress of Panama, and Wm. B. Rochester, of New York, as secretary of the commission. These nominations were confirmed by the Senate ; and an appropriation was voted by the House of Representatives, after strong opposition and much delay, to carry the contemplated measure into effect.

But the United States Government was never represented in the Panama Congress. The proceedings in the House of Representatives on this subject had been so protracted, that it was found too late for Mr. Sargeant to reach Panama in season for the meeting of the Congress, which took place on the 22nd of June, 1826. Mr. Anderson, who was then minister at Colombia, on receiving his instructions, commenced his journey to Panama ; but on reaching Carthagena he was seized with a malignant fever, which terminated his existence.

During the second session of the nineteenth Congress, the subject of commercial intercourse with the British West India Colonies was thoroughly discussed. The British Parliament had laid restrictions so onerous on the trade of the United States with these Colonies, that it could be pursued to very little profit. Bills were introduced into both houses of Congress, for the protection of the interests of American merchants, trading with the British Colonies; but the Senate and House failing to agree on the details of the proposed measures, nothing was done to effect the desired object. Congress having adjourned without passing any law to meet the restrictive measures of Great Britain, President Adams, on the 17th of March, 1827, agreeably to a law passed three years before, issued a proclamation closing the ports of the United States against vessels from the British colonies, until the restrictive measures of the British Government should be repealed.

The policy pursued by Mr. Adams toward the Indian tribes within the United States, was pacific and humane. The position they held toward the General Government was of an unsettled and embarrassing character. Enjoying a species of independence, and subject to laws of their own enactment, they were, nevertheless, dependent on the Government of the United States for protection, and were, in fact, wholly at its disposal. Near the close of Mr. Monroe's administration, in a message to Congress, on the 27th of January, 1825, he proposed a plan to remove the tribes scattered through the several States, to a tract of country west of the Mississippi, and to unite them in one nation, with some plan for their government and civilization. This proposition meeting with a decided opposition on the part of many of the Indians, was modified during Mr. Adams's administration. It finally resulted in a plan of removing west of the Mississippi such individuals among the various tribes as would consent to go under the inducements held out ; and allowing the remainder to continue in their old abode, occupying each a small tract of land. This policy has since been pursued by the General Government, and has resulted in the removal of most of the aborigines beyond the western shores of the Mississippi.

These removals, however, have been attended with no little difficulty, and at times have led to collisions which have assumed a serious aspect. An instance of this description occurred during the first year Mr. Adams occupied the presidential chair. In 1802, a compact was formed between the General Government and the State of Georgia, in which it was agreed, that in consequence of the relinquishment, on the part of Georgia, of all her claim to the land set off in the then new Mississippi Territory, the General Government, at its own expense, should obtain a relinquishment, from the Creek Indians, of all their lands within the State of Georgia, "whenever it could be peaceably done upon reasonable terms."

In compliance with this agreement, the United States had extinguished the Indian title to about fifteen millions of acres of land. At the close of Mr. Monroe's administration, over nine millions of acres were still retained by the Indians. The State authorities of

Georgia became very anxious to obtain possession of this also. At the solicitation of Gov. Troup, President Madison sent two Commissioners to make a treaty with the Creeks, for the purchase of their lands, and the removal of the Indians beyond the Mississippi. But the Creeks, having begun to appreciate and enjoy the comforts of civilization, and the advantages of the arts and sciences, which had been introduced into their midst, refused to treat on the subject, and passed a law in the General Council of their nation, forbidding, on pain of death, the sale of any of their lands. After the close of the council, a few of the Creeks, influenced by a chief named M'Intosh, met the United States Commissioners, and formed a treaty on their own responsibility, ceding to the General Government all the Creek lands in Georgia and Alabama. When intelligence of this treaty was circulated among the Indians, they were filled with indignation. Their General Council met—resolved not to sanction a treaty obtained in a manner so dishonorable and illegal—and despatched a party of Indians to the residence of M'Intosh, who immediately shot him and another chief who had signed the treaty with him.

This surreptitious treaty was transmitted to Washington, and under a misapprehension of the manner in which it was secured, was ratified by the Senate, on the 3d of March, 1825, the last day of Mr. Monroe's administration. Gov. Troup, acting under this treaty, sent surveyors into the Creek Territory, to lay out the land in lots, which were to be distributed among the white inhabitants of Georgia, by lottery. The Indians resisted this encroachment, and prepared to defend their rights by physical force—at the same time sending to Washington for protection from the General Government. The authorities of Georgia insisted upon a survey, and ordered out a body of militia to enforce it.

On hearing of this state of affairs, President Adams despatched a special agent to inquire into the facts of the case. After due investigation, the agent reported that the treaty had been obtained by bad faith and corruption, and that the Creeks were almost unanimously opposed to the cession of their lands. On receiving this report, the President determined to prevent the survey ordered by the Governor of Georgia, until the matter could be submitted to Congress, and ordered Gen. Gaines to proceed to the Creek country with a body of United States troops, to prevent collision between the Indians and the Georgia forces.

On the 5th of February, Mr. Adams transmitted a message to Congress, giving a statement of these transactions, and declaring his determination to fulfil the duty of protection the nation owed the Creeks, as guaranteed by treaty, by all the force at his command. "That the arm of military force," he continued, "will be resorted to only in the event of the failure of all other expedients provided by the laws, a

pledge has been given by the forbearance to employ
it at this time.   It is submitted to the wisdom of Congress to determine whether any further acts of legislation may be necessary or expedient to meet the
emergency which these transactions may produce."

The committee of the House of Representatives, to
which this message was referred, reported that it "is
expedient to procure a cession of the Indian lands in
the State of Georgia, and that until such a cession is
procured, the law of the land, as set forth in the treaty
at Washington, ought to be maintained by all necessary, constitutional, and legal means."   The firmness
and decision of President Adams undoubtedly prevented the unhappy consequences of a collision between the people of Georgia and the Creek Indians.
A new negotiation was opened with the Indians, by
direction of the President, which resulted in declaring
the M'Intosh treaty null and void, and in obtaining, at
length, a cession of all the lands of the Creeks within
the limits of Georgia, to the General Government.

As the friend and promoter of internal improvements, Mr. Adams was invited to be present at the
interesting ceremony of "breaking ground," on the
Chesapeake and Ohio canal, then about to be commenced, which took place on the 4th of July, 1828.
On the morning of that day, the President, the Heads
of Departments, the Foreign Ministers, the Corporations of Washington, Georgetown, and Alexandria, the

President and Directors of the Chesapeake and Ohio Canal Company, with a large concourse of citizens, embarked on board of steamboats and ascended the Potomac, to the place selected for the ceremony. On reaching the ground, a procession was formed, which moved around it so as to leave a hollow space, in the midst of a mass of people, in the centre of which was the spot marked out by Judge Wright, the Engineer of the Chesapeake and Ohio Canal Company, for the commencement of the work. A moment's pause here occurred, while the spade, destined to commence the work, was selected by the committee of arrangements, and the spot for breaking ground was precisely denoted.

At that moment the sun shone out from behind a cloud, giving an appearance of the highest animation to the scene. Amidst an intense silence, the Mayor of Georgetown handed to Gen. Mercer, the President of the Canal Company, the consecrated instrument ; which, having received, he stepped forward from the resting column, and addressed as follows the listening multitude :—

" Fellow-citizens : There are moments in the progress of time which are the counters of whole ages. There are events, the monuments of which, surviving every other memorial of human existence, eternize the nation to whose history they belong, after all other vestiges of its glory have disappeared from the globe. At such a moment have we now arrived. Such a monument we are now to found."

Turning towards the President of the United States, who stood near him, Mr. M. proceeded :—

" Mr. President : On a day hallowed by the fondest recollections, beneath this cheering (may we not humbly trust auspicious) sky, surrounded by the many thousand spectators who look on us with joyous anticipation ; in the presence of the representatives of the most polished nations of the old and new worlds ; on a spot where little more than a century ago the painted savage held his nightly orgies ; at the request of the three cities of the District of Columbia, I present to the Chief Magistrate of the most powerful Republic on earth, for the most noble purpose that was ever conceived by man, this humble instrument of rural labor, a symbol of the favorite occupation of our countrymen. May the use to which it is about to be devoted prove the precursor, to our beloved country, of improved agriculture, of multiplied and diversified arts, of extended commerce and navigation. Combining its social and moral influence with the principles of that happy constitution under which you have been called to preside over the American people, may it become a safeguard of their liberty and independence, and a bond of perpetual union !

" To the ardent wishes of this vast assembly I unite my fervent prayer to that infinite and awful Being without whose favor all human power is but vanity, that he will crown your labor with his blessing, and our work with immortality."

As soon as he had ended, the President of the United States, to whom Gen. Mercer had presented the spade, stepped forward, and, with an animation of manner and countenance which showed that his whole heart was in the thing, thus addressed the assembly of his fellow-citizens :—

" Friends and Fellow-citizens : It is nearly a full century since Berkely, bishop of Cloyne, turning towards this fair land, which we now inhabit, the eyes of a prophet, closed a few lines of poetical inspiration with this memorable prediction—

" Time's noblest empire is the last :"—

a prediction which, to those of us whose lot has been cast by Divine Providence in these regions, contains not only a precious promise, but a solemn injunction of duty, since upon our energies, and upon those of our posterity, its fulfilment will depend. For with reference to what principle could it be that Berkely proclaimed this, the last, to be the noblest empire of time? It was, as he himself declares, on the transplantation of learning and the arts to America. Of learning and the arts. The four first acts—the empires of the old world, and of former ages—the Assyrian, the Persian, the Grecian, the Roman empires—were empires of conquest, dominions of man over man. The empire which his great mind, piercing into the darkness of futurity, foretold in America, was the empire of learning and the arts,—the dominion of man over himself, and over physical nature—acquired by the inspirations of genius, and the toils of industry; not watered with the tears of the widow and the orphan; not cemented in the blood of human victims; founded not in discord, but in harmony,—of which the only spoils are the imperfections of nature, and the victory achieved is the improvement of the condition of all. Well may this be termed nobler than the empire of conquest, in which man subdues only his fellow-man.

"To the accomplishment of this prophecy, the first necessary step was the acquisition of the right of self-government, by the people of the British North American Colonies, achieved by the Declaration of Independence, and its acknowledgment by the British nation. The second was the union of all these colonies under one general confederated Government—a task more arduous than that of the preceding separation, but at last effected by the present constitution of the United States.

"The third step, more arduous still than either or both the others, vas that which we, fellow-citizens, may now congratulate ourselves, our country, and the world of man, that it is taken. It is the adaptation of the powers, physical, moral, and intellectual, of this whole Union, to the improvement of its own condition: of its moral and political condition, by wise and liberal institutions—by the cultivation of the understanding and the heart—by academies, schools, and learned institutes—by the pursuit and patronage of learning and the arts; of its physical condition, by associated labor to improve the bounties, and to supply the deficiencies of nature; to stem the torrent in its course; to level the mountain with the plain; to disarm and fetter the raging surge of the ocean. Undertakings of which the language I now hold is no exaggerated description, have become happily familiar not only to the conceptions, but to the enterprize of our countrymen. That for the commencement of which we are here assembled is eminent among the number. The project contemplates a conquest over physical nature, such as has never yet been achieved by man. The wonders of the ancient world, the pyramids of Egypt, the Colossus of Rhodes, the temple at Ephesus, the mausoleum of Artemisia, the wall of China, sink into insignificance before it :—insignificance in the mass and momentum of human labor required for the execution—insignificance in comparison of the purposes to be accomplished by the work when executed. It is, therefore, a pleasing contemplation to those sanguine and patriotic spirits who have so long looked with hope to the completion of this undertaking, that it unites the moral power and resources—first, of numerous individuals—secondly, of the corporate cities of Washington, Georgetown, and Alexandria—thirdly, of the great and powerful States of Pennsylvania, Virginia, and Maryland—and lastly, by the subscription authorized at the recent session of Congress, of the whole Union.

" Friends and Fellow-laborers. We are informed by the holy oracles of truth, that, at the creation of man, male and female, the Lord of the universe, their Maker, blessed them, and said unto them, be fruitful, and multiply, and replenish the earth, and subdue it. To subdue the earth was, therefore, one of the first duties assigned to man at his creation ; and now, in his fallen condition, it remains among the most excellent of his occupations. To subdue the earth is pre-eminently the purpose of the undertaking, to the accomplishment of which the first stroke of the spade is now to be struck. That it is to be struck by this hand, I invite you to witness.—[Here the stroke of the spade.]* And in performing this act,

---

* Attending this action was an incident which produced a greater sensation than any other that occurred during the day. The spade which the President held, struck a root, which prevented its penetrating the earth. Not deterred by trifling obstacles from doing what he had deliberately resolved to perform, Mr. Adams tried it again, with no better success. Thus foiled, he threw down the spade, hastily stripped off and laid aside his coat, and went seriously to work. The multitude around, and on the hills and trees, who could not hear, because of their

I call upon you to join me in fervent supplication to Him from whom that primitive injunction came, that he would follow with his blessing, this joint effort of our great community, to perform his will in the subjugation of the earth for the improvement of the condition of man—that he would make it one of his chosen instruments for the preservation, prosperity, and perpetuity of our Union—that he would have in his holy keeping all the workmen by whose labors it is to be completed—that their lives and their health may be precious in his sight; and that they may live to see the work of their hands contribute to the comforts and enjoyments of millions of their countrymen.

"Friends and brethren: Permit me further to say, that I deem the duty, now performed at the request of the President and Directors of the Chesapeake and Ohio Canal Company, and the Corporations of the District of Columbia, one of the most fortunate incidents of my life. Though not among the functions of my official station, I esteem it as a privilege conferred upon me by my fellow-citizens of the District. Called, in the performance of my service, heretofore as one of the representatives of my native commonwealth in the Senate, and now as a member of the executive department of the Government, my abode has been among the inhabitants of the District longer than at any other spot upon earth. In availing myself of this occasion to return to them my thanks for the numberless acts of kindness that I have experienced at their hands, may I be allowed to assign it as a motive, operating upon the heart, and superadded to my official obligations, for taking a deeper interest in their welfare and prosperity. Among the prospects of futurity which we may indulge the rational hope of seeing realized by this junction of distant waters, that of the auspicious influence which it will exercise over the fortunes of every portion of this District is one upon which my mind dwells with unqualified pleasure. It is my earnest prayer that they may not be disappointed.

"It was observed that the first step towards the accomplishment of the glorious destinies of our country was the Declaration of Independence. That the second was the union of these States under our federative Government. The third is irrevocably fixed by the

---

distance from the open space, but could see and understand, observing this action, raised a loud and unanimous cheering, which continued for some time after Mr. Adams had mastered the difficulty.

act upon the commencement of which we are now engaged. What time more suitable for this operation could have been selected than the anniversary of our great national festival ? What place more appropriate from whence to proceed, than that which bears the name of the citizen warrior who led our armies in that eventful contest to the field, and who first presided as the Chief Magistrate of our Union ? You know that of this very undertaking he was one of the first projectors; and if in the world of spirits the affections of our mortal existence still retain their sway, may we not, without presumption, imagine that he looks down with complacency and delight upon the scene before and around us ?

" But while indulging in a sentiment of joyous exultation at the benefits to be derived from this labor of our friends and neighbors, let us not forget that the spirit of internal improvement is catholic and liberal. We hope and believe that its practical advantages will be extended to every individual in our Union. In praying for the blessing of heaven upon our task, we ask it with equal zeal and sincerity upon every other similiar work in this confederacy ; and particularly upon that which, on this same day, and perhaps at this very hour, is commencing from a neighboring city. It is one of the happiest characteristics in the principle of internal improvement, that the success of one great enterprise, instead of counteracting, gives assistance to the execution of another. May they increase and multiply, till, in the sublime language of inspiration, every valley shall be exalted and every mountain and hill shall be made low ; the crooked straight, the rough places plain. Thus shall the prediction of the bishop of Cloyne be converted from prophecy into history ; and, in the virtues and fortunes of our posterity, the last shall prove the noblest empire of time."

The administration of Mr. Adams, from the first day of its existence, met with an opposition more determined, bitter, and unscrupulous than any which has ever assailed a President of the United States. It evidently was not an opposition based on well-grounded objections to his principles or his measures. Before an opportunity had been given fairly and fully to develop his policy as President, the opposition had taken its stand, and boldly declared that his administration should be overthrown at every hazard, whatever might be its policy, its integrity, or its success.   A favorite candidate, having certain elements of immense popularity with a large class of people, and supported with enthusiasm by his immediate friends, had been defeated in the previous presidential canvass, at a moment when it was thought triumphant success had been secured. Under the exasperation and excitement of this overthrow, it was determined that his more fortunate rival should be displaced at the earliest moment, at whatever cost, though his administration should prove unrivalled in patriotism, and the successful promotion of the general welfare.

The opposition did not fail to seize upon certain points, which, in the exercise of a due degree of adroitness, yielded an ample material for popular declamation and censure.   The fact that Mr. Adams had a less number of electoral votes than Gen. Jackson was greatly dwelt upon as positive evidence that the will of the people had been violated in the election of the former to the presidency—although it has since been satisfactorily ascertained that Mr. Adams had a larger number of the primary votes of the people than his prominent opponent.

The charge of " bargain and corruption," alleged against Mr. Adams and Mr. Clay, was also used as an effective weapon against the former, in the succeeding presidential canvass. Notwithstanding the charge had been promptly and emphatically denied by the parties implicated, and proof in its support fearlessly challenged—notwithstanding every attempt at evidence to fix it upon them had most signally failed, and involved those engaged therein in utter confusion of face —yet so often and so boldly was the charge repeated by designing men, so generally and continually was it reiterated by a venal press from one end of the Union to the other, that a majority of the people was driven into its belief, and the fate of Mr. Adams's administration was sealed against him.   Subsequent developments have shown, that, in the annals of political warfare, there never was a charge uttered against eminent public men, so thoroughly destitute of the shadow of truth as this.   But it answered the immediate ends of its authors.   Posterity will do ample justice to all the parties in this transaction.

Another event which operated seriously to the disadvantage of Mr. Adams, was the amalgamation of the strong Crawford party with the supporters of Gen. Jackson.   This combination threw obstacles in the way of the administration which were insurmountable. It enabled the opposition to send a majority of members to the twentieth Congress, both in the Senate and the House of Representatives.   The test of the strength of parties in the House took place on the election of Speaker.   Andrew Stevenson, of Virginia, was elected on the first ballot, by a majority of ten votes over John

W. Taylor, the administration candidate. Mr. Stevenson was a supporter of Mr. Crawford in 1824. His election to the Speaker's chair clearly indicated the union of the different sections of the opposition, and foreshadowed too evidently the overthrow of the administration of Mr. Adams.

In this state of things, with a majority of Congress against him, the President was deprived of the opportunity of carrying into execution many important measures which were highly calculated to promote the permanent benefit of the country, and which could not have failed to receive the approbation of the people. A majority of all the committees of both Houses were against him; and for the first time an administration was found without adequate strength in Congress to support its measures. In several instances the reports of committees partook of a strong partisan character, in violation of all rules of propriety and correct legislation.

The first session of the twentieth Congress, which was held immediately preceding the presidential campaign of 1828, was characterized by proceedings, which, at this day, all will unite in deciding as highly reprehensible. Instead of attending strictly to the legitimate business of the session, much of the time was spent in discussions involving the merits of the opposing candidates for the presidency, and designed to have an express bearing on the election then near at hand. Of this character was a resolution introduced into the

House of Representatives, on the 8th of January, 1828, by Mr. Hamilton, a supporter of Gen. Jackson, to inquire into the expediency of having a historical picture of the battle of New Orleans painted, and placed in the rotunda of the Capitol. This was followed by a resolution, introduced by Mr. Sloane, an administration member, requiring the Secretary of War to furnish the House with a copy of the proceedings of a court-martial ordered by Gen. Jackson, in 1814, for the trial of certain Tennessee militiamen, who were condemned and shot.

At this session of Congress may be dated the introduction of a practice which has become an evil of the greatest magnitude in the present day. Reference is had to the custom of making the halls of Congress a mere arena, where, instead of attending to the legitimate business of legislating for the benefit of the country at large, political gladiators spend much of their time in wordy contests, designed solely for the promotion of personal or party purposes, to the neglect of the interests of their constituents. From this has grown the habit of speech-making by the hour, on topics trivial in their nature, in which the people have not the slightest interest, and which, quite often, are totally foreign to the subject ostensibly in debate. Valuable time and immense treasures are thus squandered to no profitable purpose. Should not this evil be abated ?

The stern integrity of Mr. Adams, and his unyielding devotion to principle, were made to operate against him. Had he chosen to turn the vast influence at his command to the promotion of personal ends—had he unscrupulously ejected from office all political opposers, and supplied their places with others who would have labored, with all the means at their disposal, in his behalf—little doubt can be entertained that he could have secured his re-election. But he utterly refused to resort to such measures. Believing he was promoted to his high position not for his individual benefit, but to advance the welfare of the entire country, his view of duty was too elevated and pure to allow him to desecrate the trust reposed in him to personal ends. Hence the influence derived from the patronage of the General Government was turned against the administration rather than in its behalf; and the singular spectacle was presented of men exerting every nerve to overthrow Mr. Adams, who were dependent upon him for the influence they wielded against him, and for their very means of subsistence.

A hotly contested political campaign ensued in the fall of 1828. In view of the peculiar combination of circumstances, and of the means resorted to by the opposing parties to secure success, the result could be foreseen with much certainty. Gen. Jackson was elected President of the United States, and was inaugurated on the 4th of March, 1829.

Thus closed the administration of John Quincy Adams. At the call of his country he entered upon the highest station in its gift. With a fidelity and

uprightness which have not been surpassed, he discharged his important trust to the lasting benefit of all
the vital interests which tend to build up a great and
prosperous people.   And at the call of his country he
relinquished the honors of office, and willingly retired
to the private walks of life.

No man can doubt that Mr. Adams could look back
upon his labors while President with the utmost satisfaction.   " During his administration new and increased activity was imparted to those powers vested
in the Federal Government for the development of the
resources of the country, and the public revenue was
liberally expended in prosecuting those liberal measures,
to which the sanction of Congress had been deliberately given, as the settled policy of the Government.

" More than one million of dollars had been expended
in enlarging and maintaining the light-house establishment—half a million in completing the public buildings—two millions in erecting arsenals, barracks, and
furnishing the national armories—nearly the same
amount had been expended in permanent additions to
the naval establishment—upwards of three millions
had been devoted to fortifying the sea-coast—and
more than four millions expended in improving the
internal communications between different parts of the
country, and in procuring information, by scientific
surveys, concerning its capacity for further improvement.   Indeed, more had been directly effected by the
aid of Government in this respect, during Mr. Adams'

administration, than during the administrations of all his predecessors. Other sums, exceeding a million, had been appropriated for objects of a lasting character, and not belonging to the annual expense of the Government; making in the whole nearly fourteen millions of dollars expended for the permanent benefit of the country, during this administration.

"At the same time the interest on the public debt was punctually paid, and the debt itself was in a constant course of reduction, having been diminished $30,373,188 during his administration, and leaving due on the 1st of January, 1829, $58,362,136. While these sums were devoted to increasing the resources and improving the condition of the country, and in discharging its pecuniary obligations, those claims which were derived from what are termed the imperfect obligations of gratitude and humanity were not forgotten.

"More than five millions of dollars were appropriated to solace the declining years of the surviving officers of the Revolution; and a million and a half expended in extinguishing the Indian title, and defraying the expense of the removal beyond the Mississippi of such tribes as were unqualified for a residence near civilized communities, and in promoting the civilization of those who, relying on the faith of the United States, preferred to remain on the lands which were the abodes of their fathers.

"In the condition which we have described —in

peace with all the world, with an increasing revenue and with a surplus of $5,125,638 in the public treasury, —the administration of the Government of the United States was surrendered by Mr. Adams on the 3d of March, 1829."*

The "Georgia Constitutionalist" thus describes Mr. Adams' retirement from office :—"Mr. Adams is said to be in good health and spirits. The manner in which this gentleman retired from office is so replete with propriety and dignity, that we are sure history will record it as a laudable example to those who shall hereafter be required by the sovereign people to descend from exalted stations. It was a great matter with the ancients to die with decency, and there are some of our own day whose deaths are more admirable than their lives. Mr. Adams' deportment in the Presidency was lofty and proud ; but the smile with which he throws aside the trappings of power, and the graceful propriety with which he takes leave of patronage and place, are truly commendable."

* American Annual Register.

CHAPTER XI.

FEW public men in any country have possessed
attainments more varied than were those of Mr.
Adams. Every department of literature and science
received more or less of his attention—every path of
human improvement seems to have been explored by
him. As a statesman, he was unrivalled in the profundity of his knowledge. His state papers—given to
the world while Minister, Secretary of State, President,
and Member of Congress—his numerous addresses,
orations, and speeches, are astonishing in number, and
in the learning they display.* No man was more

---

* Aside from his state papers, official correspondence, and speeches,
which would make many volumes, the Literary World gives the following list of the published writings of Mr. Adams:—

"1. Oration at Boston, 1793; 2. Answer to Paine's Rights of Man,
1793; 3. Address to the Members of the Massachusetts Charitable Fire
Society; 4. Letters on Silesia; 5. Letters on Silesia, 1804; 6. Inaugural Oration at Harvard College, 1806; 7. Letters to H. G. Otis, in
reply to Timothy Pickering, 1808; 8. Review of the Works of Fisher
Ames, 1809; 9. Lectures on Rhetoric and Oratory, two volumes, 1810;

familiar with modern history, with diplomacy and international law, and the politics of America and Europe for the last two or three centuries.

In other departments he appeared equally at home. His acquaintance was familiar with the classics, and several modern languages. In oratory, rhetoric, and the various departments of belles lettres, his attainments were of more than an ordinary character. His commentaries on Desdemona, and others of Shakspeare's characters, show that he was no mean critic, in the highest walks of literature, and in all that pertains to human character.

The following interesting account of an interview with ex-President Adams, by a southern gentleman, in

10. Report on Weights and Measures, 1821; 11. Oration at Washington, 1821; 12. Duplicate Letters; the Fisheries and the Mississippi, 1822; 13. Oration to the citizens of Quincy, 1831; 14. Oration on the Death of James Monroe, 1831; 15. Dermot McMorrogh, or the Conquest of Ireland, 1832; 16. Letters to Edward Livingston, on Free Masonry, 1833; 17. Letters to William L. Stone, on the entered apprentice's oath, 1833; 18. Oration on the Life and Character of Lafayette, 1835; 19. Oration on the Life and Character of James Madison, 1836; 20. The Characters of Shakspeare, 1837; 21. Oration delivered at Newburyport, 1837; 22. Letters to his Constituents of the Twelfth Congressional District of Massachusetts, 1837; 23. The Jubilee of the Constitution, 1839; 24. A Discourse on Education, delivered at Braintree, 1840; 25. An Address at the Observatory, Cincinnati, 1843.

Among the unpublished works of Mr. Adams, besides his Diary, which extends over half a century, and would probably make some two dozen stout octavos, are Memoirs of the earlier Public and Private Life of John Adams, second President of the United States, in three volumes; Reports and Speeches on Public Affairs; Poems, including two new cantos of Dermot McMorrogh, a Translation of Oberon, and numerous Essays and Discourses."

1834, affords some just conceptions of the versatility
of his genius, and the profoundness of his erudition :—

" Yesterday, accompanied by my friend T., I paid a visit to the
venerable ex-President, at his residence in Quincy. A violent rain
setting in as soon as we arrived, gave us from five to nine o'clock
to listen to the learning of this man of books. His residence is a
plain, very plain one : the room into which we were ushered, (the
drawing-room, I suppose,) was furnished in true republican style.
It is probably of ancient construction, as I perceived two beams
projecting from the low ceiling, in the manner of the beams in a
ship's cabin. Prints commemorative of political events, and the old
family portraits, hung about the room ; common straw matting
covered the floor, and two candlesticks, bearing sperm candles,
ornamented the mantle-piece. The personal appearance of the ex-
President himself corresponds with the simplicity of his furniture.
He resembles rather a substantial, well-fed farmer, than one who
has wielded the destinies of this mighty Confederation, and been
bred in the ceremony and etiquette of an European Court. In fact,
he appears to possess none of that sternness of character which
you would suppose to belong to one a large part of whose life has
been spent in political warfare, or, at any rate, amidst scenes requiring a vast deal of nerve and inflexibility.

" Mrs. Adams is described in a word —a lady. She has all the
warmth of heart and ease of manner that mark the character of the
southern ladies, and from which it would be no easy matter to dis-
tinguish her.

" The ex-President was the chief talker. He spoke with infinite
ease, drawing upon his vast resources with the certainty of one
who has his lecture before him ready written. The whole of his
conversation, which steadily he maintained for nearly four hours,
was a continued stream of light. Well contented was I to be a
listener. His subjects were the architecture of the middle ages ; the
stained glass of that period ; sculpture, embracing monuments particularly. On this subject his opinion of Mrs. Nightingale's monument in Westminster Abbey, differs from all others that I have
seen or heard. He places it above every other in the Abbey, and
observed in relation to it, that the spectator ' saw nothing else.'
Milton, Shakspeare, Shenstone, Pope, Byron, and Southey were in

turn remarked upon. He gave Pope a wonderfully high character, and remarked that one of his chief beauties was the skill exhibited in varying the cesural pause—quoting from various parts of his author, to illustrate his remarks more fully. He said very little on the politics of the country. He spoke at considerable length of Sheridan and Burke, both o whom he had heard, and could describe with the most graphic effect. He also spoke of Junius ; and it is remarkable that he should place him so far above the best of his contemporaries. He spoke of him as a bad man ; but maintained, as a writer, that he had never been equalled.

" The conversation never flagged for a moment ; and on the whole, I shall remember my visit to Quincy, as amongst the most instructive and pleasant I ever passed."

As a theologian, Mr. Adams was familiar with the tenets of the various denominations which compose the great Christian family, and acquainted with the principal arguments by which they support their peculiar views. While entertaining decided opinions of his own, which he did not hesitate to avow on all proper occasions, he was tolerant of the sentiments of all who differed from him. He deemed it one of the most sacred rights of every American citizen, and of every human being, to worship God according to the dictates of his own conscience, without let or hindrance, our laws equally tolerating, and equally protecting every sect.

In the most abstruse sciences he was equally at home. His report to Congress, while Secretary of State, on Weights and Measures was very elaborate, and evinced a deep and careful research into this important but most difficult subject. That report was of the utmost value. Adopting the philosophical and unchangeable basis of the modern French system of mensuration, an arc of the meridian, it laid the foundation for the accurate manipulations and scientific calculations of the late Professor Hassler, which have furnished an unerring standard of Weights and Measures to the people of this country. In a very learned notice of " Measures, Weights, and Money," by Col. Pasley, Royal Engineer, F. R. S., published in London, in 1834, he pays the following well-merited compliment to Mr. Adams :—

" I cannot pass over the labors of former writers, without acknowledging in particular, the benefit which I have derived, whilst investigating the historical part of my subject, from a book printed at Washington, in 1821, as an official Report on Weights and Measures, made by a distinguished American statesman, Mr. John Quincy Adams, to the Senate of the United States, of which he was afterwards President. This author has thrown more light into the history of our old English weights and measures, than all former writers on the same subject. His views of historical facts, even where occasionally in opposition to the reports of our own Parliamentary Committees, appear to me to be the most correct. For my own part, I confess that I do not think I could have seen my way into the history of English weights and measures, in the feudal ages, without his guidance."

To his other accomplishments Mr. Adams added that of a poet. His pretensions in this department were humble, yet many of his productions, thrown off hastily, no doubt, during brief respites from severer labors, possess no little merit. A few specimens will not be uninteresting to the reader.

The following stanzas are from a hymn by Mr. Adams for the celebration of the 4th of July, 1831. at Quincy, Mass. :—

" Sing to the Lord a song of praise ;
    Assemble, ye who love his name ;
Let congregated millions raise
    Triumphant glory's loud acclaim.
From earth's remotest regions come ;
    Come, greet your Maker, and your King ;
With harp, with timbrel, and with drum,
    His praise let hill and valley sing.

*   *   *   *   *   *   *

" Go forth in arms ; Jehovah reigns ;
    Their graves let foul oppressors find ;
Bind all their sceptred kings in chains ;
    Their peers with iron fetters bind.
Then to the Lord shall praise ascend ;
    Then all mankind, with one accord,
And freedom's voice, till time shall end,
    In pealing anthems, praise the Lord."

The lines which follow were inscribed to the sun-dial under the window of the hall of the House of Representatives, at Washington :—

" Thou silent herald of Time's silent flight !
    Say, couldst thou speak, what warning voice were thine ?
    Shade, who canst only show how others shine !
Dark, sullen witness of resplendent light
In day's broad glare, and when the noontide bright
    Of laughing fortune sheds the ray divine,
    Thy ready favors cheer us—but decline
The clouds of morning and the gloom of night.
Yet are thy counsels faithful, just and wise ;
    They bid us sieze the moments as they pass—

Snatch the retrieveless sunbeam as it flies,
  Nor lose one sand of life's revolving glass—
Aspiring still, with energy sublime,
  By virtuous deeds to give eternity to Time."

It is seldom that lines more pure and beautiful can be found, than the following on the death of children:—

" Sure, to the mansions of the blest
  When infant innocence ascends,
Some angel brighter than the rest
  The spotless spirit's flight attends.

" On wings of ecstacy they rise,
  Beyond where worlds material roll,
Till some fair sister of the skies
  Receives the unpolluted soul.

" There at the Almighty Father's hand,
  Nearest the throne of living light,
The choirs of infant seraphs stand,
  And dazzling shine, where all are bright.

" The inextinguishable beam,
  With dust united at our birth,
Sheds a more dim, discolored gleam,
  The more it lingers upon earth :

" Closed is the dark abode of clay,
  The stream of glory faintly burns,
Nor unobscured the lucid ray
  To its own native fount returns :

" But when the Lord of mortal breath
  Decrees his bounty to resume,
And points the silent shaft of death,
  Which speeds an infant to the tomb,

" No passion fierce, no low desire,
 Has quenched the radiance of the flame ;
Back to its God the living fire
 Returns, unsullied, as it came."

The heart which could turn aside from the stern
conflicts of the political world, and utter sentiments so
chaste and tender, must have been the residence of the
sweetest and noblest emotions of man.

Having taken final leave, as he believed, of the duties
of public life, and retired to the beloved shades of
Quincy, it was the desire and intention of Mr. Adams
to devote the remainder of his days to the peaceful
pursuits of literature. It had long been his purpose,
whenever opportunity should offer, to write a history of
the life and times of his venerated father, " the elder
Adams." His heart was fixed on this design, and
some introductory labors had been commenced. But
an overruling Providence had a widely different work
in preparation for him.

If Mr. Adams had been permitted to follow the bent
of his own feelings at that time—if he had continued in
the retirement he had so anxiously sought as a rest
from the toils of half a century—the brightest page of
his wonderful history would have remained forever un-
written. He would have been remembered as a dis-
creet and trusty diplomatist, an able statesman, a successful politician, a capable President, and an honest
and honorable man ! This would, indeed, have been

a measure of renown with which most men would have been content, and which few of the most fortunate sons of earth can ever attain. He was abundantly satisfied with it. He asked for nothing more—he expected nothing more this side the grave. But it was not enough ! Fame was wreathing brighter garlands, a more worthy chaplet, for his brow. A higher, nobler task was before him, than any enterprize which had claimed his attention. His long and distinguished career—his varied and invaluable experience—had been but a preparation to enable him to enter upon the real work of life for which he was raised up.

The world did not yet know John Quincy Adams Long as he had been before the public, the mass had thus far failed to read him aright. Hitherto circumstances had placed him in collision with aspiring men. He stood in their way to station and power. There was a motive to conceal his virtues and magnify his faults. He had never received from his opposers the smallest share of credit really due to him for patriotism, self-devotion, and purity of purpose. Even his most devoted friends did not fully appreciate these qualities in him. During his long public service, he had ever been an object of hatred and vituperation to a class of minds utterly incapable of estimating his talents or comprehending his high principles of action. In the heat of political struggles, no abuse, no defamation, were too great to heap upon him. Misrepresentation, duplicity, malignity, did their worst. Did he utter a patriotic sentiment, it was charged to hypocrisy and political cunning. Did he do a noble deed, worthy to be recorded in letters of gold—sacrificing party predilections and friendship to support the interest of his country, and uphold the reputation and dignity of its Government—it was attributed to a wretched pandering for the emoluments of office. Did he endeavor to exercise the powers entrusted to him as President in such a manner as to preserve peace at home and abroad, develope the internal resources of the nation, improve facilities for transportation and travel, protect and encourage the industry of the country, and in every department promote the permanent prosperity and welfare of the people—it was allowed to be nothing more than the arts of an intriguer, seeking a re-election to the Presidency. Yea, it was declared in advance, that, "if his administration should be as pure as the angels in heaven," it should be overthrown. Did he exhibit the plain simplicity of a true republican in his dress and manners, and economy in all his expenditures, it was attributed to parsimony and meanness! A majority of his countrymen had been deceived as to his principles and character, and sacrificed him politically on the altar of prejudice and party spirit.

Throughout his life he had ever been a lover of man and of human freedom—the best friend of his country —the most faithful among the defenders of its institutions—a sincere republican, and a true man. But blinded by political prejudice, a large portion of his fellow-citizens refused the boon of credit for these qualities. It remained for another stage of his life, another field of display, to correct them of this error, and to vindicate his character. It was requisite that he should step down from his high position, disrobe himself of office, power and patronage, place himself beyond the reach of the remotest suspicion of a desire for political preferment and emolument, to satisfy the world that John Quincy Adams had from the beginning, been a pure-hearted patriot, and one of the noblest sons of the American Confederacy. His new career was to furnish a luminous commentary on his past life, and to convince the most sceptical, of the justice of his claim to rank among the highest and best of American patriots. Placed beyond the reach of any gift of office from the nation, with nothing to hope for, and nothing to fear in this respect, he was to write his name in imperishable characters, so high on the tablets of his country's history and fame, as to be beyond the utmost reach of malignity or suspicion! The door which led to this closing act of his dramatic life, was soon opened.

On returning to Quincy, one of the first things which received the attention of Mr. Adams, was the discharge of a filial duty towards his deceased parents, in the erection of a monument to their memory. The elder Adams in his will, among other liberal bequests, had left a large legacy to aid in the erection of a new

Unitarian church in Quincy.   The edifice was completed, and ex-President J. Q. Adams caused the monument to his father and mother to be erected within the
walls.   It was a plain and simple design, consisting of a
tablet, having recessed pilasters at the sides, with a base
moulding and cornice ; the whole supported by trusses
at the base.   The material of which it was made was
Italian marble ; and the whole was surmounted by a
fine bust of John Adams, from the chisel of Greenough,
the American artist, then at Rome.   The inscription,
one of the most feeling, appropriate, and classical
specimens extant, was as follows :—

" LIBERTATEM AMICITTAM FIDEM RETINEBIS.
D. O. M.*
Beneath these Walls
Are deposited the Mortal Remains of
JOHN ADAMS,
Son of John and Susanna (Boyalston) Adams,
Second President of the United States.
Born 19–30 October, 1735.
On the fourth of July, 1776,
He pledged his Life, Fortune, and Sacred Honor
To the INDEPENDENCE OF HIS COUNTRY.
On the third of September, 1783,
He affixed his Seal to the definitive Treaty with Great Britain,
Which acknowledged that Independence,
And consummated the redemption of his pledge.
On the fourth of July, 1826,
He was summoned
To the Independence of Immortality,
And to the JUDGMENT OF HIS GOD.
This House will bear witness to his Piety :
This Town, his Birth-place, to his Munificence :
History to his Patriotism :
Posterity to the Depth and Compass of his Mind.

---

* *Deo, Optimo, Maximo*—to God, the Best and Greatest.

At his side
Sleeps till the Trump shall sound,
ABIGAIL,
His beloved and only Wife,
Daughter of William and Elizabeth (Quincy) Smith.
In every relation of Life, a pattern
Of Filial, Conjugal, Maternal, and Social Virtue.
Born 11–22 November, 1744.
Deceased 28 October, 1818,
Aged 74.

———

Married 25 October, 1764.
During a union of more than half a century,
They survived, in Harmony of Sentiment, Principle and Affection,
The Tempests of Civil Commotion ;
Meeting undaunted, and surmounting
The Terrors and Trials of that Revolution
Which secured the Freedom of their Country ;
Improved the Condition of their Times;
And brightened the Prospects of Futurity
To the Race of Man upon Earth.

———

PILGRIM :

From lives thus spent thy earthly Duties learn ;
From Fancy's Dreams to active Virtue turn :
Let Freedom, Friendship, Faith thy Soul engage,
And serve, like them, thy Country and thy Age."

Mr. Adams had remained in the retirement of Quincy but little more than a single year, when the following paragraph appeared in the public prints throughout the country :—

" Mr. Adams, late President of the United States, is named as a candidate for Congress, from the district of Massachusetts now represented by Mr. Richardson, who declines a re-election."

It would be difficult to describe the surprise created by this announcement, in every quarter of the Union.

Speculation was at fault. Would he accept or reject such a nomination? By a large class it was deemed impossible that one who had occupied positions so elevated—who had received the highest honors the nation could bestow upon him—would consent to serve the people of a single district, in a capacity so humble, comparatively, as a Representative in Congress. Such a thing was totally unheard of. The people, however, of the Plymouth congressional district in which he resided, met and duly nominated him for the proposed office. All doubts as to his acceptance of the nomination were speedily dispelled by the appearance of a letter from Mr. Adams, in the Columbian Sentinel, Oct., 15, 1830, in which he says :—

"If my fellow-citizens of the district should think proper to call for such services as it may be in my power to render them, by representing them in the twenty-second Congress, I am not aware of any sound principle which would justify me in withholding them. To the manifestations of confidence on the part of those portions of the people who, at two several meetings, have seen fit to present my name for the suffrages of the district, I am duly and deeply sensible."

In due time the election was held, and Mr. Adams was returned to Congress, by a vote nearly unanimous. From that time forward for seventeen years, and to the hour of his death, he occupied the post of Representative in Congress from the Plymouth district, in Massachusetts, with unswerving fidelity, and distinguished honor.

There can be no doubt that many of the best friends

of Mr. Adams seriously questioned the propriety of his
appearing as a Representative in the halls of Congress.
It was a step never before taken by an ex-President of
the United States.   They apprehended it might be de-
rogatory to his dignity, and injurious to his reputation
and fame, to enter into the strifes, and take part in the
litigations and contentions which characterize the national House of Representatives.   Moreover, they were
fearful that in measuring himself, as he necessarily must,
in the decline of life, with younger men in the prime
of their days, who were urged by the promptings of
ambition to tax every capacity of their nature, he might
injure his well-earned reputation for strength of intellect, eloquence and statesmanship.   But these mis-
givings were groundless.   In the House of Representatives, as in all places where Mr. Adams was
associated with others, he arose immediately to the
head of his compeers.   So far from suffering in his
reputation, it was immeasurably advanced during his
long congressional career.   New powers were developed—new traits of character were manifested—new
and repeated instances of devotion to principle and the
rights of man were made known—which added a
brighter lustre to his already widely-extended fame.
He exhibited a fund of knowledge so vast and profound
—a familiarity so perfect with nearly every topic which
claimed the attention of Congress—he could bring forth
from his well-replenished storehouse of memory so vast
an array of facts, shedding light upon subjects deeply

obscured to others—displayed such readiness and power
in debate, pouring out streams of purest eloquence, or
launching forth the most scathing denunciations when
he deemed them called for—that his most bitter opposers, while trembling before his sarcasm, and dread-
ing his assaults, could not but grant him the meed of
their highest admiration. Well did he deserve the
title conferred upon him by general consent, of "the
Old Man Eloquent!"

Had Mr. Adams followed the bent of his own inclinations—had he consulted simply his personal ease
and comfort—he would probably never have appeared
again in public life. Having received the highest dis
tinctions his country could bestow upon him, blessed
with an ample fortune, and possessing all the elements
of domestic comfort, he would have passed the evening
of his earthly sojourn in peaceful tranquillity, at the
mansion of his fathers in Quincy. But it was one of
the sacred rules in this distinguished statesman's life, to
yield implicit obedience to the demands of duty. His
immediate neighbors and fellow-citizens called him to
their service in the national councils. He was conscious of the possession of talents, knowledge, experience, and all the qualifications which would enable
him to become highly useful, not only in acting as the
representative of his direct constituents, but in promoting the welfare of our common country. This
conviction once becoming fixed in his mind, decided
his course. He felt he had no choice left but to com-

ply unhesitatingly with the demand which had been made upon his patriotism. In adopting this resolution —in consenting, after having been once at the head of the National Government, to assume again the labors of public life in a subordinate station, wholly divested of power and patronage, urged by no influence but the claims of duty, governed by no motive but a simple desire to serve his country and promote the well-being of his fellow-man—Mr. Adams presented a spectacle of moral sublimity unequalled in the annals of nations !

For many years Mr. Adams was a member, and one of the Vice Presidents, of the American Bible Society. In reply to an invitation to attend its anniversary in 1830, he wrote the following letter :—

" Sir :—Your letter of the 22d of March was duly received; and while regreting my inability to attend personally at the celebration of the anniversary of the institution, on the 13th of next month, I pray you, sir, to be assured of the gratification which I have experienced in learning the success which has attended the benevolent exertions of the American Bible Society.

" In the decease of Judge Washington, they have lost an able and valuable associate, whose direct co-operation, not less than his laborious and exemplary life, contributed to promote the cause of the Redeemer. Yet not for him, nor for themselves by the loss of him, are they called to sorrow as without hope; for lives like his shine but as purer and brighter lights in the world, after the lamp which fed them is extinct, than before.

" The distribution of Bibles, if the simplest, is not the least efficacious of the means of extending the blessings of the Gospel to the remotest corners of the earth; for the Comforter is in the sacred volume : and among the receivers of that million of copies distributed by the Society, who shall number the multitudes awakened thereby, with good will to man in their hearts, and with the song of the Lamb upon their lips?

"The hope of a Christian is inseparable from his faith. Whoever believes in the divine inspiration of the holy Scriptures, must hope that the religion of Jesus shall prevail throughout the earth. Never since the foundation of the world have the prospects of mankind been more encouraging to that hope than they appear to be at the present time. And may the associated distribution of the Bible proceed and prosper, till the Lord shall have made 'bare his holy arm in the eyes of all the nations; and all the ends of the earth shall see the salvation of our God.'

"With many respects to the Board of Managers, please to accept the good wishes of your friend and fellow-citizen,

"JOHN QUINCY ADAMS."

On the 4th of July, 1831, at half past three o'clock in the afternoon, the venerable JAMES MONROE, fifth President of the United States, departed life, aged 73 years. He died at the residence of his son-in-law, Samuel L. Gouverneur, Esq., in the city of New York. His decease had been for some days expected; but life lingered until the anniversary of his country's independence, when his spirit took its departure to a better world. Throughout the United States, honors were paid to his memory by hoisting of flags at half mast, the tolling of bells, firing of minute guns, the passing of resolutions, and delivery of eulogies. He was, emphatically, a great and good man, respected and beloved by the people of all parties, without exception. There are few instances in the history of the world, of more remarkable coincidences than the death of three Presidents of the United States, who took most prominent parts in proclaiming and achieving the independ-

ence of our country, on the anniversary of the day
when the declaration of that independence was made to
the world. The noise of the firing of cannon, in celebrating the day, caused the eyes of the dying Monroe to
open inquiringly. When the occasion of these rejoicings was communicated to him, a look of intelligence
indicated that he understood the character of the day.

At this anniversary of our National Independence,
Mr. Adams delivered an oration before the citizens of
Quincy. It was an able and eloquent production.
The following were the concluding paragraphs. In
reference to nullification, which was threatened by
some of the Southern States, he said:—

" The event of a conflict in arms, between the Union and one of
its members, whether terminating in victory or defeat, would be but
an alternative of calamity to all. In the holy records of antiquity,
we have two examples of a confederation ruptured by the sever-
ance of its members, one of which resulted, after three desperate
battles, in the extermination of the seceding tribe. And the vic-
torious people, instead of exulting in shouts of triumph, came to the
house of God, and abode there till even, before God; and lifted up
their voices, and wept sore, and said,—O Lord God of Israel *why* is
this come to pass in Israel, that there should be to-day one tribe lacking in Israel? The other was a successful example of resistance
against tyrannical taxation, and severed forever the confederacy,
the fragments forming separate kingdoms; and from that day their
history presents an unbroken series of disastrous alliances, and
exterminating wars—of assassinations, conspiracies, revolts, and
rebellions, until both parts of the confederacy sunk into tributary
servitude to the nations around them; till the countrymen of David
and Solomon hung their harps upon the willows of Babylon, and'
were totally lost amidst the multitudes of the Chaldean and Assyrian
monarchies, ' the most despised portion of their slaves.'

" In these mournful memorials of their fate, we may behold the sure, too sure prognostication of our own, from the hour when force shall be substituted for deliberation, in the settlement of our constitutional questions. This is the deplorable alternative—the extirpation of the seceding member, or the never-ceasing struggle of two rival confederacies, ultimately bending the neck of both under the yoke of foreign domination, or the despotic sovereignty of a conqueror at home. May heaven avert the omen! The destinies, not only of our posterity, but of the human race, are at stake.

" Let no such melancholy forebodings intrude upon the festivities of this anniversary. Serene skies and balmy breezes are not congenial to the climate of freedom. Progressive improvement in the condition of man, is apparently the purpose of a superintending Providence. That purpose will not be disappointed. In no delusion of national vanity, but with a feeling of profound gratitude to the God of our fathers, let us indulge in the cheering hope and belief, that our country and her people have been selected as instruments for preparing and maturing much of the good yet in reserve for the welfare and happiness of the human race. Much good has already been effected by the solemn proclamation of our principles—much more by the illustration of our example. The tempest which threatens desolation may be destined only to purify the atmosphere. It is not in tranquil ease and enjoyment that the active energies of mankind are displayed. Toils and dangers are trials of the soul. Doomed to the first by his sentence at the fall, man by submission converts them into pleasures. The last are, since the fall, the conditions of his existence. To see them in advance, to guard against them by all the suggestions of prudence, to meet them with the composure of unyielding resistance, and to abide with firm resignation the final dispensation of Him who rules the ball—these are the dictates of philosophy—these are the precepts of religion—these are the principles and consolations of patriotism—these remain when all is lost—and of these is composed the spirit of independence—the spirit embodied in that beautiful personification of the poet, which may each of you, my countrymen, to the last hour of his life, apply to himself,—

> 'Thy spirit, Independence, let me share,
> Lord of the lion heart, and eagle eye!
> Thy steps I follow, with my bosom bare,
> Nor heed the storm that howls along the sky.'

" In the course of nature, the voice which now addresses you must soon cease to be heard upon earth. Life and all which it inherits lose their value as it draws towards its close. But for most of you, my friends and neighbors, long and many years of futurity are yet in store. May they be years of freedom—years of prosperity—years of happiness, ripening for immortality ! But, were the breath which now gives utterance to my feelings the last vital air I should draw, my expiring words to you and your children should be, *Independence and Union forever !*"

A few weeks subsequent to the death of ex-President Monroe, Mr. Adams delivered an interesting and able eulogy on his life and character, before the public authorities of the city of Boston, in Faneuil Hall. In drawing to a conclusion, he used the following language :—

" Our country, by the bountiful dispensations of a gracious Heaven, is, and for a series of years has been, blessed with profound peace. But when the first father of our race had exhibited before him, by the archangel sent to announce his doom, and to console him in his fall, the fortunes and misfortunes of his descendants, he saw that the deepest of their miseries would befal them while favored with all the blessings of peace ; and in the bitterness of his anguish he exclaimed :—

' Now I see
Peace to corrupt, no less than war to waste.'

" It is the very fervor of the noonday sun, in the cloudless atmosphere of a summer sky, which breeds

'the sweeping whirlwind's sway,
That, hushed in grim repose, expects his evening prey.'

" You have insured the gallant ship which ploughs the waves, freighted with your lives and your children's fortunes, from the fury of the tempest above, and from the treachery of the wave beneath. Beware of the danger against which you can alone insure yourselves —the latent defect of the gallant ship itself. Pass but a few short days, and forty years will have elapsed since the voice of him who addresses you, speaking to your fathers from this hallowed spot, gave for you, in the face of Heaven, the solemn pledge, that if, in the course of your career on earth, emergencies should arise, calling for the exercise of those energies and virtues which, in times of tranquillity and peace remain by the will of Heaven dormant in the human bosom, you would prove yourselves not unworthy the sires who had toiled, and fought, and bled, for the independence of the country. Nor has that pledge been unredeemed. You have maintained through times of trial and danger the inheritance of freedom, of union, of independence bequeathed you by your forefathers. It remains for you only to transmit the same peerless legacy, unimpaired, to your children of the next succeeding age. To this end, let us join in humble supplication to the Founder of empires and the Creator of all worlds, that he would continue to your posterity the smiles which his favor has bestowed upon you ; and, since ' it is not in man that walketh to direct his steps,' that he would enlighten and lead the advancing generation in the way they should go. That in all the perils, and all the mischances which may threaten or befall our United Republic, in after times, he would raise up from among your sons deliverers to enlighten her councils, to defend her freedom, and if need be, to lead her armies to victory. And should the gloom of the year of independence ever again overspread the sky, or the metropolis of your empire be once more destined to smart under the scourge of an invader's hand,* that there never may be found wanting among the children of your country, a warrior to bleed, a statesman to counsel, a chief to direct and govern, inspired with all the virtues, and endowed with all the faculties which have been so signally displayed in the life of JAMES MONROE."

---

* Alluding to the burning of the city of Washington, in the war of 1812.

CHAPTER XII.

MR. ADAMS took his seat in the House of Representatives without ostentation, in December, 1831. His
appearance there produced a profound sensation. It
was the first time an ex-President had ever entered
that Hall in the capacity of a member. He was received
with the highest marks of respect. It presented a
singular spectacle to behold members of Congress
who, when Mr. Adams was President, had charged him
with every species of political corruption, and loaded
his name with the most opprobrious epithets, now
vieing with one another in bestowing upon him the
highest marks of respect and confidence. That which
they denied the President, they freely yielded to the
MAN. It was the true homage which virtue and
patriotism must ever receive—more honorable, and far
more grateful to its object, than all the servility and

flattery which power and patronage can so easily purchase.

The degree of confidence reposed in Mr. Adams was manifested by his being placed at once at the head of the Committee on Manufactures. This is always a responsible station ; but it was peculiarly so at that time. The whole Union was highly agitated on the subject of the tariff. The friends of domestic manufactures at the North, insisted upon high protective duties, to sustain the mechanical and manufacturing interests of the country against a ruinous foreign competition. The Southern States resisted these measures as destructive to their interests, and remonstrated with the utmost vehemence against them—in which they were joined by a large portion of the Democratic party throughout the North. Mr. Adams, with enlarged views of national unity and general prosperity, counselled moderation to both parties. As Chairman of the Committee on Manufactures, he strove to produce such a compromise between the conflicting interests, as should yield each section a fair protection, and restore harmony and fraternity among the people.

So important were Mr. Adams' services deemed in the Committee on Manufactures, that, on proposing to resign his post as Chairman, to fulfil other duties which claimed his attention, he was besought by all parties to relinquish his purpose. Mr. Cambreleng, of N. Y., a political opponent of Mr. Adams, said, " It was not a pleasant duty to oppose the request of any member of the House, particularly one of his character. He did so with infinite regret in the present instance ; and he certainly would not take such a course, but for the important consequences that might result from assenting to the wishes of the distinguished gentleman from Massachusetts. He had reached the conclusion, not without infinite pain and reluctance, that the harmony, *if not the existence of our Confederacy*, depends, at this crisis, upon the arduous, prompt, and patriotic efforts of a few eminent men. He believed that much might be done by the gentleman from Massachusetts."

In the same tone of high compliment, Mr. Barbour, of Virginia, said, " that to refuse anything that could be asked by the gentleman from Massachusetts gave him pain, great pain. He said it was with unaffected sincerity he declared, that the member from Massachusetts (with whom he was associated in the committee) had not only fulfilled all his duties with eminent ability, in the committee, but in a spirit and temper that commanded his grateful acknowledgments, and excited his highest admiration. Were it permitted him to make a personal appeal to the gentleman, he would have done so in advance of this motion. He would have appealed to him as a patriot, as a statesman, as a philanthropist, and above all as an American, feeling the full force of all his duties, and touched by all their incentives to lofty action—to forbear this request."

These complimentary appeals were well deserved by Mr. Adams, and show most emphatically the high position he occupied in the esteem and confidence of the entire House of Representatives, on becoming a member thereof. But, with the modesty of true greatness, it was painful to him to hear these encomiums uttered in his own presence. He arose, and begged the House, in whatever further action it might take upon the subject, to refrain from pursuing this strain. " I have been most deeply affected," he said, " by what has already passed. I have felt, in the strongest manner, the impropriety of my being in the House while such remarks were made ; being very conscious that sentiments of an opposite kind might have been uttered with far more propriety, and have probably been withheld in consequence of my presence."

Mr. Adams carried with him into Congress all his previous habits of industry and close application to business. He was emphatically a hard worker. Few men spent more hours in the twenty-four in assiduous labor. He would take no active part in any matter— would engage in the discussion of no topic—and would not commit himself on any question—until he had sounded it to its nether depths, and explored all its ramifications, all its bearings and influences, and had thoroughly become master of the subject. To gain this information no toil was too great, no application too severe. It was in this manner that he was enabled to overwhelm with surprise his cotemporaries in Congress, by the profundity of his knowledge. No subject could be started, no question discussed, on which he was not perfectly at home. Without hesitation or mistake, he could pour forth a stream of facts, dates, names, places, accompanied with narrations, anecdotes, reflections and arguments, until the matter was thoroughly sifted and laid bare in all its parts and properties, to the understanding of the most casual observer. The tenacity and correctness of his memory was proverbial. Alas, for the man who questioned the correctness of his statements, his facts, or dates. Sure discomfiture awaited him. His mind was a perfect calendar, a store-house, a mine of knowledge, in relation to all past events connected with the history of his country and his age.

In connection with his other exemplary virtues, Mr. Adams was prompt, faithful, unwearied, in the discharge of all his public duties. The oldest member of the House, he was at the same time the most punctual —the first at his post ; the last to retire from the labors of the day. His practice in these respects could well put younger members to the blush. While many others might be negligent in their attendance, sauntering in idleness, engaged in frivolous amusements, or even in dissipation, he was always at his post. No call of the House was necessary—no Sergeant-at-arms need be despatched—to bring him within the Hall of Representatives. He was the last to move an adjournment, or to adopt any device to consume time or neglect the public business for personal convenience or gratification. In every respect he was a model legislator. His example can be most profitably imitated by those who would arise to eminence in the councils of the nation.

" My seat was, for two years, by his side, and it would have scarcely more surprised me to miss one of the marble columns of the Hall from its pedestal than to see his chair empty. * * * I shall, perhaps, be pardoned for introducing here a slight personal recollection, which serves, in some degree, to illustrate his habits. The sessions of the last two days of (I think) the twenty-third Congress, were prolonged, the one for nineteen, and the other for seventeen hours. At the close of the last day's session, he remained in the hall of the House the last seated member of the body. One after another, the members had gone home ; many of them for hours. The hall—brilliantly lighted up, and gaily attended, as was, and perhaps is still, the custom at the beginning the last evening of a session—had become cold, dark, and cheerless. Of the members who remained, to prevent the public business from dying for want of a quorum, most but himself were sinking from exhaustion, although they had probably taken their meals at the usual hours, in the course of the day. After the adjournment, I went up to Mr. Adams' seat, to join company with him, homeward ; and as I knew he came to the House at eight o'clock in the morning, and it was then past midnight, I expressed a hope that he had taken some refreshment in the course of the day. He said he had not left his seat ; but *holding up a bit of hard bread in his fingers*, gave me to understand in what way he had sustained nature."*

The following reminiscence will further illustrate Mr. Adams' habits of industry and endurance at a later day, as well as show his views in regard to the famous " Expunging Resolution."

" On a cold and dreary morning, in the month of January, 1837, I went to the capitol of the United States, at a very early hour, to write out a very long speech I had reported for an honorable gentleman, who wished to look well in print ; and on entering the hall

---

* Edward Everett.

of the House of Representatives, I found Mr. Adams, as early as the hour was, in his seat, busily engaged in writing. He and myself were the only persons present; even the industrious Mr. Follansbee, the then doorkeeper, had not made his appearance, with his assistants and pages, to distribute copies of the journal and the usual documents.

"As I made it a rule never to speak to Mr. Adams, unless he spoke first, I said nothing; but took my seat in the reporters' gallery, and went to work. I had written about half an hour, when the venerable statesman appeared at my desk, and was pleased to say that I was a very industrious man. I thanked him for the compliment, and, in return, remarked, that, as industrious as I might be, I could not keep pace with him, 'for,' said I, 'I found you here, sir, when I came in.'

"'I believe I was a little early, sir,' he replied; 'but, as there is to be a closing debate to-day, in the Senate, on the expunging resolution, which I feel inclined to hear, I thought I would come down at an unusual hour, this morning, and dispatch a little writing before the Senate was called to order.'

"'Do you think the expunging resolution will be disposed of to-day?' I inquired.

"'I understand it will,' he rejoined. 'I hope so, at least,' he added, 'for I think the country has already become weary of it, and is impatient for a decision. It has already absorbed more time than should have been devoted to it.'

"'It will pass, I suppose, sir?'

"'Oh, certainly; and by a very decided majority. The administration is too strong for the opposition; and the affair will call up a strict party vote. Of course Mr. Clay's resolution will be expunged, and the journal will not be violated.'

"I was somewhat surprised at the remark, and, in return, observed that I had always understood that it was on the constitutional ground, that the expunging process could not be effected without destroying the journal, that the opponents of the measure had based themselves.

"'It is true, sir, that that has been the grave and somewhat tenable argument in the Senate; but it is a fallacy, after all,' he replied. 'The constitution, sir, it is true, renders it imperative on both Houses to keep a correct journal of its proceedings; and all this can be done, and any portion of it may be expunged, without violating that instrument. For instance, sir, a resolution is adopted to-day, is entered on the journal, and to-morrow is expunged—and still the journal remains correct, and the constitution is not violated. For the act by which the expungation is effected is recorded on the journal; the expunged resolution becomes a matter of record, and thus everything stands fair and correct. The constitution is a sacred document, and should not be violated; but how often is it strictly adhered to, to the very letter? There are, sir, some men in the world who make great parade about their devotion to the "*dear constitution,*"—men, sir, who make its sacred character a hobby, and who, nevertheless, are perfectly reckless of its violation, if the ends of party are to be accomplished by its abjuration.'

"There was a degree of sarcasm blended with his enunciation of the 'dear constitution,' which induced me to think it possible that he intended some personal allusion when he repeated the words. In this I might, and might not, have erred.

"'In what way, Mr. Adams,' I inquired, 'is this expunging process to be accomplished? Is the objectionable resolution to be erased from the journal with a pen; or is the leaf that contains it to be cut out?'

"'Neither process is to be resorted to, as I understand it,' he replied. 'The resolution will remain in the book; black lines will be drawn around it, and across it from right angles, and the word "expunged," will be written on the face of it. It will, to all intents and purposes, still stand on the face of the book. There are precedents in parliamentary journalism for the guidance of the Senate, and I suppose they will be adopted.'

"He then proceeded to give me a very graphic and interesting description of an expunging process that took place in the British Parliament in the reign of James the First, of England, which I would repeat, if time and space allowed. He detained me a long time, in narrating precedents, and commenting on them; and then abruptly bringing the subject to a close, left me to pursue my labors.

"Soon after the House had been called to order, immediately after the chaplain had said his prayers—for that was a ceremonial that Mr. Adams always observed—I saw him leave his seat, and proceed, as I supposed, to the Senate chamber. After an hour or two had elapsed, I went into the Senate, and there found him, standing outside of the bar, listening, with all imaginable attention, to Mr. Felix Grundy, who was delivering himself of some brief remarks he had to utter on the subject.

"At nine o'clock in the evening, as I fumbled my way through the badly-lighted rotunda, having just escaped from a caucus that had been holding 'a secret session,' in the room of the committee on public lands, I descried a light issuing from the vestibule of the Senate chamber, which apprized me that 'the most dignified body on earth' was still in session. Impelled by a natural curiosity, I proceeded towards the council chamber of the right reverend signors; and, just as I reached the door, Mr. Adams stepped out. I inquired if the resolution had been disposed of.

"'No, sir,' he replied; 'nor is it probable that it will be to-night! A Senator from North Carolina is yet on the floor; and, as it does not appear likely that he will yield it very soon, and as I am somewhat faint and weary, I think I shall go home.'

"The night was very stormy. Snow was falling fast; the moon, which had

'———— not yet fill'd her horns,'

had receded beneath the western horizon; and, as the capitol was but sadly lighted, I offered my services to the venerable sage of Quincy, and at the same time asked leave to conduct him to his dwelling.

"'Sir,' said he, 'I am indebted to you for your proffered kindness; but I need not the service of any one. I am somewhat advanced in life, but not yet, by the blessing of God, infirm; or what Doctor Johnson would call "superfluous;" and you may recollect what old Adam says in the play of "As you like it:"

"For in my youth I never did apply
Hot and rebellious liquors in my blood."'

"For the first time in my life, I found Mr. Adams a little inclined to be facetious; and I was glad of it—for it was to me a kind of assurance that my presence was not absolutely unwelcome.

"The salutation being over, and Mr. Adams having consented that I should see him down the steps of the capitol, I proceeded onward, and soon found myself, with my revered convoy, in the vicinity of the western gate of the capitol grounds. 'The wind whistled a dismal tale,' as we trudged onward, looking in vain for a cab; and the snow and sleet, which, early in the day, had mantled the earth, was now some twelve inches deep on Pennsylvania avenue. I insisted on going onward; but Mr. Adams objected, and bidding me good night somewhat unceremoniously, told me, almost in as many words, that my farther attendance was unwelcome.

" As I left him, he drew his ' Boston wrapper' still closer around him, hitched up his mittens, and with elastic step breasted a wintry storm that might have repelled even the more elastic movement of juvenility, and wended up the avenue. Although I cannot irreverently say that he

'Whistled as he went, for want of thought,'

I fancy that his mind was so deeply imbued with the contemplation of affairs of state, and especially in contemplating the expunging resolution, that he arrived at his home long before he was aware that he had threaded the distance between the capitol and the Presidential square."*

Although elected to the House of Representatives as a Whig, and usually acting with that party, yet Mr. Adams would never acknowledge that fealty to party could justify a departure from the conscientious discharge of duty. He went with his party as far as he believed his party was right and its proceedings calculated to promote the welfare of the country. But no party claims, no smiles nor frowns, could induce him to sanction any measure which he believed prejudicial to the interest of the people. Hence, during his congressional career, the Whigs occasionally found him a decided opposer of their policy and measures, on questions where he deemed they had mistaken the true

* Reminiscences of the late John Quincy Adams, by an Old Colony Man.—*New York Atlas.*

course.   In this he was but true to his principles, char
acter, and whole past history.   It was not that he loved
his political party or friends less, but that he loved what
he viewed as conducive to the welfare of the nation,
more.

The same principle of action governed him in reference to his political opponents.   In general he threw
his influence against the administration of Gen. Jackson, under a sincere conviction that its policy was injurious to the welfare of our common country.   But to
every measure which he could sanction, he did not
hesitate to yield the support of all his energies.

An instance of this description occurred in relation
to the treaty of indemnity with France.   For nearly
forty years, negotiations had been pending in vain with
the French Government, to procure an indemnity for
spoliations of American commerce, during the French
Revolution and Republic.   On the 4th of July, 1831,
Mr. Rives, the American Minister to France, succeeded
in concluding a treaty with that country, securing to
American merchants an indemnity of five millions of
dollars.   But although the treaty was duly ratified by
both Governments, the French Chamber of Deputies
obstinately refused, for several years, to vote an appropriation of money to fulfil its stipulations.   In 1835,
Gen. Jackson determined on strong measures to bring
the French Government to the discharge of its obligations.   He accordingly sent a message to Congress,
recommending, in the event of further delay on the

part of France, that *letters of marque and reprisal* be issued against the commerce of France, and at the same time instructed Mr. Edward Livingston, our Minister at that day at the Court of St. Cloud, to demand his passports, and retire to London. In all these steps, which resulted in bringing France to a speedy fulfilment of the treaty, Mr. Adams yielded his unreserved support to the administration. He believed Gen. Jackson, in resorting to compulsory measures, was pursuing a course called for alike by the honor and the interest of the country, and he did not hesitate to give him a cordial support, notwithstanding he was a political opponent. In a speech made by Mr. Adams on the subject, in the House of Representatives, he said :—

" Sir, if we do not unite with the President of the United States in an effort to compel the French Chamber of Deputies to carry out the provisions of this treaty, we shall become the scorn, the contempt, the derision and the reproach of all mankind! Sir, this treaty has been ratified on both sides of the ocean; it has received the sign manual of the sovereign of France, through His Imperial Majesty's principal Minister of State; it has been ratified by the Senate of this Republic; it has been sanctioned by Almighty God; and still we are told, in a voice potential, in the other wing of this capitol, that the arrogance of France,—nay, sir, not of France, but of her Chamber of Deputies —the insolence of the French Chambers, must be submitted to, and we must come down to the *lower* degradation of re-opening negotiations to attain that which has already been acknowledged to be our due! Sir, is this a specimen of your boasted chivalry? Is this an evidence of the existence of that heroic valor which has so often led our arms on to glory and immortality? Re-open negotiation, sir, with France? Do it, and soon you will find your flag insulted, dishonored, and trodden in the dust by the pigmy States of Asia and Africa—by the very banditti of the earth. Sir, the only negotiations, says the President of the United States, that he would encounter, should be at the cannon's mouth!"

The effect produced by this speech was tremendous on all sides; and, for a while, the House was lost in the excitement it afforded. The venerable orator took his seat; and, as he sank into it, the very walls shook with the thundering applause he had awakened.

On the 28th of June, 1836, the venerable ex-President JAMES MADISON, departed life at Montpelier, Va., in the eighty-sixth year of his age. He had filled a prominent place in the history of our Government, from its first organization. As a statesman, he was unsurpassed in critical acumen, in profundity of knowledge, in an understanding of constitutional Government, and its adaptation to the rights and interests of the people. His writings are an invaluable legacy to his countrymen, and will be studied and quoted for ages to come. "His public acts were a noble commentary upon his political principles—his private life an illustration of the purest virtues of the heart."

When a message from the President, announcing the death of Mr. Madison, was received in the House of Representatives, Mr. Adams arose and said:—

"By the general sense of the House, it is with perfect propriety that the delegation from the commonwealth of Virginia have taken the lead in the melancholy duty of proposing the measures suitable to be adopted as testimonials of the vereration due, from the Legislature of the Union, to the memory of the departed patriot and sage, the native of their soil, and the citizen of their community.

"It is not without some hesitation, and some diffidence, that I have risen to offer in my own behalf, and in that of my colleagues upon this floor, and of our common constituents, to join our voice, at once of mourning and exultation, at the event announced to both Houses of Congress, by the message from the President of the United States—of mourning at the bereavement which has befallen our common country, by the decease of one of her most illustrious sons—of exultation at the spectacle afforded to the observation of the civilized world, and for the emulation of after times, by the close of a life of usefulness and of glory, after forty years of service in trusts of the highest dignity and splendor that a confiding country could bestow, succeeded by twenty years of retirement and private life, not inferior, in the estimation of the virtuous and the wise, to the honors of the highest station that ambition can ever attain.

"Of the public life of James Madison what could I say that is not deeply impressed upon the memory and upon the heart of every one within the sound of my voice? Of his private life, what but must meet an echoing shout of applause from every voice within this hall? Is it not in a pre-eminent degree by emanation from his mind, that we are assembled here as the representatives of the people and the States of this Union? Is it not transcendently by his exertions that we all address each other here by the endearing appellation of countrymen and fellow-citizens? Of that band of benefactors of the human race, the founders of the Constitution of the United States, James Madison is the last who has gone to his reward. Their glorious work has survived them all. They have transmitted the precious bond of union to us, now entirely a succeeding generation to them. May it never cease to be a voice of admonition to us, of our duty to transmit the inheritance unimpaired to our children of the rising age.

"Of the personal relations of this great man, which gave rise to the long career of public service in which twenty years of my own life has been engaged, it becomes me not to speak. The fulness of the heart must be silent, even to the suppression of the overflowings of gratitude and affection."

To the year 1835, the career of Mr. Adams in

Congress had been marked by no signal display of characteristics peculiar to himself, other than such as the world had long been familiar with in his previous history. He had succeeded in maintaining his reputation for patriotism, devotion to principle, political sagacity and wisdom, and his fame as a public debater and eloquent speaker. But no new development of qualities unrecognized before had been made. From that year forward, however, he placed himself in a new attitude before the country, and entered upon a career which eclipsed all his former services, and added a lustre to his fame which will glow in unrivalled splendor as long as human freedom is prized on earth. It can hardly be necessary to state that allusion is here made to his advocacy of the Right of Petition, and his determined hostility to slavery. At an age when most men would leave the stormy field of public life, and retire to the quiet seclusion of domestic comfort, these great topics inspirited Mr. Adams with a renewed vigor. With all the ardor and zeal of youth, he placed himself in the front rank of the battle which ensued, plunged into the very midst of the melee, and, with a dauntless courage, that won the plaudits of the world, held aloft the banner of freedom in the Halls of Congress, when other hearts quailed and fell back ! He led "the forlorn hope" to the assault of the bulwarks of slavery, when the most sanguine believed his almost superhuman labors would be all in vain. In these contests a spirit blazed out from his noble soul which electrified the nation with admiration. In his intrepid bearing amid these scenes he fully personified the couplet quoted in one of his orations :—

" Thy spirit, Independence, let me share,
    Lord of the lion heart and eagle eye !
Thy steps I follow, with my bosom bare,
    Nor heed the storm that howls along the sky."

The first act in the career of Mr. Adams as a Member of Congress, was in relation to slavery. On the 12th of December, 1831, it being the second week of the first session of the twenty-second Congress, he presented fifteen petitions, all numerously signed, from sundry inhabitants of Pennsylvania, praying for the abolition of slavery and the slave trade in the District of Columbia. In presenting these petitions, Mr. Adams remarked, that although the petitioners were not of his immediate constituents, yet he did not deem himself at liberty to decline presenting their petitions, the transmission of which to him manifested a confidence in him for which he was bound to be grateful. From a letter which had accompanied the petitions, he inferred that they came from members of the Society of Friends or Quakers ; a body of men, he declared, than whom there was no more respectable and worthy class of citizens—none who more strictly made their lives a commentary on their professions ; a body of men comprising, in his firm opinion, as much of human virtue, and as little of human infirmity, as any other equal number of men, of any denomination, upon the face of the globe.

The petitions for the abolition of the slave trade in the District of Columbia, Mr. Adams considered relating to a proper subject for the legislation of Congress. But he did not give his countenance to those which prayed for the abolition of slavery in that District. Not that he would approbate the system of slavery; for he was, and in fact had been through life, its most determined foe. But he believed the time had not then arrived for the discussion of that subject in Congress. It was his settled conviction that a *premature* agitation of slavery in the national councils would greatly retard, rather than facilitate, the abolition of that giant evil—" as the most salutary medicines," he declared in illustration, " unduly administered, were the most deadly of poisons."

The position taken by Mr. Adams, in presenting these petitions, was evidently misunderstood by many, and especially by Abolitionists. They construed it into a disposition on his part to sanction, or at least to succumb unresistingly, to the inhumanity and enormity of the slave institution. In this conclusion they signally erred. Mr. Adams, by birth, education, all the associations of his life, and the fixed principles of his moral and political character, was an opposer of slavery in every form. No man felt more keenly the wretched absurdity of professing to base our Government on the " self-evident truth, that all men are created *equal*, and endowed by their Creator with an unalienable right to life, *liberty*, and the pursuit of happiness"—of proclaiming our Union the abode of liberty, the "home of the free," the asylum of the oppressed—while holding in our midst millions of fellow-beings manacled in hopeless bondage! No man was more anxious to correct this disgraceful misnomer, and wipe away its dark stain from our national escutcheon at the earliest practicable moment. But he was a statesman of profound knowledge and far-reaching sagacity. He possessed the rare quality of being able to "bide his time" in all enterprizes. Great as he felt the enormity of American slavery to be, he would not, in seeking to remove it, select a time so unseasonable, and adopt measures so unwise, as would result, Samson-like, in removing the pillars of our great political fabric, and crushing the glorious Union, formed by the wisdom and cemented by the blood of our Revolutionary Fathers, into a mass of ruins.

Believing there was a time to withhold and a time to strike, he would patiently wait until the sentiment of the American people became sufficiently ripened, under the increasing light and liberality of the age, to permit slavery to be lawfully and peaceably removed, while the Union should remain unweakened and untouched—the pride of our hearts, the admiration of the world. Hence, in his early career, he saw no propitious moment for such a work. While discharging the duties of U. S. Senator, Secretary of State, and President, an attempt in that direction would have resulted in an aggravation of the evils of slavery, and

a strengthening of the institution.   Nor on first entering Congress did he conceive the time to be fully come
to engage in that agitation of the momentous subject,
which, when once commenced in earnest, would never
cease until either slavery would be abolished, as far as
Congress possessed constitutional power, or the Union
become rent in twain !   But he evidently saw that
time was at hand—even at the door—and he prepared
himself for the contest.

In 1835, the people of Texas took up arms in open
rebellion against the Government of Mexico.   That
Province had been settled chiefly by emigrants from
the Southern and Southwestern States.   Many of
them had taken their slaves with them.   But the
Mexican Government, to their enduring honor be it
said, abolished slavery throughout that Republic.   The
ostensible object of the Texian insurrection was to
resist certain schemes of usurpation alleged against
Santa Anna, at that time President of Mexico.   At the
present day, however, after having witnessed the entire progress and consummation of the scheme, it is
abundantly evident, that from the beginning there was
a deliberate and well-digested plan to re-establish
slavery in Texas—annex that province to the United
States—and thus immensely increase the slave territory and influence in the Union.

At the first blast of the Texian bugle, thousands of
volunteers from the slaveholding States rushed to the

standard of " the lone star." Agents were sent to the
United States to create an interest in behalf of Texas
—the most inflammatory appeals were made to the people of the Union—and armed bodies of American citizens were openly formed in the South, and transported
without concealment to the seat of the insurrection.
President Jackson reminded the inhabitants of the
United States of their obligations to observe neutrality in
the contest between Mexico and its rebellious province.
At the same time, Gen. Gaines, with a body of U. S.
troops, was ordered to take up a position within the
borders of Texas. The avowed object of this movement was to protect the people of the Southwestern
frontiers from the incursions of Indian tribes in the
employment of Mexico. But the presence of such a
body of troops could not but exert an influence favorable to the measures and objects of Texas ; and besides, it afterwards appeared the Indians had no disposition to take sides with Mexico, or to make any
depredations on the territories of the United States.
A call was made on Congress for an appropriation of
a million of dollars to carry on these military operations, the entire tendency of which was to encourage
Texas in its attempt to throw off the Mexican allegiance and re-establish slavery.

The source from whence the authorities of Texas
were confidently looking for assistance, and the ulterior
object at which they were aiming in their insurrection
—viz.: annexation to the United States, and thus add-

ing territory and strength to the institution of slavery
—are clearly revealed in the following extracts from a
letter addressed by Gen. Houston, commander of the
Texian forces, to Gen. Dunlap, of Nashville, Tenn :—

"*Near Sabine, July*, 2, 1836.

" To Gen. Dunlap :

Sir :—Your favor of the 1st of June reached me last evening.
I regret so much delay will necessarily result before you can reach
us. We will need your aid, and that speedily. The enemy, in large
numbers, are reported to be in Texas. * * * * * The army with which
they first entered Texas is broken up and dispersed by desertion
and other causes. If they get another army of the extent proposed,
it must be composed of new recruits, and men pressed into service.
They will not possess the mechanical efficiency of discipline which
gives the Mexican troops the only advantage they have. They will
easily be routed by a very inferior force. *For a portion of that
force, we shall be obliged to look to the United States!* It cannot
reach us too soon. There is but one feeling in Texas, in my opinion, and that is, to establish the independence of Texas, and to be
attached to the United States! * * * * * March as speedily as
possible, with all the aid you can bring, and I doubt not but you
will be gratified with your reception and situation."

The whole plan succeeded beyond the anticipation
of its most sanguine projectors. Aided by men and
means from the United States, Texas established its
independence—organized a government—incorporated
slavery into its constitution so thoroughly as to guard
against the remotest attempt ever to remove it—and
by a process unsurpassed in the annals of political
intrigue, in due time became annexed to the North
American Union. In this accession of a territory
from which several large States will eventually be

carved out, the slave power of the United States obtained a signal advantage, of which it will not be backward to avail itself in the time of its need. A faithful history of this entire movement is yet to be written.

Mr. Adams, with his well-known and long-tried sagacity, saw at a glance the whole design of the originators of the Texas insurrection. While most people were averse to the belief that a project was seriously on foot to sever a large and free province from the Mexican Republic and annex it to the Union as slave territory, he read the design in legible characters from the beginning. In a speech made in the House of Representatives, in May, 1836, in reference to the call for a million of dollars, for purposes already stated, Mr. Adams unriddled the Texian project with the vision of a prophet.

"Have we not seen American citizens," said Mr. Adams, "going from all parts of the country to carry on the war of this province against the united Government of Mexico? Who were those who fell at Alamo? Who are now fighting under the command of the hero* of Texian fame? And have we not been called upon in this House, to recognize Texian independence? It seems that Gen. Gaines considers this a war in defence of 'our Texians.'"

Mr. Cambreleng explained that the word "neighbors," had been accidentally omitted in Gen. Gaines' dispatch.

Mr. Adams continued:—" Was this an intention to conquer Texas,

---

* General Houston.

to re-establish that slavery which had been abolished by the United Mexican States ? If that was the case, and we were to be drawn into an acknowledgment of their independence, and then, by that preliminary act, by that acknowledgment, if we were upon their application to admit Texas to become a part of the United States, then the House ought to be informed of it. I shall be for no such war, nor for making any such addition to our territory. * * * * * * I hope Congress will take care to go into no war for the re-establishment of slavery where it has been abolished—that they will go into no war in behalf of ' our Texians,' or ' our Texian neighbors'— and that they will go into no war with a foreign power, without other cause than the acquisition of territory."

In a speech delivered a few days subsequent to the above, Mr. Adams used the following language :—

" It is said that one of the earliest acts of this administration was a proposal, made at a time when there was already much ill-humor in Mexico against the United States, that she should cede to the United States a very large portion of her territory—large enough to constitute nine States equal in extent to Kentucky. It must be confessed that a device better calculated to produce jealousy, suspicion, ill-will and hatred, could not have been contrived. It is further affirmed that this overture, offensive in itself, was made precisely at the time when a swarm of colonists from these United States, were covering the Mexican border with land-jobbing, and with slaves, introduced in defiance of Mexican laws, by which slavery had been abolished throughout the Republic. The war now raging in Texas is a Mexican civil war, and a war for the re-establishment of slavery where it was abolished. It is not a servile war, but a war between slavery and emancipation, and every possible effort has been made to drive us into the war on the side of slavery."

" When, in the year 1836, resolutions to recognize the independence of Texas came up in the House of Representatives, Mr. Adams opposed them with great energy and eloquence, and pro voked a most ardent and violent debate. Mr. Waddy Thompson, then a Representative in Congress, and subsequently Minister to Mexico, advocated the passage of the resolutions; and, in doing so, said that Mr. Adams, in negotiating the Florida treaty, actually ceded to Mexico the whole of Texas, a province that was part and parcel of this Union.

" Mr. Adams immediately arrested the speech of Mr. Thompson, and denied the impeachment. Mr. Thompson rejoined, and, to strengthen his position, quoted some remarks Gen. Jackson had made on the subject, confirmatory of the charge of having sacrificed the national domain, in the Florida negotiation.

"Mr. Adams replied with great warmth; and went into a minute and interesting narrative of the whole transaction. Among other things, he said that, before the Florida treaty was signed, he took it to Gen. Jackson, to obtain his opinion of it; and that it was unconditionally approved by him.

" Mr. Thompson was surprised at the announcement of this fact. It weakened his position very materially; and he resumed his seat a defeated antagonist. So said the House of Representatives, with scarcely the exception of a member.

"Mr. Adams continued his defence. ' At that time,' said he, ' General Jackson was in this city, on exciting business connected with the Seminole war; and, after the treaty had been concluded, and only wanted the signatures of the contracting parties, the then President of the United States directed me to call on General Jackson, in my official capacity as Secretary of State, and obtain his opinion in reference to boundaries. I did call. General Jackson, sir, was at that time holding his quarters in the hotel at the other end of the avenue, *now* kept by Mr. Azariah Fuller, but *then* under the management of Jonathan McCarty. The day was exceedingly warm, and, on entering General Jackson's parlor, I found him much exhausted by excitement, and the intensity of the weather. I made known to him the object of my visit; when he replied that I would greatly oblige him if I would excuse him from looking into the matter then. "Leave the papers with me, sir, till to-morrow, or the next day, and I will examine them." I did leave them, sir; and the next day called for the hero's opinion and decision. Sir, I recollect the occurrence perfectly well; General Jackson was still unwell; and the papers, with an accompanying map, were spread before him. With his cane, sir, he pointed to the boundaries, as they had been agreed upon by the parties; and, sir, with a very emphatic expression, which I need not repeat, he affirmed them.'

" This debate, whilst yet warm from the hands of the reporters, reached General Jackson; and was at once pressed upon his attention. Its contradiction and refutation were deemed matters of paramount importance. The old soldier did not hesitate long to act in the matter, and speedily there appeared in the Globe newspaper a letter, signed Andrew Jackson, denying, in unqualified and unconditional terms, everything that Mr. Adams had uttered. He denied having been in Washington at the time Mr. Adams designated; but afterwards, being convinced that he was in error, in this fact only he corrected himself, but denied most positively that he had seen the Florida treaty, or Mr. Adams, at the time of its negotiation, or that he had had the remotest agency or connection with the transaction.

" Mr. Adams responded, and appealed to his diary, where everything was set forth with the utmost precision and accuracy. The year, day of the month, and of the week, and the very hour of the day, all were faithfully recorded.

" The affair produced much sensation at Washington; and even the most determined advocates of General Jackson believed that he, and not Mr. Adams, was in error. No one would, or could for a moment, believe that Mr. Adams ' had made a false report.'

" Whilst this controversy was pending, I called at the Presidential mansion, one afternoon, when General Jackson, strange to say, happened to be alone. He said that he was very glad to see me, because he would like to hear, from one who had an opportunity of seeing more of the press than he *saw*, what was the exact state of public opinion, in regard to the controversy.

" ' As far as I am capable of judging, Mr. President,' I replied, ' the people appear to be unanimous in the opinion that there is a misunderstanding, a misapprehension, between you and Mr. Adams; for no one imagines, for a moment, that either of you would misrepresent facts! Mr. Adams is a man of infinite method; he is generally accurate, and, in this instance, it appears that he is sustained by his diary.'

" ' His diary! don't tell me anything more about his diary! Sir, that diary comes up on all occasions—one would think that its pages were as immutable as the laws of the Medes and Persians! Sir, that diary will be the death of me! I wonder if James Monroe kept a *diary!* If he did, it is to be hoped that it will be looked to, to see if it contains anything about this Adams and Don Onis treaty. Sir, I did not see it ; I was *not* consulted about it.'

"The old hero was exceedingly vehement, and was proceeding to descant with especial violence, when he was interrupted by the entrance of Mr. Secretary Woodbury, and I never heard another word about the matter. A question of veracity between the parties was raised, and was never adjudicated. Both went down to the grave before any definite light was cast on the subject ; but the world had decided that General Jackson was in error.*

---

* Reminiscences of the late John Quincy Adams, by an Old Colony Man.

CHAPTER XIII.

MR. ADAMS PRESENTS PETITIONS FOR THE ABOLISHMENT OF SLAVERY—OPPOSITION OF SOUTHERN MEMBERS—EXCITING SCENES IN THE HOUSE OF REPRESENTATIVES—MARKS OF CONFIDENCE IN MR. ADAMS.

In the meantime, during the years 1836 and 1837, the public mind in the Northern States, became fully aroused to the enormities of American slavery—its encroachments on the rights and interests of the free States—the undue influence it was exercising in our national councils—and the evident determination to enlarge its borders and its evils, by the addition of new and large territories. Petitions for the abolition of slavery and the slave trade in the District of Columbia and the Territories, began to pour into Congress, from every section of the East and North. These were generally presented by Mr. Adams. His age and experience—his well-known influence in the House of Representatives—his patriotism, and his intrepid advocacy of human freedom—inspired the confidence of the people of the free States, and led them to entrust to him their petitions. With scrupulous fidelity he performed the duty thus imposed upon him. Whoever petitions might come from—whatever the nature of their prayer—whether for such objects as he could sanction or not—if they were clothed in respectful language, Mr. Adams felt himself under an imperative obligation to present them to Congress. For several sessions at this period, few days passed without his presenting more or less petitions having some relation to the subject of slavery.

The southern members of Congress became alarmed at these demonstrations, and determined to arrest them, even at the sacrifice, if need be, of the right of petition —the most sacred privilege of freemen. On the 8th of Feb., 1836, a committee was raised by the House of Representatives, to take into consideration what disposition should be made of petitions and memorials for the abolition of slavery and the slave trade, in the District of Columbia, and report thereon. This committee consisted of Messrs. Pinckney of South Carolina, Hamer of Ohio, Pierce of New Hampshire, Hardin of Kentucky, Jarvis of Maine, Owens of Georgia, Muhlenberg of Pennsylvania, Dromgoole of Virginia, and Turrill of New York. On the 18th of May, the committee made a lengthy and unanimous report through Mr. Pinckney, recommending the adoption of the following resolutions :—

"Resolved, That Congress possesses no constitutional authority to interfere in any way with the institution of slavery in any of the States of this Confederacy.

"Resolved, That Congress ought not to interfere in any way with slavery in the District of Columbia.

"And whereas, It is extremely important and desirable that the agitation of this subject should be finally arrested, for the purpose of restoring tranquillity to the public mind, your committee respectfully recommend the adoption of the following additional resolution, viz. :—

" Resolved, That all petitions, memorials, resolutions, propositions or papers, relating in any way, or to any extent whatever, to the subject of slavery, or the abolition of slavery, shall, without being either printed or referred, be laid upon the table, and that no further action whatever shall be had thereon."

When the first of these resolutions was taken up, Mr. Adams said, if the House would allow him five minutes' time, he would prove the resolution to be untrue. His request was denied.

On the third resolution Mr. Adams refused to vote, and sent to the Speaker's chair the following declaration, demanding that it should be placed on the journal of the House, there to stand to the latest posterity :—

" I hold the resolution to be a direct violation of the Constitution of the United States, of the rules of this House, and of the rights of my constituents."

Notwithstanding the rule embodied in this resolution virtually trampled the right of petition into the dust, yet it was adopted by the House, by a large majority. But Mr. Adams was not to be deterred by this arbitrary restriction, from a faithful discharge of his duty as a representative of the people. Petitions on the subject of slavery continued to be transmitted to him in increased numbers. With unwavering firmness—against a bitter and unscrupulous opposition, exasperated to the highest pitch by his pertinacity—amidst a perfect tempest of vituperation and abuse—he persevered in presenting these petitions, one by one, to the amount sometimes of two hundred in a day—demanding the action of the House on each separate petition.

His position amid these scenes was in the highest degree illustrious and sublime. An old man, with the weight of years upon him, forgetful of the elevated stations he had occupied, and the distinguished honors received for past services, turning away from the repose which age so greatly needs, and laboring, amidst scorn and derision, and threats of expulsion and assassination, to maintain the sacred right of petition for the poorest and humblest in the land—insisting that the voice of a free people should be heard by their representatives, when they would speak in condemnation of human slavery and call upon them to maintain the principles of liberty embodied in the immortal Declaration of Independence—was a spectacle unwitnessed before in the history of legislation. A few specimens of these transactions will enable the reader to judge of the trials Mr. Adams was compelled to endure in the discharge of his duties, and also of his moral courage and indomitable perseverance, amid the most appalling circumstances.

On the 6th of Jan., 1837, Mr. Adams presented the petition of one hundred and fifty women, whom he stated to be the wives and daughters of his immediate constituents, praying for the abolition of slavery in the District of Columbia, and moved that the petition be read.

Mr. Glascock objected to its reception.

Mr. Parks moved that the preliminary motion, on the reception of the petition, be laid on the table, which was carried.

Mr. Adams said, that if he had understood the decision of the Speaker in this case, it was not the petition itself which was laid upon the table, but the motion to receive. In order to save the time of the House, he wished to give notice that he should call up that motion, for decision, every day, so long as he should be permited to do so by the House; because he should not consider his duty accomplished so long as the petition was not received, and so long as the House had not decided that it would not receive it.

Mr. Pinckney rose to a question of order, and inquired if there was now any question pending before the House?

The Speaker said, he had understood the gentleman from Massachusetts as merely giving notice of a motion hereafter to be made. In doing so, it certainly was not in order to enter into debate.

Mr. Adams said, that so long as freedom of speech was allowed to him as a member of that House, he would call up that question until it should be decided.

Mr. Adams was called to order.

Mr. A. said, he would then have the honor of presenting to the House the petition of two hundred and twenty-eight women, the wives and daughters of his immediate constituents; and as a part of the speech which he intended to make, he would take the liberty of reading the petition. It was not long, and would not consume much time.

Mr. Glascock objected to the reception of the petition.

Mr. Adams proceeded to read, that the petitioners, inhabitants of South Weymouth, in the State of Massachusetts, " impressed with the sinfulness of slavery, and keenly aggrieved by its existence in a part of our country over which Congress ——"

Mr. Pinckney rose to a question of order. Had the gentleman from Massachusetts a right, under the rule, to read the petition?

The Speaker said, the gentleman from Massachusetts had a right to make a statement of the contents of the petition.

Mr. Pinckney desired the decision of the Speaker as to whether a gentleman had a right to read a petition.

Mr. Adams said he was reading the petition as a part of his speech, and he took this to be one of the privileges of a member of the House. It was a privilege he would exercise till he should be deprived of it by some positive act.

The Speaker repeated that the gentleman from Massachusetts had a right to make a brief statement of the contents of the petition. It was not for the Speaker to decide whether that brief statement should be made in the gentleman's own language, or whether he should look over the petition, and take his statement from that.

Mr. Adams.—At the time my friend from South Carolina——

The Speaker said the gentleman must proceed to state the contents of the petition.

Mr. Adams.—I am doing so, sir.

The Speaker.—Not in the opinion of the chair.

Mr. Adams.—I was at this point of the petition—"Keenly aggrieved by its existence in a part of our country over which Congress possesses exclusive jurisdiction in all cases whatsoever ——"

Loud cries of " Order," " Order !"

Mr. Adams.—"Do most earnestly petition your honorable body ——"

Mr. Chambers of Kentucky rose to a point of order.

Mr. Adams.—"Immediately to abolish slavery in the District of Columbia ——"

Mr. Chambers reiterated his call to order, and the Speaker directed Mr. Adams to take his seat.

Mr. Adams proceeded with great rapidity of enunciation, and in a very loud tone of voice—"*And to declare every human being free who sets foot upon its soil !*"

The confusion in the hall at this time was very great. The Speaker decided that it was not in order for a member to read a petition, whether it was long or short.

Mr. Adams appealed from any decision which went to establish the principle that a member of the House should not have the power to read what he chose. He had never before heard of such a thing. If this practice was to be reversed, let the decision stand upon record, and let it appear how entirely the freedom of speech was suppressed in this House. If the reading of a paper was to be suppressed in his person, so help him God, he would only consent to it as a matter of record.

Mr. Adams finished the petition. The petitioners " respectfully announce their intention to present the same petition yearly before this honorable body, that it might at least be a memorial in the holy cause of human freedom that they had done what they. could."

These words were read amidst tumultuous cries for "order," from every part of the House. The petition was finally received, and laid upon the table.

Other scenes of a still more exciting character soon occurred.

On the 7th of February, 1837, after Mr. Adams had offered some two hundred or more abolition petitions, he came to a halt; and, without yielding the floor, employed himself in packing up his budget. He was about resuming his seat, when he took up a paper, and hastily glancing at it, exclaimed, in a shrill tone—

"Mr. Speaker, I have in my possession a petition of a somewhat extraordinary character; and I wish to inquire of the chair if it be in order to present it."

"If the gentleman from Massachusetts," said the Speaker, "will inform the chair what the character of the petition is, it will probably be able to decide on the subject."

"Sir," ejaculated Mr. Adams, "the petition is signed by eleven slaves of the town of Fredericksburgh, in the county of Culpepper, in the state of Virginia. It is one of those petitions which, it has occurred to my mind, are not what they purport to be. It is signed partly by persons who cannot write, by making their marks, and partly by persons whose handwriting would manifest that they have received the education of slaves. The petition declares itself to be from slaves, and I am requested to present it. I will send it to the chair."

The Speaker (Mr. Polk,) who habitually extended to Mr. Adams every courtesy and kindness imaginable, was taken by surprise, and found himself involved in a dilemma. Giving his chair one of those *hitches* which ever denoted his excitement, he said that a petition from slaves was a novelty, and involved a question that he did not feel called upon to decide. He would like to take time to consider it; and, in the meantime, would refer it to the House.

The House was very thin at the time, and little attention was paid to what was going on, till the excitement of the Speaker attracted the attention of Mr. Dixon H. Lewis, of Alabama, who impatiently, and under great excitement, rose and inquired what the petition was.

Mr. Speaker afforded the required information. Mr. Lewis, forgetting all discretion, whilst he frothed at the mouth, turned towards

Mr. Adams, and ejaculated at the top of his voice, " By G–d, sir, this is not to be endured any longer !"

" Treason ! treason !" screamed a half dozen other members. " Expel the old scoundrel ; put him out ; do not let him disgrace the House any longer !"

" Get up a resolution to meet the case," exclaimed a member from North Carolina.

Mr. George C. Dromgoole, who had acquired a very favorable reputation as a parliamentarian, was selected as the very man who, of all others, was most capable of drawing up a resolution that would meet and cover the emergency. He produced a resolution with a preamble, in which it was stated, substantially, that, whereas the Hon. John Quincy Adams, a representative from Massachusetts, had presented to the House of Representatives a petition signed by negro slaves, thus " giving *color to an idea*" that bondmen were capable of exercising the right of petition, it was " Resolved, That he be taken to the bar of the House, and be censured by the Speaker thereof."

Mr. Haynes said, the true motion, in his judgment, would be to move that the petition be rejected.

Mr. Lewis hoped that no motion of that kind would come from any gentleman from a slaveholding section of the country.

Mr. Haynes said he would cheerfully withdraw his motion.

Mr. Lewis was glad the motion was withdrawn. He believed that the House should punish severely such an infraction of its decorum and its rules ; and he called on the members from the slaveholding States to come forward now and demand of the House the punishment of the gentleman from Massachusetts.

Mr. Grantland, of Georgia, would second the motion, and go all lengths in support of it.

Mr. Lewis said, that if the House would inflict no punishment for such flagrant violations of its dignity as this, it would be better for the Representatives from the slaveholding States to go home at once.

Mr. Alford said, if the gentleman from Massachusetts intended to present this petition, the moment it was presented he should move, as an act of justice to the South, which he in part represented, and which he conceived had been treated with indignity, that it be taken from the House and burnt ; and he hoped that every man who was a friend to the constitution, would support him. There must be an end to this constant attempt to raise excitement, or the Union could not exist much longer. The moment any man should disgrace the Government under which he lived, by presenting a petition from *slaves*, praying for emancipation, he hoped that petition would, by order of the House, be committed to the flames.

Mr. Waddy Thompson moved the following resolution:—

"Resolved, That the Hon. John Quincy Adams, by the attempt just made by him to introduce a petition purporting on its face to be from slaves, has been guilty of a gross disrespect to this House, and that he be instantly brought to the bar, to receive the severe censure of the Speaker."

The idea of bringing the venerable ex-President to the bar, like a culprit, to receive a reprimand from a comparatively youthful Speaker, would be a spectacle so disgraceful, and withal so absurd, that the proposition met with no favor. An easier way to reprimand was devised. Mr. Haynes introduced the following resolution:—

"Resolved, That John Quincy Adams, a Representative from the State of Massachusetts, has rendered himself justly liable to the severest censure of this House, and is censured accordingly, for having attempted to present to the House the petition of slaves."

Several other resolutions and propositions, from members of slaveholding States, were submitted to the House; but none proved satisfactory even to themselves. Mr. Adams, unmoved by the tempest which raged around him, defended himself, and the integrity of his purpose, with the distinguished ability and eloquence which characterized all his public labors.

"In regard to the resolutions now before the House," said he, "as they all concur in naming me, and in charging me with high crimes and misdemeanors, and in calling me to the bar of the House to answer for my crimes, I have thought it was my duty to remain silent, until it should be the pleasure of the House to act either on one or the other of these resolutions. I suppose that if I shall be brought to the bar of the House, I shall not be struck mute by the previous question, before I have an opportunity to say a word or two in my own defence. * * * * * *

"Now, as to the fact what the petition was for, I simply state to the gentleman from Alabama, (Mr. D. H. Lewis,) who has sent to

the table a resolution assuming that this petition was for the abolition of slavery—I state to him that he is mistaken. He must
amend his resolution ; for if the House should choose to read this
petition, I can state to them they would find it something very much
the reverse of that which the resolution states it to be. And if the
gentleman from Alabama still chooses to bring me to the bar of
the House, he must amend his resolution in a very important particular ; for he may probably have to put into it, that my crime has
been for attempting to introduce the petition of slaves that slavery
should *not* be abolished. * * * * * *

" Sir, it is well known, that from the time I entered this House,
down to the present day, I have felt it a sacred duty to present any
petition, couched in respectful language, from any citizen of the
United States, be its object what it may ; be the prayer of it that in
which I could concur, or that to which I was utterly opposed. It
is for the sacred right of petition that I have adopted this course.
* * * * * * * * Where is your law which says that the mean, and the
low, and the degraded, shall be deprived of the right of petition, if
their moral character is not good ? Where, in the land of freemen,
was the right of petition ever placed on the exclusive basis of
morality and virtue ? Petition is *supplication*—it is *entreaty*—it is
prayer! And where is the degree of vice or immorality which
shall deprive the citizen of the right to *supplicate* for a boon, or to
pray for mercy? Where is such a law to be found ? It does not
belong to the most abject despotism ! There is no absolute monarch
on earth, who is not compelled, by the constitution of his country, to
receive the petitions of his people, whosoever they may be. The
Sultan of Constantinople cannot walk the streets and refuse to receive petitions from the meanest and vilest of the land. This is the
law even of despotism. And what does your law say ? Does it
say that, before presenting a petition, you shall look into it, and
see whether it comes from the virtuous, and the great, and the
mighty ? No sir ; it says no such thing. The right of petition belongs to *all.* And so far from refusing to present a petition because
it might come from those low in the estimation of the world, it would
be an additional incentive, if such incentive were wanting.

" But I must admit," continued Mr. Adams, sarcastically, " that
when *color* comes into the question, there may be other considerations. It is possible that this House, which seems to consider it

so great a crime to attempt to offer a petition from slaves, may, for aught I know, say that freemen, if not of the *carnation*, shall be deprived of the right of petition, in the sense of the House."

When southern members saw that, in their haste, they had not tarried to ascertain the nature of the petition, and that it prayed for the *perpetuation*, instead of the *abolition* of slavery, their position became so ludicrous, that their exasperation was greatly increased. At the time the petition was announced by Mr. Adams, the House was very thin; but the excitement it produced soon filled it; and, besides, the *sergeant-at-arms* had been instructed to arrest and bring in all absentees. The excitement commenced at about one o'clock, and continued until seven o'clock in the evening, when the House adjourned. Mr. Adams stood at his desk, resolutely refusing to be seated till the matter was disposed of, alleging that if he were guilty, he was not entitled to a seat among high and honorable men. When Mr. Droomgoole's resolution was read to the House for its consideration, Mr. Adams yielded to it one of those sarcastic sneers which he was in the habit of giving, when provoked to satire; and said—" Mr. Speaker, if I understand the resolution of the honorable gentleman from Virginia, it charges me with being guilty of 'giving *color* to *an idea!*' " The whole House broke forth in one common irrepressible peal of laughter. The Droomgoole resolution was actually laughed out of existence. The House now found that it had got itself in a dilemma,—that Mr. Adams was too much for it; and, at last, adjourned, leaving the affair in the position in which they found it.

For several days this subject continued to agitate the House. Mr. Adams not only warded off the virulent attacks made upon him, but carried the war so effectually into the camp of his enemies, that, becoming heartily tired of the contest, they repeatedly endeavored to get rid of the whole subject by laying it on the table. To this Mr. Adams objected. He insisted that it should be thoroughly canvassed. Immense excitement ensued. Call after call of the House was made. Mr. Henry A. Wise, who was, at the time, engaged on the Reuben Whitney affair, was sent for, with an accompanying message that the stability of the Union was in danger!

Breathless, and impatient, Mr. Wise made his appearance, and inquired what was the matter. He was informed.

" And is that all ?" ejaculated Mr. Wise. " The gentleman from

Massachusetts has presented a petition signed by slaves! Well, sir, and what of that? Is anybody harmed by it? Sir, in my opinion, slaves are the very persons who should petition. Mine, sir, pray to me, and I listen to them; and shall not the feeble supplicate? Sir, I see no danger,—the country, I believe, is safe."

At length the exciting subject was brought to a termination, by the passage of the following preamble and resolutions; much softened, it will be seen, in comparison with the measures first proposed:—

"An inquiry having been made by an honorable gentleman from Massachusetts, whether a paper which he held in his hand, purporting to be a petition from certain slaves, and declaring themselves to be slaves, came within the order of the House of the 18th of January,* and the said paper not having been received by the Speaker, he stated that in a case so extraordinary and novel, he would take the advice and counsel of the House.

"Resolved, That this House cannot receive said petition without disregarding its own dignity, the rights of a large class of citizens of the South and West, and the Constitution of the United States.

"Resolved, That slaves do not possess the right of petition secured to the citizens of the United States by the constitution."

The slave petition is believed to have been a counterfeit, manufactured by certain members from slaveholding States, and was sent to Mr. Adams by the way of experiment —with the double design of ascertaining if he could be imposed upon; and, if the deception succeeded, those who got it up were curious to know if the venerable statesman would redeem his pledge, and present a petition, no matter who it came from. He was too wily not to detect the plot at the outset; he knew that all was a hoax; but, he resolved to present the paper, and then turn the tables on its authors.†

On the 20th of December, 1838, Mr. Adams presented a petition praying for the establishment of international relations with the Republic of Hayti, and moved that it be referred to the Committee

* This order was the same as that adopted by the House on the 18th of May, 1836. See p. 281.

† Reminiscences of the late John Quincy Adams, by an Old Colony Man.

on Foreign Affairs, with instructions to consider and report thereon. This motion was opposed with great warmth by members from slaveholding States. Mr. Adams was repeatedly interrupted during the delivery of the brief speech he made on the occasion.

Mr. Bynum insisted that the gentleman from Massachusetts should take his seat, under the rule. If, however, he was permitted to proceed, Mr. B. hoped some gentleman of the slaveholding portion of the House would be allowed to answer him.

Mr. Adams.—Sir, I hope so. Only open our mouths, gentlemen; that is all we ask, and you may answer as much as you please.

Mr. Bynum.—I object to the gentleman proceeding further with his observations, except by consent of the House. If we have rules we had better either obey them or burn them.

The House voted, by 114 to 47, to allow Mr. Adams to proceed.

In continuing his speech, Mr. Adams said, that even admitting the object of the petitioners is abolition, as has been alleged, they had the right to petition for that too; for every individual in the country had a right to be an abolitionist. The great men of the Revolution were abolitionists, and if any man denies it, I will prove it.

Mr. Wise.—I deny it.

The Speaker said this was out of order.

Mr. Adams.—I feel obliged to the gentleman from Virginia for giving me the invitation, and I will now prove what I say.

The Speaker said this did not form any part of the question before the House.

Mr. Adams.—George Washington, *in articulo mortis*, by his last will and testament, before God, his Creator, emancipated his slaves.

Mr. Wise.—Because he had no children.

The Speaker again interposed, and said the gentleman could not go into that question. It was entirely out of order.

Mr. Adams.—I did but accept the invitation of the gentleman from Virginia. I do not wish to go further. I simply take the position that George Washington was an abolitionist in the most extensive sense of the term; and I defy any man in this House to the discussion, and to prove to the contrary if he can.

The Speaker called Mr. Adams to order.

Mr. Adams.—Well, sir, I was stating the high authority which is to be found for the principles of abolition. Does the gentleman from Virginia deny that Thomas Jefferson was an abolitionist?

Mr. Wise.—I do.

The Speaker again interposed.

Mr. Adams.—Well, sir, then I come back to my position, that every man in this country has a right to be an abolitionist, and that in being so he offends no law, but, in my opinion, obeys the most sacred of all laws.

The motion to instruct the committee, was finally laid upon the table.

Mr. Adams was evidently anxious to engage in a legitimate discussion, in the House of Representatives, of the subject of slavery in all its bearings, influences, and results. Such a discussion, coolly and deliberately entered upon, by men of the most distinguished abilities in the nation, could not but have been pregnant with lasting good, not only to the North, but also to the South and the entire country. To afford opportunity for a dignified and profitable investigation of this momentous topic, Mr. Adams, on the 25th of Feb., 1839, proposed the following amendments to the Constitution of the United States :—

" *Resolved, by the Senate and House of Representatives in Congress assembled,* two-thirds of both Houses concurring therein, That the following amendments to the Constitution of the United States be proposed to the several States of the Union, which, when ratified by three-fourths of the legislatures of said States, shall become and be a part of the Constitution of the United States :—

" 1. From and after the 4th day of July, 1842, there shall be throughout the United States no hereditary slavery; but on and after that day, every child born within the United States, their territories or jurisdiction, shall be born free.

" 2. With the exception of the territory of Florida, there shall henceforth never be admitted into this Union, any State, the constitution of which shall tolerate within the same the existence of slavery.

" 3. From and after the 4th day of July, 1845, there shall be neither slavery nor slave trade, at the seat of Government of the United States."

Instead of meeting and canvassing, in a manly and honorable manner, the vitally important question involved in these propositions, the slaveholding Representatives objected to its coming before the House for consideration, in any form whatever. In this instance, as in most others, where the merits of slavery are involved, the supporters of that institution manifested a timidity, a want of confidence in its legitimacy, of the most suspicious nature. If slavery is lawful and defensible—if it violates no true principle among men, no human right bestowed by the Creator—if it can be tolerated and perpetuated in harmony with republican institutions and our Declaration of Independence—if its existence in the bosom of the Confederacy involves no incongruity, and is calculated to promote the prosperity and stability of the Union, or the welfare of the slaveholding States themselves—these are facts which can be made evident to the world, by the unsurpassed abilities of southern statesmen. Why, then, object to a candid and fearless investigation of the subject? But if slavery is the reverse of all this— if it is a moral poison, contaminating and blighting everything connected with it, and containing the seeds of its own dissolution sooner or later—why should wise, sagacious politicians, prudent and honest men, and conscientious Christians, shut their eyes and turn away from a fact so appalling and so dangerous. No man of intelligence can hope, in this age of the world, to perpetuate that which is wrong and destructive, by bravado and threatening—by refusing to look it in the face, or to allow others to scrutinize it. Error must pass away. Truth, however unpalatable, or however it may be obscured for a season, must eventually triumph. The very exertions of its supporters to perpetuate wrong, will but hasten its death.

> " Truth, crushed to earth, will rise again ;
> Th' eternal years of God are hers :
> But Error, wounded, writhes with pain,
> And dies among her worshippers."

Notwithstanding the course Mr. Adams felt himself compelled to pursue led him frequently into collision with a large portion of the Members of the House of Representatives, and caused them sometimes, in the heat of excitement, to forget the deference due his age, his experience, and commanding abilities, yet there was ever a deep, under-current feeling of veneration for him, pervading all hearts. Those who were excited to the highest pitch of frenzy by his proceedings, could not but admire the singleness of his purpose, and his undaunted courage in discharging his duties. On all subjects aside from slavery, his influence in the House has never been surpassed. Whenever he arose to speak, it was a signal for a general abandonment of listlessness and inattention. Members dropped their

newspapers and pamphlets—knots of consulting politicians in different parts of the Hall were dissolved—
Representatives came hastily in from lobbies, com-
mittee-rooms, the surrounding grounds—and all eagerly
clustered around his chair to listen to words of wisdom, patriotism, and truth, as they dropped burning
from the lips of " the old man eloquent !" The confidence placed in him in emergencies, was unbounded.
A case in point is afforded in the history of the difficulty occasioned by the double delegation from New
Jersey.

On the opening of the 26th Congress, in December, 1839, in
consequence of a two-fold delegation from New-Jersey, the House
was unable, for some time, to complete its organization, and presented to the country and the world the perilous and discreditable
aspect of the assembled Representatives of the people, unable to form
themselves into a constitutional body.   On first assembling, the
House has no officers, and the Clerk of the preceding Congress acts,
by usage, as chairman of the body, till a Speaker is chosen.   On
this occasion, after reaching the State of New Jersey, the acting
Clerk declined to proceed in calling the roll, and refused to entertain any of the motions which were made for the purpose of extri-
cating the House from its embarrassment.   Many of the ablest and
most judicious members had addressed the House in vain, and there
was nothing but confusion and disorder in prospect.

The fourth day opened, and still confusion was triumphant.
But the hour of disenthrallment was at hand, and a scene was
presented which sent the mind back to those days when Cromwell
uttered the exclamation—" Sir Harry Vane ! wo unto you, Sir Harry
Vane !"—and in an instant dispersed the famous Rump Parliament.

Mr. Adams, from the opening of this scene of confusion and
anarchy, had maintained a profound silence.   He appeared to be
engaged most of the time in writing.   To a common observer, he
seemed to be reckless of everything around him—but nothing, not
the slightest incident, escaped him.   The fourth day of the struggle

had now commenced; Mr. Hugh H. Garland, the Clerk, was directed to call the roll again.

He commenced with Maine, as was usual in those days, and was proceeding toward Massachusetts. I turned, and saw that Mr. Adams was ready to get the floor at the earliest moment possible. His keen eye was riveted on the Clerk; his hands clasped the front edge of his desk, where he always placed them to assist him in rising. He looked, in the language of Otway, like the

> " ———————— fowler, eager for his prey."

"New Jersey!" ejaculated Mr. Hugh H. Garland, "and the Clerk has to repeat that ———— "

Mr. Adams sprang to the floor!

"I rise to interrupt the Clerk," was his first ejaculation.

"Silence, silence," resounded through the hall; "hear him, hear him! Here what he has to say; hear John Quincy Adams!" was the unanimous ejaculation on all sides.

In an instant, the most profound silence reigned throughout the Hall—you might have heard a leaf of paper fall in any part of it—and every eye was riveted on the venerable Nestor of Massachusetts—the purest of statesmen, and the noblest of men! He paused for a moment; and, having given Mr. Garland a

> " ———————————— withering look!"

he proceeded to address the multitude:

"It was not my intention," said he, "to take any part in these extraordinary proceedings. I had hoped that this House would succeed in organizing itself; that a Speaker and Clerk would be elected, and that the ordinary business of legislation would be progressed in. This is not the time, or place, to discuss the merits of the conflicting claimants for seats from New Jersey; that subject belongs to the House of Representatives, which, by the constitution, is made the ultimate arbiter of the qualifications of its members. But what a spectacle we here present! We degrade and disgrace ourselves; we degrade and disgrace our constituents and the country. We do not, and cannot organize; and why? Because the Clerk of this House, the mere Clerk, whom we create, whom we employ, and whose existence depends upon our will, usurps the *throne*, and sets us, the Representatives, the vicegerents of the whole

American people, at defiance, and holds us in contempt! And what is this Clerk of yours? Is he to control the destinies of sixteen millions of freemen? Is he to suspend, by his mere negative, the functions of Government, and put an end to this Congress? He refuses to call the roll! It is in your power to compel him to call it, if he will not do it voluntarily. [Here he was interrupted by a member, who said that he was authorized to say that compulsion could not reach the Clerk, who had avowed that he would resign, rather than call the State of New Jersey.] Well, sir, then let him resign," continued Mr. Adams, " and we may possibly discover some way by which we can get along, without the aid of his all-powerful talent, learning and genius. If we cannot organize in any other way—if this Clerk of yours will not consent to our discharging the trusts confided to us by our constituents, then let us imitate the example of the Virginia House of Burgesses, which, when the colonial Governor Dinwiddie ordered it to disperse, refused to obey the imperious and insulting mandate, and, *like men* ———— "

The multitude could not contain or repress their enthusiasm any longer, but saluted the eloquent and indignant speaker, and intercepted him with loud and deafening cheers, which seemed to shake the capitol to its centre. The very Genii of applause and enthusiasm seemed to float in the atmosphere of the Hall, and every heart expanded with an indescribable feeling of pride and exultation. The turmoil, the darkness, the very " chaos of anarchy," which had, for three successive days, pervaded the American Congress, was dispelled by the magic, the talismanic eloquence of a single man; and, once more the wheels of Government and of Legislation were put in motion.*

Having, by this powerful appeal, brought the yet unorganized assembly to a perception of its hazardous position, he submitted a motion requiring the acting Clerk to proceed in calling the roll. This and similar motions had already been made by other members. The difficulty was, that the acting Clerk declined to entertain them. Accordingly, Mr. Adams was immediately interrupted by a burst of voices demanding, " How shall the question be put?" " Who will put the question?" The voice of Mr. Adams was heard above the tumult, " I intend to put the question myself!" That word brought order out of chaos. There was the master mind.

---

* Reminiscences—by an Old Colony Man.

As soon as the multitude had recovered itself, and the excitement of irrepressible enthusiasm had abated, Mr. Richard Barnwell Rhett, of South Carolina, leaped upon one of the desks, waved his hand, and exclaimed :

" I move that the Honorable John Quincy Adams take the chair of the Speaker of this House, and officiate as presiding officer, till the House be organized by the election of its constitutional officers ! As many as are agreed to this will say *ay ;* those ———"

He had not an opportunity to complete the sentence—" those who are not agreed, will say *no,*"—for one universal, deafening, thundering *ay*, responded to the nomination.

Hereupon, it was moved and ordered that Lewis Williams, of North Carolina, and Richard Barnwell Rhett, conduct John Quincy Adams to the chair.

Well did Mr. Wise, of Virginia, say, " Sir, I regard it as the proudest hour of your life ; and if, when you shall be gathered to your fathers, I were asked to select the words which, in my judgment, are best calculated to give at once the character of the man, I would inscribe upon your tomb this sentence, ' I will put the question myself.' "*

---

* In a public address, Mr. Adams once quoted the well known words of Tacitus, Annal. vi. 39—" *Par negotiis neque supra*"—applying them to a distinguished man, lately deceased. A lady wrote to inquire whence they came. Mr. Adams informed her, and added, that they could not be adequately translated in less than seven words in English. The lady replied that they might be well translated in five—*Equal to, not above, duty*—but better in three—JOHN QUINCY ADAMS.—*Massachusetts Quarterly Review.*

CHAPTER XIV.

It would be impossible, in the limit prescribed to
these pages, to detail the numerous scenes and occur-
rences of a momentous nature, in which Mr. Adams
took a prominent part during his services in the House
of Representatives. The path he marked out for himself at the commencement of his congressional career,
was pursued with unfaltering fidelity to the close of
life. His was the rare honor of devoting himself, unreservedly, to his legitimate duties as a Representative
of the people while in Congress, and to nothing else.
He believed the halls of the Capitol were no place for
political intrigue ; and that a member of Congress, instead of studying to shape his course to make political
capital or to subserve party ends, should devote himself rigidly and solely to the interests of his constitu-

LIFE OF JOHN QUINCY ADAMS.

ents. His practice corresponded with his theory. His speeches, his votes, his entire labors in Congress, were confined strictly to practical subjects, vitally connected with the great interests of our common country, and had no political or party bearing, other than such as truth and public good might possess.

His hostility to slavery and the assumptions and usurpations of slave power in the councils of the nation, continued to the day of his death. At the commencement of each session of Congress, he demanded that the infamous "gag rule," which forbid the presentation of petitions on the subject of slavery, should be abolished. But despite its continuance, he persisted in handing in petitions from the people of every class, complexion and condition. He did not hesitate to lay before the House of Representatives a petition from Haverhill, Mass., for *the dissolution of the Union!* Although opposed in his whole soul to the prayer of the petitioners, yet he believed himself sacredly bound to listen with due respect to every request of the people, when couched in respectful terms.

In vain did the supporters of slavery endeavor to arrest his course, and to seal his lips in silence. In vain did they threaten assassination—expulsion from the House—indictment before the grand jury of the District of Columbia. In vain did they declare that he should " be made amenable to *another tribunal,* [mob-law] and as an incendiary, be brought to condign punishment." " My life on it," said a southern member.

"if he presents that petition from slaves, we shall yet see him within the walls of the penitentiary." All these attempts at brow-beating moved him not a tittle. Firm he stood to his duty, despite the storms of angry passion which howled around him, and with withering rebukes repelled the assaults of hot-blooded opponents, as the proud old headland, jutting far into ocean's bosom, tosses high, in worthless spray, the dark mountain billows which in wrath beat upon it.

"Do the gentlemen from the South," said he, "think they can frighten me by their threats? If that be their object, let me tell them, sir, *they have mistaken their man*. I am not to be frightened from the discharge of a sacred duty, by their indignation, by their violence, nor, sir, by all the grand juries in the universe. I have done only my duty; and I shall do it again under the same circumstances, even though they recur to-morrow."

> "Though aged, he was so iron of limb,
> None of the youth could cope with him;
> And the foes whom he singly kept at bay,
> Outnumbered his thin hairs of silver grey."

Nor was Mr. Adams without encouragement in his trying position. His immediate constituents, at their primary meetings, repeatedly sent up a cheering voice in strong and earnest resolutions, approving heartily his course, and urging him to perseverance therein. The Legislatures of Massachusetts and Vermont, rallied to his support. In solemn convocation they protested against the virtual annihilation of the right of petition—against slavery and the slave trade in the District of Columbia—gave their entire sanction to the principles advocated by Mr. Adams, and pledged their countenance to all measures calculated to sustain them.

Large bodies of people in the Eastern, Northern, and Middle States, sympathized with him in his support of the most sacred of privileges bestowed on man. Representative after Representative were sent to Congress, who gathered around him, and co-operated with him in his holy warfare against the iron rule which slavery had been enabled to establish in the national Legislature. With renewed energy he resisted the mighty current which was undermining the foundations of the Republic, and bearing away upon its turbid waters the liberties of the people. And he resisted not in vain.

The brave old man lived to see his labors, in this department of duty, crowned with abundant success. One after another the cohorts of slavery gave way before the incessant assaults, the unwearied perseverance, of Mr. Adams, and the faithful compeers who were sent by the people to his support. At length, in 1845, the obnoxious "gag rule" was rescinded, and Congress consented to receive, and treat respectfully, all petitions on the subject of slavery. This was a moral triumph which amply compensated Mr. Adams for all the labors he had put forth, and for all the trials he had endured to achieve it.

Yes; he " lived to hear that subject which of all others had been forbidden an entrance into the Halls of Congress, fairly broached. He lived to listen, with a delight all his own, to a high-souled, wholehearted speech on the slave question, from his colleague, Mr. Palfrey — a speech, of which it is not too high praise to say, that it would not have disparaged the exalted reputation of Mr. Adams, had he made it himself. Aye, more, he lived to see the whole House of Representatives—the members from the South, not less than those from the North, attentive and respectful listeners to that speech of an hour's length, on the political as well as moral aspect of slavery in this Republic. What a triumph! At the close of it, the moral conqueror exclaimed, ' God be praised ; the seals are broken, the door is open.' "*

If anything were wanting to crown the fame of Mr. Adams, in the last days of life, with imperishable honor, or to add, if possible, new brilliancy to the beams of his setting sun, it is found in his advocacy of the freedom of the Amistad slaves.

A ship-load of negroes had been stolen from Africa, contrary to the law of nations, of humanity and of God, and surreptitiously smuggled, in the night, into the Island of Cuba. This act was piracy, according to the law of Spain, and of all Governments in Christendom, and the perpetrators thereof, had they been detected, would have been punished with death. Immediately after the landing of these unfortunate Africans, about thirty-six of them were purchased of the slave-pirates, by two Spaniards named Don Jose Ruiz and Don Pedro Montes, who shipped them for Guanaja, Cuba, in the schooner " *Amistad.*" When three days out from Havana, the Africans rose, killed the captain and crew, and took possession of the vessel—sparing the lives of their purchasers, Ruiz and Montes. This

* Rev. S. J. May.

transaction was unquestionably justifiable on the part of the negroes. They had been stolen from their native land—had fallen into the hands of pirates and robbers, and reduced to abject slavery. According to the first law of nature—the law of self-defence—implanted in the bosom of every human being by the Creator, they were justified in taking any measures necessary to restore them to the enjoyment of that freedom which was theirs by birthright.

The negroes being unable to manage the schooner, compelled Ruiz and Montes to navigate her, and directed them to shape her course for Africa; for it was their design to return to their native land. But they were deceived by the two Spaniards, who brought the schooner to the coast of the United States, where she was taken possession of by Lieut. Gedney, of the U. S. surveying brig Washington, a few miles off Montauk Point, and brought into New London, Conn. The two Spaniards claimed the Africans as their property; and the Spanish Minister demanded of the President of the United States, that they be delivered up to the proper authorities, and taken back to Havana, to be tried for piracy and murder. The matter was brought before the District Court of Connecticut.

In the mean time President Van Buren ordered the U. S. schooner Grampus, Lieut. John S. Paine, to repair to New Haven, to be in readiness to convey the Africans to Havana, should such be the decision of the Court. But the Court decided that the Government of the United States had no authority to return them into slavery ; and directed that they be conveyed in one of our public ships to the shores of Africa, from whence they had but recently been torn away. From this decision the U. S. District Attorney appealed to the Supreme Court of the United States.

These transactions attracted the attention of the whole people of the Union, and naturally excited the sympathy of the masses, *pro* and *con*, as they were favorable or unfavorable to the institution of slavery. Who should defend, in the Supreme Court, these poor outcasts—ignorant, degraded, wretched—who, fired with a noble energy, had burst the shackles of slavery, and by a wave of fortune had been thrown into the midst of a people professing freedom, yet keeping their feet on the necks of millions of slaves? The eyes of all the friends of human rights turned instinctively to JOHN QUINCY ADAMS. Nor were their expectations disappointed. Without hesitation he espoused the cause of the Amistad negroes. At the age of seventy-four, he appeared in the Supreme Court of the United States to advocate their cause. He entered upon this labor with the enthusiasm of a youthful barrister, and displayed forensic talents, a critical knowledge of law, and of the inalienable rights of man, which would have added to the renown of the most eminent jurists of the day.

" When he went to the Supreme Court, after an absence of thirty years, and arose to defend a body of

friendless negroes, torn from their home and most un-
justly held in thrall—when he asked the Judges to
excuse him at once both for the trembling faults of age
and the inexperience of youth, having labored so long
elsewhere that he had forgotten the rules of court—
when he summed up the conclusion of the whole matter, and brought before those judicial but yet moisten-
ing eyes, the great men whom he had once met there—
Chase, Cushing, Martin, Livingston, and Marshal himself; and while he remembered that they were 'gone,
gone, all gone,' remembered also the eternal Justice
that is never gone—the sight was sublime. It was
not an old patrician of Rome, who had been Consul,
Dictator, coming out of his honored retirement at the
Senate's call, to stand in the Forum to levy new
armies, marshal them to victory afresh, and gain
thereby new laurels for his brow; but it was a plain
citizen of America, who had held an office far greater
than that of Consul, King, or Dictator, his hand red-
dened by no man's blood, expecting no honors, but
coming in the name of justice, to plead for the slave,
for the poor barbarian negro of Africa, for Cinque and
Grabbo, for their deeds comparing them to Harmodius
and Aristogeiton, whose classic memory made each
bosom thrill. That was worth all his honors—it was
worth while to live fourscore years for that."*

This effort of Mr. Adams was crowned with complete success. The Supreme Court decided that the

* Theodore Parker.

Africans were entitled to their freedom, and ordered them to be liberated.   In due time they were enabled, by the assistance of the charitable, to sail for Africa, and take with them many of the implements of civilized life.   They arrived in safety at Sierre Leone, and were allowed once more to mingle with their friends, and enjoy God's gift of freedom, in a *Pagan* land— having fortunately *escaped* from a cruel and life-long bondage, in the midst of a *Christian* people.

In reply to a letter requesting Mr. Adams to write out his argument in this case, he concludes as follows : " I shall endeavor, as you desire, to write out, in full extent, my argument before the Court, in which all this was noticed and commented upon.   If it has no other effect, I hope it will at least have that of admonishing the free people of this Union to keep perpetually watchful eyes upon every act of their executive administration, having any relation to the subject of slavery."

In availing the country of the benefit of the " Smithsonian Bequest," and in founding the " Smithsonian Institute" at Washington, Mr. Adams took an active part. He repeatedly called the attention of Congress to the subject, until he succeeded in causing a bill to be passed providing for the establishment of the Institute. He was appointed one of the Regents of the Institute, which office he held until his death.

In the summer of 1843, Mr. Adams visited Lebanon Springs, N. Y., for the benefit of his health, which had become somewhat impaired, and also the health of a cherished member of his family. He designed to devote only four or five days to this journey ; but he was so highly pleased with the small portion of the State of New York he saw at Lebanon Springs, that he was induced to proceed further. He visited Saratoga, Lake George, - Lower Canada, Montreal and Quebec. Returning, he ascended the St. Lawrence and the Lakes as far as Niagara Falls and Buffalo, and by the way of Rochester, Auburn, Utica and Albany, sought his home in Quincy with health greatly improved.

Although Mr. Adams had many bitter enemies— made so by his fearless independence, and the stern integrity with which he discharged the public duties entrusted to him—yet in the hearts of the people he ever occupied the highest position. They not only respected and admired the politician, the statesman, but they venerated the MAN! they loved him for his purity, his philanthropy, his disinterested patriotism, his devotion to freedom and human rights. All this was manifested during his tour through New York. It was marked in its whole extent by demonstrations of the highest attention and respect from people of all parties. Public greetings, processions, celebrations, met him and accompanied him at every step of his journey. Never since the visit of La Fayette, had

such an anxious desire to honor a great and good man
been manifested by the entire mass of the people.
His progress was one continued triumphal procession.
"I may say," exclaimed Mr. Adams, near the close of
his tour, "without being charged with pride or vanity,
I have come not alone, for the whole people of the
State of New York have been my companions!"

At Buffalo he was received with every possible
demonstration of respect. The national ensign was
streaming from an hundred masts, and the wharves,
and the decks and rigging of the vessels, were crowded
by thousands anxious to catch a glimpse of the renowned statesman and patriot, who was greeted by
repeated cheers. Hon. Millard Fillmore addressed
him with great eloquence. The following is the conclusion of his speech:—

"You see around you, sir, no political partisans seeking to promote some sinister purpose; but you see here assembled the people
of our infant city, without distinction of party, sex, age, or condition—all, all anxiously vieing with each other to show their
respect and esteem for your public services and private worth.
Here are gathered, in this vast multitude of what must appear to
you strange faces, thousands whose hearts have vibrated to the
chord of sympathy which your written speeches have touched.
Here is reflecting age, and ardent youth, and lisping childhood, to
all of whom your venerated name is as dear as household words —
all anxious to feast their eyes by a sight of that extraordinary and
venerable man, of whom they have heard, and read, and thought so
much —all anxious to hear the voice of that ' old man eloquent,' on
whose lips wisdom has distilled her choicest nectar. Here, sir, you
see them all, and read in their eager and joy-gladdened countenances,
and brightly-beaming eyes, a welcome—a thrice-told, heart-felt,
soul-stirring welcome to 'the man whom they delight to honor.'"

Mr. Adams responded to this speech in a strain of most interesting remarks. He commenced as follows :—

"I must request your indulgence for a moment's pause to take breath. If you inquire why I ask this indulgence, it is because I am so overpowered by the eloquence of my friend, the chairman of the Committee of Ways and Means, (whom I have been so long accustomed to refer to in that capacity, that, with your permission, I will continue so to denominate him now,) that I have no words left to answer him. For so liberal has he been in bestowing that eloquence upon me which he himself possesses in so eminent a degree, that while he was ascribing to me talents so far above my own consciousness in that regard, I was all the time imploring the god of eloquence to give me, at least at this moment, a few words to justify him before you in making that splendid panegyric which he has been pleased to bestow upon me ; and that the flattering picture which he has presented to you, may not immediately be defaced before your eyes by what you should hear from me. * * * * * *

In concluding his remarks he said :—" Of your attachment to moral principle I have this day had another and pleasing proof in the dinner of which I have partaken in the steamer, in which, by your kindness, I have been conveyed to this place. It was a sumptuous dinner, but at which *temperance* was the presiding power. I congratulate you on the evidence there exhibited of your attachment to moral principle, in your co-operation in that great movement which is promoting the happiness and elevation of man in every quarter of the globe.

"And here you will permit me to allude to an incident which has occurred in my recent visit to Canada, in which I perceived the co-operation of the people of that Province in the same great moral reformation. While at Quebec, I visited the falls of Montmorenci, a cataract which, but for yours, would be among the greatest wonders of nature. In going to it, I passed through the parish of Beauport, and there, by the side of the way, I saw a column with an inscription upon its pedestal, which I had the curiosity to stop and read. It was erected by the people of Beauport in gratitude to the Virgin, for her goodness in promoting the cause of temperance in that parish. Perhaps I do not sufficiently sympathize with the people of Beauport in attributing to the Virgin so direct an influence upon this moral reform; but in the spirit with which they erected that monument I do most cordially sympathize with them. For, under whatever influence the cause may be promoted, the cause itself can never fail to make its votaries wiser and better men. I cannot make a speech. My heart is too full, and my voice too feeble. Farewell! And with that farewell, may the blessings of heaven be upon you throughout your lives!"

Mr. Adams was greatly delighted with his visit to Niagara Falls. A letter-writer thus describes it :—

" Mr. Adams seems incapable of fatigue, either physical or mental. After a drive in the morning to Lewiston, he stopped, on his return to the Falls, at the whirlpool. The descent to the water's edge, which is not often made, is, as you will remember, all but vertical, down a steep of some three hundred and sixty feet. One of the party was about going down, when Mr. Adams remarked that he would accompany him. Gen. Porter and the other gentlemen present remonstrated, and told him it was a very severe undertaking for a young and hearty man, and that he would find it, in such a hot day, quite impracticable. He seemed, however, to know his capacities; and this old man, verging on four score years, not only made the descent, but clambered over almost impracticable rocks along the margin of the river, to obtain the various views presented at different points. The return was not easy, but he was quite adequate to the labor; and after resting a few minutes at the summit, resumed his ride, full of spirits and of animated and instructive conversation. After dinner, he crossed over to Goat Island, and beheld the cataract from the various points, and continued his explorations until all was obscured by darkness. He seemed greatly impressed by the wonderful contrast presented by the scene of rage and repose—of the wild and furious dashing of the mighty river down the rapids, with its mad plunge over the precipice—and the sullen stillness of the abyss of waters below. I wish I could repeat to you his striking conversation during these rambles, replete with brilliant classical allusions, historical illustrations, and the most minute, and as it seemed to me, universal information. * * * * * * I sincerely concur with the worthy captain of one of our steamboats, who said to me the other day,—' Oh, that we could take the *engine* out of the old " Adams," and put it into a new hull !' "

During his visit at the Falls, Mr. Adams, on a Sabbath morning, accompanied by Gen. Porter, visited the remnant of the Tuscarora Indians, and attended divine service in their midst. At the conclusion of the sermon, Mr. Adams made a brief address to the Indians, which is thus described by the letter-writer alluded to above :—

" Mr. Adams alluded to his advanced age, and said this was the first time he had ever looked upon their beautiful fields and forests —that he was truly happy to meet them there and join with them in the worship of our common Parent—reminded them that in years past he had addressed them from the position which he then occupied, in language, at once that of his station and his heart, as ' his children'—and that now, as a private citizen, he hailed them in terms of equal warmth and endearment, as his ' brethren and sisters.' He alluded, with a simple eloquence which seemed to move the Indians much, to the equal care and love with which God regards all his children, whether savage or civilized, and to the common destiny which awaits them hereafter, however various their lot here. He touched briefly and forcibly on the topics of the sermon which they had heard, and concluded with a beautiful and touching benediction upon them."

At Rochester immense multitudes assembled to receive Mr. Adams. He was welcomed in an eloquent address from the Mayor of the city. The following are a few extracts from the reply of Mr. Adams :—

" Mr. Mayor and Fellow-citizens :—I fear you expect from me a speech. If it were in my power, oppressed as I am with mingled astonishment and gratitude at what I have experienced and now see of your kindness, to make a speech, I would gratify you with one adorned with all the chaste yet simple eloquence which are combined in the address to which you have just listened from your worthy Mayor. But it is not in my power. You may probably think there is some affection on my part, in pretending inability to address you, knowing as many of you do, that I have often addressed assemblies like this. But I hope for greater indulgence from you than this. I trust you will consider that I have seen and spoken to multitudes like that now before me, but that these multitudes had frowning faces. Those I could meet, and to those I could speak. But to you, whose every face is expressive of generous affection—to you, in whose every countenance I see kindness and friendship—I cannot speak. It is too much for me. It overcomes my powers of speech. It is a new scene to me. * * * * * *

" Amongst the sentiments which I have expressed, and the observations which I have made during my brief tour through this portion of your State, it was impossible for me to forego a constant comparison with what New York was in other days, and what it is now. I first set my feet upon the soil of the now Empire State, in 1785. I then visited the city of New York,—at that time a town of 18,000 inhabitants. I tarried, while in that city, at the house of John Jay—a man whom I name, and whom all will remember, as one of the most illustrious of the distinguished patriots who carried our beloved country through the dark period of the Revolution. Mr. Jay, the Secretary of Foreign Affairs, under the Congress of the Federation, was laying the foundation of a house in Broadway, but which was separated by the distance of a quarter of a mile from any other dwelling. At that time, being eighteen years of age, I received an invitation to visit western New York; and I have regretted often, but never more than now, that I had not accepted that invitation. Oh ! what would I not have given to have seen this part of this great State then, that I might be able to contrast it with what it now is. * * * * *

" It has seemed to me as if in this region the God of nature intended to make a more sublime display of his power, than in any other portion of the world. He has done so in physical nature—in the majestic cataract, whose sound you can almost hear—in forest and in field —in the mind of man among you. In what has been accomplished to make your city what it is, the aged have done the most. The middle aged may say we will improve upon what has been done; and the young, we shall accomplish still more than our fathers. That, fellow-citizens, was the boast in the ancient Spartan procession—a procession which was divided into three classes—the old, the middle-aged, and the young. They had a saying which each class repeated in turn. The aged said—

> ' We have been, in days of old,
> Wise and gentle, brave and bold.'

The middle-aged said—

> ' We, in turn, your place supply;
> Who doubts it, let them come and try.'

And the boys said—

> ' Hereafter, at our country's call,
> We promise to surpass you all.'

And so it will be with you—each in your order."

At Auburn every possible token of respect was paid to the venerable statesman. A committee consisting of ex-Gov. Seward, Judge Conklin, Judge Miller, Luman Sherwood, P. H. Perry, S. A. Goodwin, James C. Wood, and J. L. Doty, Esqs., proceeded to Canandaigua to meet Mr. Adams. At half past nine o'clock in the evening, Mr. Adams, accompanied by the committee, arrived in Auburn. He was received by a torch-light procession, composed of the Auburn Guards, the Firemen, and an immense concourse of citizens, and conducted to the mansion of Gov. Seward, where he thus briefly addressed the people :—

" Fellow-citizens :—Notwithstanding the glow with which these brilliant torch-lights illuminate my welcome among you, I can only acknowledge your kindness, on this occasion, by assuring you that to-morrow morning, by the light of the blessed sun, I hope to take every one of you by the hand, and express feelings too strong for immediate utterance."

On the following morning at six o'clock, Mr. Adams visited the State Prison, and made many inquiries concerning the discipline of the prison, and its success in the prevention of crime and reformation of offenders. At 9 o'clock he met the citizens in the First Presbyterian church, where he was addressed by Gov. Seward, as follows :—

" Sir :—I am charged with the very honorable and most agreeable duty, of expressing to you the reverence and affectionate esteem of my fellow-citizens, assembled in your presence.

" A change has come over the spirit of your journey, since your steps have turned towards your ancestral sea-side home. An excursion to invigorate health impaired by labors, too arduous for age, in the public councils, and expected to be quiet and contemplative, has become one of fatigue and excitement. Rumors of your advance escape before you, and a happy and grateful community rise up in their clustering cities, towns, and villages, impede your way with demonstrations of respect and kindness, and convert your unpretending journey into a triumphal progress. Such honors frequently attend public functionaries, and such an one may sometimes find it difficult to determine how much of the homage he receives is paid to his own worth, how much proceeds from the habitual reverence of good republican citizens to constituted elective authority, and how much from the spirit of venal adulation.

" You, sir, labor under no such embarrassment. The office you hold, though honorable, is purely legislative, and such as we can bestow by our immediate suffrage on one of ourselves. You conferred personal benefits sparingly when you held the patronage of the nation. That patronage you have relinquished, and can never regain. Your hands will be uplifted often, during your remaining days, to invoke blessings on your country, but never again to distribute honors or reward among your countrymen. The homage

paid you, dear sir, is sincere, for it has its sources in the just sentiments and irrepressible affections of a free people, their love of
truth, their admiration of wisdom, their reverence for virtue, and
their gratitude for beneficence.

" Nor need you fear that enthusiasm exaggerates your title to the
public regard.   Your fellow-citizens, in spite of political prudence,
could not avoid honoring you on grounds altogether irrespective of
personal merit.   John Adams, who has gone to receive the reward
of the just, was one of the most efficient and illustrious founders of
this Empire, and afterwards its Chief Ruler.   The son of such a
father would, in any other age, and even in this age, in any other
country than this, have been entitled, by birth alone, to a sceptre.
We not merely deny hereditary claims to civil trust, but regard
even hereditary distinction with jealousy.   And this circumstance
enhances justly the estimate of your worth.   For when before has
it happened that in such a condition of society the son has, by mere
civic achievement, attained the eminence of such a sire, and effaced
remembrance of birth by justly acquired renown ?

" The hand we now so eagerly grasp, was pressed in confidence
and friendship by the Father of our Country.   The wreath we place
on your honored brow, received its earliest leaves from the hand of
Washington.   We cannot expect, with the agency of free and universal suffrage, to be always governed by the wise and the good.
But surely your predecessors in the Chief Magistracy, were men
such as never before successively wielded power in any State.
They differed in policy as they must, and yet, throughout their several dynasties, without any sacrifice of personal independence, and
while passing from immature youth to ripened age, you were coun-
sellor and minister to them all.   We seem therefore, in this interview with you, to come into the presence of our departed chiefs ;
the majestic shade of Washington looks down upon us ; we hear the
bold and manly eloquence of the elder Adams ; and we listen to the
voices of the philosophic and sagacious Jefferson, the refined and
modest Madison, and the generous and faithful Monroe.

" A life of such eminent patriotism and fidelity found its proper
reward in your elevation to the eminence from which you had justly
derived so many honors.   Although your administration of the government is yet too recent for impartial history, or unbounded eulogy,

our grateful remembrance of it is evinced by the congratulations you now receive from your fellow-citizens.

" But your claims to the veneration of your countrymen do not end here.   Your predecessors descended from the Chief Magistracy to enjoy, in repose and tranquillity, honors even greater than those which belonged to that eminent station.   It was reserved for you to illustrate the important truths, that offices and trusts are not the end of public service, but are merely incidents in the life of the true American citizen; that duties remain when the highest trust is resigned; and that there is scope for a pure and benevolent ambition beyond even the Presidency of the United States of America.

" You have devoted the energies of a mind unperverted, the learning and experience acquired through more than sixty years, and even the influence and fame derived from your high career of public service, to the great cause of universal liberty.   The praises we bestow are already echoed back to us by voices which come rich and full across the Atlantic, hailing you as the indefatigable champion of humanity—not the humanity which embraces a single race or clime, but that humanity which regards the whole family of MAN.   Such salutations as these cannot be mistaken.   They come not from your contemporaries, for they are gone—you are not of this generation, but of the PAST, spared to hear the voice of POSTERITY.   The greetings you receive come up from the dark and uncertain FUTURE.   They are the whisperings of posthumous FAME—fame which impatiently awaits your departure, and which, spreading wider and growing more and more distinct, will award to JOHN QUINCY ADAMS a name to live with that of WASHINGTON !"

The audience expressed their sympathy with this address by long and enthusiastic cheering.   When order was restored, Mr. Adams rose, evidently under great and unaffected embarrassment.

He replied to the speech in an address of about half an hour, during which the attention of his audience was riveted upon the speaker, with intense interest

and affection. He declared the embarrassment he felt
in speaking. He was sensible that his fellow-citizens
had laid aside all partizan feelings in coming up to
greet him. He desired to speak what would not
wound the feelings of any one. He was grateful,
deeply grateful, to them all. But on what subject of
public interest could a public man speak, that would
find harmony among an intelligent, thinking people?
There were such subjects, but he could not speak of
them.

The people of Western New York had always been
eminently just and generous to him, and had recently
proved their kindness on various occasions, by inviting
him to address the State Agricultural Society on
agriculture. But his life had been spent in the closet,
in diplomacy, or in the cabinet ; and he had not learned
the practice, or even the theory of agriculture. After
what he had seen of the harvests of Western New
York, bursting with food for the sustenance of man, for
him to address the people of such a district on agriculture, would be as absurd as the vanity of the rhetorician
who went to Carthage to instruct Hannibal in the art of
war. He had been solicited to address the young. In
his life time he had been an instructor of youth, and,
strange as from his present display they might think it, he
had instructed them in the art of eloquence. And there
was no more honorable office on earth than instructing
the young. But the schools and seminaries had passed
him, while he was engaged in other pursuits ; and for

him now to attempt to instruct the young of this generation, would evince only the garrulousness of age.

He had been invited to discourse on internal improvement; but that was a subject he feared to touch. On one point, however, all men agreed. All were in favor of internal improvement. But there was a balance between the reasonable sacrifices of this generation, and the burden it had a right to cast upon posterity, and every individual might justly claim to hold his balance for himself. One thing, however, he was sure he might assume with safety. In looking over the State of New York, upon its canals and railroads, which brought the borders of the State into contiguity, and its citizens in every part into communion with each other, he was sure that all rejoiced, and might well glory in what had been accomplished.

Mr. A. said he had read and endeavored to inform himself concerning prison discipline, a subject deeply interesting to the peace, good order, and welfare of society; but after his examination of the penitentiary here, he was satisfied that he was yet a learner, instead of being able to give instruction on that important subject.

He had been asked to enlist in the growing army of temperance, and discourse on that cause, so deeply cherished by every well wisher of our country. And he would cheerfully speak; but other and more devoted men had occupied the field, and what was left for him to say on temperance? In passing through Catholic

Lower Canada he saw a column erected to the Virgin
Mary, in gratitude for her promotion of the temperance
cause. If indeed the blessed Virgin did lend her aid
to that great work, it would almost win him to worship
at her shrine, although he belonged to that class of
people who rejected the invocation of saints.

He felt, therefore, that he had no subject on which
to address them, but himself and his own public life.
The experience of an old man, related by himself,
would, he feared, be more irksome than profitable.

"What, then, am I to say? I am summoned here
to speak, and to reply to what has been said to me by
my respected friend, your late Chief Magistrate. And
what is the theme he has given me? It is myself.
And what can I say on such a subject? To know
that he entertains, or that you entertain for me the
sentiments he has expressed, absolutely overpowers
me. I cannot go on. The only answer I can make,
is a declaration, that during my public service, now
protracted to nearly the age of eighty, I have endeavored to serve my country honestly and faithfully.
How imperfectly I have done this, none seem so sensible as myself. I must stop. I can only repeat
thanks, thanks, thanks to you, one and all, and implore
the blessings of God upon you and your children."

At the conclusion of this reply, Mr. Adams was
introduced to a large number of the ladies and gentlemen assembled in the church. He then returned to
the American Hotel, where he remained an hour,

receiving the visits of the citizens of the adjoining towns. At 11 o'clock the Auburn Guards escorted Mr. Adams and the committee, followed by a large procession, to the car-house. Accompanied by Gov. Seward, Judge Miller, Hon. Christopher Morgan, the committee, Auburn Guards, and a number of the citizens of Auburn, he was conveyed in an extra train of cars, in an hour and five minutes, to Syracuse.

At Syracuse, at Utica, at Albany, the same spontaneous outgushing manifestations of respect and affection met him that had hitherto attended his journey in every populous place through which he passed. In his reply to the address of Mr. Barnard, at Albany, he concluded in the following words :—

"Lingering as I am on the stage of public life, and, as many of you may think, lingering beyond the period when nature calls for repose—while I remain in the station which I now occupy in the Congress of the United States, if you, my hearers, as an assembly, or if any one among you, as an individual, have any object or purpose to promote, or any end to secure that he believes can in any way advance his interests or increase his happiness, then, in the name of God, I ask you *to send your petitions to me!* (Tremendous cheering.) I hope this is not trespassing too far on politics. (Laughter, and cheers.) I unhesitatingly promise you, one and all, that if I can in any way serve you in that station, I will do it most cheerfully ; regarding it as the choicest blessing of God, if I shall thus be enabled to make some just return for the kind attentions which you have this day bestowed upon me."

In his route homeward, Mr. Adams was received and entertained in a very handsome manner by the people of Pittsfield, Mass. He was addressed by Hon.

George N. Briggs, who alluded, in eloquent terms, to his long and distinguished public services. Mr. Adams, in reply, spoke of the scenes amidst which he had passed his early youth, and of the influence which they exerted in forming his character and shaping his purposes. "In 1775," said he, "the minute men from a hundred towns in the province were marching, at a moment's warning, to the scene of opening war. Many of them called at my father's house in Quincy, and received the hospitality of John Adams. All were lodged in the house which the house would contain ; others in the barns, and wherever they could find a place. There were then in my father's kitchen *some dozen or two of pewter spoons;* and I well recollect going into the kitchen and seeing some of the men engaged *in running those spoons into bullets for the use of the troops !* Do you wonder," said he, "that a boy of seven years of age, who witnessed this scene, should be a patriot ?"

In the fall of the same year, Mr. Adams received an invitation from the Cincinnati Astronomical Society, to visit that city, and assist in the ceremony of laying the corner stone of an observatory, to be erected on an eminence called Mount Ida. The invitation was accepted. On his journey to Cincinnati, the same demonstrations of respect, the same eagerness to honor the aged patriarch were manifested in the various cities and towns through which he passed, as on his summer tour.

The ceremony of laying the corner stone took place on the 9th of November, 1843. Mr. Adams delivered an address on the occasion, replete with eloquence, wisdom, philosophy, and religion. The following beautiful extract will afford a specimen :—

" The various difficult, and, in many respects, opposite motives which have impelled mankind to the study of the stars, have had a singular effect in complicating and confounding the recommendation of the science. Religion, idolatry, superstition, curiosity, the thirst for knowledge, the passion for penetrating the secrets of nature, the warfare of the huntsman by night and by day against the beast of the forest and of the field, the meditations of the shepherd in the custody and wanderings of his flocks, the influence of the revolving seasons of the year, and the successive garniture of the firmament upon the labors of the husbandman, upon the seed time and the harvest, the blooming of flowers, the ripening of the vintage, the polar pilot of the navigator, and the mysterious magnet of the mariner—all, in harmonious action, stimulate the child of earth and of heaven to interrogate the dazzling splendors of the sky, to reveal to him the laws of their own existence.

" He has his own comforts, his own happiness, his own existence, identified with theirs. He sees the Creator in creation, and calls upon creation to declare the glory of the Creator. When Pythagoras, the philosopher of the Grecian schools, conceived that more than earthly idea of ' the music of the spheres'—when the great dramatist of nature could inspire the lips of his lover on the moonlight green with the beloved of his soul, to say to her :—

> ' Sit, Jessica.—Look how the floor of Heaven
> Is thick inlaid with pattens of bright gold !
> There's not the smallest orb which thou beholdest,
> But in his motion like an angel sings,
> Still choiring to the young eyed cherubim !'

" Oh, who is the one with a heart, but almost wishes to cast off this muddy vesture of decay, to be admitted to the joy of listening to the celestial harmony !"

CHAPTER XV.

THE last time Mr. Adams appeared in public in
Boston, he presided at a meeting of the citizens of that
city, in Faneuil Hall. "A man had been kidnapped
in Boston—kidnapped at noon-day, 'on the high road
between Faneuil Hall and old Quincy,' and carried
off to be a slave! New England hands had seized
their brother, sold him into bondage forever, and his
children after him. A meeting was called to talk the
matter over, in a plain way, and look in one another's
faces. Who was fit to preside in such a case? That
old man sat in the chair in Faneuil Hall. Above him
was the image of his father and his own; around him
were Hancock and the other Adams, and Washington,
greatest of all. Before him were the men and women
of Boston, met to consider the wrongs done to a miserable negro slave. The roof of the old Cradle of Liberty

spanned over them all. Forty years before, a young
man and a Senator, he had taken the chair at a meeting called to consult on the wrong done to American
seamen, violently impressed by the British from an
American ship of war—the unlucky Chesapeake. Now
an old man, clothed with half a century of honors, he
sits in the same Hall, to preside over a meeting to consider the outrage done to a single slave. One was the
first meeting of citizens he ever presided over; the
other was the last: both for the same object—the defence of the eternal right!"*

Few men retain the health and vigor with which
Mr. Adams was blessed in extreme old age. When
most others are decrepit and helpless, he was in the
enjoyment of meridian strength and energy, both of
body and mind, and could endure labors which would
prostrate many in the prime of manhood. An instance
of his powers of endurance is furnished in his journey
to Washington, to attend the opening of Congress,
when in the 74th year of his age. On Monday morning
he left Boston, and the same evening delivered a lecture
before the Young Men's Institute, in Hartford, Conn.
The next day he proceeded to New Haven, and in the
evening lectured before a similar Institute in that city.
Wednesday he pursued his journey to New York, and
in the evening lectured before the New York Lyceum,
in the Broadway Tabernacle. Thursday evening he

* Theodore Parker.

delivered an address before an association in Brooklyn ; and on Friday evening delivered a second lecture before the New York Lyceum. Here were labors which would seriously tax the constitution of vigorous youth ; and yet Mr. Adams performed them with much comparative ease.

His great longevity, and his general good health, must be attributed, in no small degree, to his abstemious and temperate habits, early rising, and active exercise. He took pleasure in athletic amusements, and was exceedingly fond of walking. During his summer residence in Quincy, he has been known to walk to his son's residence in Boston (seven miles,) before breakfast. "While President of the United States, he was probably the first man up in Washington, lighted his own fire, and was hard at work in his library, while sleep yet held in its obliviousness the great mass of his fellow-citizens." He was an expert swimmer, and was in the constant habit of bathing, whenever circumstances would permit. Not unfrequently the first beams of the rising sun, as they fell upon the beautiful Potomac, would find Mr. Adams buffeting its waves with all the sportiveness and dexterity of boyhood, while a single attendant watched upon the shore. When in the Presidency, he sometimes made a journey from Washington to Quincy on horseback, as a simple citizen, accompanied only by a servant.

More than four score years had sprinkled their

frosts upon his brow, and still he was in the midst of his usefulness. Promptly at his post in the Hall of Representatives stood the veteran sentinel, watching vigilantly over the interests of his country. With an eye undimmed by age, a quick ear, a ready hand, an intellect unimpaired, he guarded the citadel of liberty, ever on the alert to detect, and mighty to repel, the approach of the foe, however covert or however open his attacks. Never did the Union, never did freedom, the world, more need his services than now. A large territory, of sufficient extent to form several States, had been blighted by slavery, and annexed to the United Sates. A sanguinary and expensive war, growing out of this strengthening of the slave power, had just terminated, adding to the Union still larger territories—now free soil indeed, but furnishing a field for renewed battles between slavery and liberty. New revolutions were about to break forth in Europe, to convulse the Eastern Hemisphere, and cause old thrones to totter and fall!

How momentous the era! How deeply fraught with the prosperity of the American Republic—with the progress of man—the freedom of nations—the happiness of succeeding generations! How could he, who for years had prominently and nobly stood forth, as the leader of the hosts contending for the rights and the liberties of humanity, be spared from his post at such a juncture? Who could put on his armor?—who wield his weapons?—who "lead a forlorn hope," or

mount a deadly breach in battles which might yet
be waged between the sons of freedom and the propa-
gators of slavery ?   But the loss was to be experienced.
A wise and good Providence had so ordered.   The
sands of his life had run out.   A voice from on high
called him away from earth's stormy struggles, to
bright and peaceful scenes in the spirit land.   He
could no longer tarry.   Death found the faithful veteran at his post, with his harness on.   How applicable
the words of Scott, on the departure of Pitt :—

> " Hadst thou but lived, though stripp'd of power,
>   A watchman on the lonely tower,
>   Thy thrilling trump had roused the land,
>   When fraud or danger were at hand ;
>   By thee, as by the beacon-light,
>   Our pilots had kept course aright ;
>   As some proud column, though alone,
>   Thy strength had propp'd the tottering throne.
>   Now is the stately column broke,
>   The beacon-light is quenched in smoke,
>   The trumpet's silver sound is still,
>   The warder silent on the hill !
>   O think how, to his latest day,
>   When death, just hovering, claimed his prey,
>   With Palinure's unaltered mood,
>   Firm at his dangerous post he stood ;
>   Each call for needful rest repell'd,
>   With dying hand the rudder held,
>   Till, in his fall, with fateful sway,
>   The steerage of the realm gave way."

It has been supposed by some that the remote cause
of Mr. Adams's death was a severe injury he received
by a fall in the House of Representatives, in June,

1840. The accident is thus described by an eye witness :—

" It had been a very warm day, and the debates had partaken of extraordinary excitement, when, a few moments before sunset, the House adjourned, and most of the members had sought relief from an oppressive atmosphere, in the arbors and recesses of the adjoining Congressional gardens.

" At that time I held a subordinate clerkship in the House, which usually confined me, the larger portion of the day not devoted to debate, to one of the committee rooms ; whilst the balance of the day I occupied as a reporter.

" Mr. Adams was always the first man in the House, and the last man out of it ; and, as I usually detained myself an hour or more after adjournment, in writing up my notes, I often came in contact with him. He was pleased to call at my desk very often, before he went home, and indulge in some incidental, unimportant conversation. On the day referred to, just as the sun was setting, and was throwing his last rays through the murky hall, I looked up, and saw Mr. Adams approaching. He had almost reached my desk, and had uplifted his hand in friendly salutation, when he pitched headlong, some six or eight feet, and struck his head against the sharp corner of an iron rail that defended one of the entrance aisles leading to the circle within the bar, inflicting a heavy contusion on his forehead, and rendering him insensible. I instantly leaped from my seat, took the prostrate sufferer in my arms, and found that he was in a state of utter stupor and insensibility. Looking around for aid, I had the good fortune to find that Col. James Munroe, of the New York delegation, had just returned to his desk to procure a paper he had forgotten, when, giving the alarm, he flew to the rescue, manifesting the deepest solicitude for the welfare of the venerable statesman. Follansbee, the doorkeeper, with two or more of his pages, came in next ; and after we had applied a plentiful supply of cold water to the sufferer, he returned to consciousness, and requested that he might be taken to his residence. In less than five minutes, Mr. Moses H. Grinnell, Mr. George H. Profit, Mr. Ogden Hoffman, and Col. Christopher Williams, of Tennessee, were called in, a carriage was procured, and Mr. Adams was being conveyed to his residence in President

Square, when, it being ascertained that his shoulder was dislocated, the carriage was stopped at the door of the private hotel of Col. Munroe, in Pennsylvania Avenue, between Eleventh and Twelfth streets; the suffering, but not complaining statesman, was taken out, and surgical aid instantly put in requisition. Doctor Sewall was sent for; when it was ascertained that the left shoulder-joint was out of the socket; and, though Mr. Adams must have suffered intensely, he complained not—did not utter a groan or a murmur.

"More than an hour elapsed before the dislocated limb could be adjusted; and to effect which, his arm endured, in a concentrated and continued wrench or pull, many minutes at a time, the united strength of Messrs. Grinnell, Munroe, Profit, and Hoffman. Still Mr. Adams uttered not a murmur, though the great drops of sweat that rolled down his furrowed cheeks, or stood upon his brow, told but too well the physical agony he endured. As soon as his arm was adjusted, he insisted on being carried home, and his wishes were complied with.

"The next morning I was at the capitol at a very early hour, attending to some writing. I thought of, and lamented the accident that had befallen Mr. Adams, and had already commenced writing an account of it to a correspondent. At that instant I withdrew my eyes from the paper on which I was writing, and saw Mr. Adams standing a foot or two from me, carefully examining the carpeting. 'Sir,' said he, 'I am looking for that place in the matting that last night tripped me. If it be not fastened down, it may kill some one.' And then he continued his search for the trick-string matting."

Mr. Adams after this accident did not enjoy as sound health as in previous years, yet was more active and vigorous than the majority of those who attain to his age. But on the 20th of November, 1846, he experienced the first blow of the fatal disease which eventually terminated his existence.

On the morning of that day, while sojourning at the residence of his son, in Boston, preparing to depart for

Washington, he was walking out with a friend to visit
a new Medical College, and was struck with paralysis
by the way.   This affliction confined him several
weeks, when he obtained sufficient strength to proceed
to Washington, and enter upon his duties in the House
of Representatives.   He viewed this attack as the
touch of death.   An interregnum of nearly four months
occurs in his journal.   The next entry is under the
head of "Posthumous Memoir."   After describing his
recent sickness, he continues :—"From that hour I
date my decease, and consider myself, for every useful
purpose, to myself and fellow-creatures, dead;   and
hence I call this, and what I may hereafter write, a
posthumous memoir."

Although he was after this, regular in his attendance
at the House of Representatives, yet he did not mingle
as freely in debate as formerly.   He passed the following summer, as usual, at his seat in Quincy.   In November, he left his native town for Washington, to
return no more in life !

On Sunday, the 20th of February, 1848, he appeared
in unusual health.   In the forenoon he attended public
worship at the capitol, and in the afternoon at St.
John's church.   At nine o'clock in the evening he
retired with his wife to his library, where she read to
him a sermon of Bishop Wilberforce, on Time—" hovering, as he was, on the verge of eternity !"   This
was the last night he passed beneath his own roof.

Monday, the 21st, he rose at his usual very early

hour, and engaged in his accustomed occupations with his pen. An extraordinary alacrity pervaded his movements, and the cheerful step with which he ascended the steps of the capitol was remarked by his attendants. He occupied a portion of the forenoon in composing a few stanzas of poetry, at the request of a friend, and had signed his name twice for members who desired to obtain his autograph.

Mr. Chase had introduced a resolution of thanks to Generals Twiggs, Worth, Quitman, Pillow, Shields, Pearce, Cadwalader, and Smith, for their services in the Mexican war, and awarding them gold medals. Mr. Adams was in his seat, and voted on the two questions preliminary to ordering its engrossment, with an uncommonly emphatic tone of voice. About half past one o'clock, P. M., as the Speaker had risen to put another question to the House, the proceedings were suddenly interrupted by cries of " Stop !—stop !—Mr. Adams !" There was a quick movement towards the chair of Mr. Adams, by two or three members, and in a moment he was surrounded by a large number of Representatives, eagerly inquiring—" What's the matter ?"— " Has he fainted ?"—" Is he dead ?" JOHN QUINCY ADAMS, while faithful at his post, and apparently about to rise to address the Speaker, had sunk into a state of unconsciousness ! He had been struck a second time with paralysis. The scene was one of intense excitement. Pallor, anxiety, alarm, were depicted on every countenance. " Take him out,"—" Bring water,"—

exclaimed several voices. He had been prevented from falling to the floor by a member from Ohio, whose seat was near his—Mr. Fisher—who received him in his arms. Immediately Mr. Grinnell, one of his colleagues from Massachusetts, was by his side, keeping off a press of anxious friends, and bathing his face with iced water.

"He was immediately lifted into the area in front of the Clerk's table. The Speaker instantly suggested that some gentleman move an adjournment, which being promptly done, the House adjourned. A sofa was brought, and Mr. Adams, in a state of perfect helplessness, though not of entire insensibility, was gently laid upon it. The sofa was then taken up and borne out of the Hall into the Rotunda, where it was set down, and the members of both Houses, and strangers, who were fast crowding around, were with some difficulty repressed, and an open space cleared in its immediate vicinity; but a medical gentleman, a member of the House, (who was prompt, active, and self-possessed throughout the whole painful scene,) advised that he be removed to the door of the Rotunda opening on the east portico, where a fresh wind was blowing. This was done; but the air being chilly and loaded with vapor, the sofa was, at the suggestion of Mr. Winthrop, once more taken up and removed to the Speaker's apartment, the doors of which were forthwith closed to all but professional gentlemen and particular friends."

The features of the dying patriarch were almost as rigid as though in death ; but there was a serenity in his countenance which betokened an absence of pain. There were five physicians, members of the House, present, viz. :—Drs. Newell, Fries, Edwards, Jones of Georgia, and Lord. These gentlemen were unremitting in their attentions. Drs. Lindsley and Thomas, of the city, were also immediately called in. Under the advice of the medical gentlemen present, he was cupped, and mustard plasters were applied, which seemed to afford some relief. Reviving a little and recovering consciousness, Mr. Adams inquired for his wife. She was present, but in extreme illness, and suffering the most poignant sorrow. After a few moments' interval he relapsed again into unconsciousness. A correspondent of the New York Express describes as follows the progress of these melancholy events :—

" *Half past one o'clock.*—Mr. Benton communicated to the Senate the notice of the sudden illness of Mr. Adams, and moved an adjournment of that body.

" *Quarter to two.*—Mr. Adams has several physicians with him, but exhibits no signs of returning consciousness. The report is that he is sinking.

" *Two o'clock.*—Mr. Giddings informs me that he shows signs of life. He has just now attempted to speak, but cannot articulate a word. Under medical advice he has submitted to leeching.

" *Half past two.*—Mrs. Adams and his niece and nephew are with him, and Mr. A. is no worse. The reports, however, are quite contradictory, and many despair of his recovery.

" *Three o'clock.*—None but the physicians and the family are present, and the reports again become more and more doubtful. The physicians say that Mr. Adams may not live more than an hour, or he may live two or three days.

"His right side is wholly paralyzed, and the left not under control, there being continually involuntary motions of the muscles. Everything which medical aid can do, has been done for his relief. Briefly, just now, by close attention, he seemed anxious to 'thank the officers of the House.' Then, again, he was heard to say—'*This is the last of earth!* I AM CONTENT!' These were the last words which fell from the lips of 'the old man eloquent,' as his spirit plumed its pinions to soar to other worlds."

Mr. Adams lay in the Speaker's room, in a state of apparent unconsciousness, through the 22d and 23d, —Congress, in the meantime, assembling in respectful silence, and immediately adjourning from day to day. The struggles of contending parties ceased—the strife for interest, place, power, was hushed to repose. Silence reigned through the halls of the capitol, save the cautious tread and whispered inquiry of anxious questioners. The soul of a sage, a patriot, a Christian, is preparing to depart from the world!—no sound is heard to ruffle its sweet serenity!—a calmness and peace, fitting the momentous occasion, prevail around!

The elements of life and death continued their uncertain balance, until seven o'clock, on the evening
of the 23d, when the spirit of JOHN QUINCY ADAMS
bade adieu to earth forever, and winged its flight to God.

> " Give forth thy chime, thou solemn bell,
>   Thou grave, unfold thy marble cell ;
>   O earth ! receive upon thy breast,
>   The weary traveller to his rest.

> " O God ! extend thy arms of love,
>   A spirit seeketh thee above !
>   Ye heav'nly palaces unclose,
>   Receive the weary to repose."

The tidings of Mr. Adams' death flew on electrical
wings to every portion of the Union.   A statesman, a
philanthropist, a father of the Republic, had fallen.   A
nation heard, and were dissolved in tears !

In the history of American statesmen, none lived a
life so long in the public service—none had trusts so
numerous confided to their care—none died a death
so glorious.   Beneath the dome of the nation's capitol ;
in the midst of the field of his highest usefulness, where
he had won fadeless laurels of renown ; equipped with
the armor in which he had fought so many battles for
truth and freedom, he fell beneath the shaft of the king
of terrors.   And how bright, how enviable the reputation he left behind !   As a man, pure, upright, benevolent, religious —his hand unstained by a drop of human
blood ; uncharged, unsuspected of crime, of premedi-
tated wrong, of an immoral act, of an unchaste word

—as a statesman, lofty and patriotic in all his purposes; devoted to the interests of the people; sacredly exercising all power entrusted to his keeping for the good of the public alone, unmindful of personal interest and aggrandizement; an enthusiastic lover of liberty; a faithful, fearless defender of the rights of man! The sun of his life in its lengthened course through the political heavens, was unobscured by a spot, undimmed by a cloud; and when, at the close of the long day, it sank beneath the horizon, the whole firmament glowed with the brilliancy of its reflected glories! Rulers, statesmen, legislators! study and emulate such a life—seek after a character so beloved, a death so honorable, a fame so immortal. Like him—

> " So live, that when thy summons comes to join
> The innumerable caravan, that moves
> To the pale realms of shade, where each shall take
> His chamber in the silent halls of death,
> Thou go not, like the quarry-slave at night,
> Scourged to his dungeon; but, sustained, and soothed
> By an unfaltering trust, approach thy grave,
> Like one who wraps the drapery of his couch
> About him, and lies down to pleasant dreams."

On the day succeeding Mr. Adams' death, when the two Houses of Congress met, the full attendance of members, and a crowded auditory, attested the deep desire felt by all to witness the proceedings which would take place in relation to the death of one who had long occupied so high a place in the councils of the Republic. As soon as the House of Representatives was called to order, the Speaker, (the Hon. Robert C. Winthrop of Massachusetts,) rose, and in a feeling manner addressed the House as follows :—

" *Gentlemen of the House of Representatives of the United States :* It has been thought fit that the Chair should announce officially to the House, an event already known to the members individually, and which has filled all our hearts with sadness. A seat on this floor has been vacated, toward which all eyes have been accustomed to turn with no common interest. A voice has been hushed forever in this Hall, to which all ears have been wont to listen with profound reverence. A venerable form has faded from our sight, around which we have daily clustered with an affectionate regard. A name has been stricken from the roll of the living statesmen of our land, which has been associated, for more than half a century, with the highest civil service, and the loftiest civil renown.

" On Monday, the 21st instant, JOHN QUINCY ADAMS sunk in his seat, in presence of us all, by a sudden illness, from which he never recovered ; and he died, in the Speaker's room, at a quarter past seven o'clock last evening, with the officers of the House and the delegation of his own Massachusetts around him.

" Whatever advanced age, long experience, great ability, vast learning, accumulated public honors, a spotless private character, and a firm religious faith, could do, to render any one an object of interest, respect, and admiration, they had done for this distinguished person ; and interest, respect, and admiration, are but feeble terms to express the feelings with which the members of this House and the people of the country have long regarded him.

" After a life of eighty years, devoted from its earliest maturity to the public service, he has at length gone to his rest. He has been privileged to die at his post ; to fall while in the discharge of his duties ; to expire beneath the roof of the capitol ; and to have his last scene associated forever, in history, with the birthday of that illustrious patriot, whose just discernment brought him first into the service of his country.

" The close of such a life, under such circumstances, is not an event for unmingled emotions. We cannot find it in our hearts to regret, that he has died as he has died. He himself could have desired no other end. 'This is the end of earth,' were his last words, uttered on the day on which he fell. But we might also hear him exclaiming, as he left us—in a language hardly less familiar to him than his native tongue—'*Hoc est, nimirum, magis feliciter de vitâ migrare, quam mori.*'

"It is for others to suggest what honors shall be paid to his memory. No acts of ours are necessary to his fame. But it may be due to ourselves and to the country, that the national sense of his character and services should be fitly commemorated."

Mr. Holmes of South Carolina arose and addressed the House in most eloquent strains. The following are extracts from his eulogy :—

"The mingled tones of sorrow, like the voice of many waters, have come unto us from a sister State—Massachusetts weeping for her honored son. The State I have the honor in part to represent once endured, with yours, a common suffering, battled for a common cause, and rejoiced in a common triumph. Surely, then, it is meet that in this, the day of your affliction, we should mingle our griefs.

"When a great man falls, the nation mourns; when a patriarch is removed, the people weep. Ours, my associates, is no common bereavement. The chain which linked our hearts with the gifted spirits of former times, has been rudely snapped. The lips from which flowed those living and glorious truths that our fathers uttered, are closed in death! Yes, my friends, Death has been among us! He has not entered the humble cottage of some unknown, ignoble peasant; he has knocked audibly at the palace of a nation! His footstep has been heard in the Hall of State! He has cloven down his victim in the midst of the councils of a people! He has borne in triumph from among you the gravest, wisest, most reverend head! Ah! he has taken him as a trophy who was once chief over many States, adorned with virtue, and learning, and truth; he has borne at his chariot-wheels a renowned one of the earth.

"There was no incident in the birth, the life, the death of Mr. Adams, not intimately woven with the history of the land. Born in the night of his country's tribulation, he heard the first murmurs of discontent; he saw the first efforts for deliverance. Whilst yet a little child, he listened with eagerness to the whispers of freedom as they breathed from the lips of her almost inspired apostles : he caught the fire that was then kindled ; his eye beamed with the first ray ; he watched the day spring from on high, and long before he departed from earth, it was graciously vouchsafed unto him to behold the effulgence of her noontide glory. * * * * * * *

"He disrobed himself with dignity of the vestures of office, not to retire to the shades of Quincy, but, in the maturity of his intellect, in the vigor of his thought, to leap into this arena, and to continue, as he had begun, a disciple, an ardent devotee at the temple of his country's freedom. How, in this department, he ministered to his country's wants, we all know, and have witnessed. How often we have crowded into that aisle, and clustered around that now vacant desk, to listen to the counsels of wisdom, as they fell from the lips of the venerable sage, we can all remember, for it was but of yesterday. But what a change ! How wondrous ! how sudden ! 'Tis like a vision of the night. That form which we beheld but a few days since, is now cold in death !

"But the last Sabbath, and in this hall, he worshipped with others. Now his spirit mingles with the noble army of martyrs, and the just made perfect, in the eternal adoration of the living God. With him " this is the end of earth." He sleeps the sleep that knows no waking. He is gone—and forever ! The sun that ushers in the morn of that next holy day, while it gilds the lofty dome of the capitol, shall rest with soft and mellow light upon the consecrated spot beneath whose turf forever lies the PATRIOT FATHER and the PATRIOT SAGE !"

The following resolutions were unanimously passed by the House of Representatives :—

"Resolved, That this House has heard with the deepest sensibility, of the death in this capitol of JOHN QUINCY ADAMS, a Member of the House from the State of Massachusetts.

"Resolved, That, as a testimony of respect for the memory of this distinguished statesman, the officers and members of the House will wear the usual badge of mourning, and attend the funeral in his hall on Saturday next, at 12 o'clock.

"Resolved, That a committee of thirty be appointed to superintend the funeral solemnities.

"Resolved, That the proceedings of this House in relation to the death of JOHN QUINCY ADAMS be communicated to the family of the deceased by the Clerk.

"Resolved, That the seat in this hall just vacated by the death of the late JOHN QUINCY ADAMS be unoccupied for thirty days, and that it, together with the hall, remain clothed with the symbol of mourning during that time.

"Resolved, That the Speaker appoint one member of this House from each State and Territory, as a committee to escort the remains of our venerable friend, the Honorable JOHN QUINCY ADAMS, to the place designated by his friends for his interment.

"Resolved, That this House, as a further mark of respect for the memory of the deceased, do adjourn to Saturday next, the day appointed for the funeral."

In the Senate, after a formal annunciation of the death of Mr. Adams, in a message from the House of Representatives, Mr. Davis, of Massachusetts, arose and delivered a feeling address, on the life and services of the deceased patriot. The following are extracts :—

"Mr. President : By the recent affliction of my colleague, (Mr. Webster,) a painful duty devolves upon me. The message just delivered from the House proves that the hand of God has been again among us. A great and good man has gone from our midst. If, in speaking of JOHN QUINCY ADAMS, I can give utterance to the language of my own heart, I am confident I shall meet with a response from the Senate.

"He was born in the then Province of Massachusetts, while she was girding herself for the great revolutionary struggle which was then before her. His parentage is too well known to need even an allusion; yet I may be pardoned if I say, that his father seemed born to aid in the establishment of our free Government, and his mother was a suitable companion and co-laborer of such a patriot. The cradle hymns of the child were the songs of liberty. The power and competence of man for self-government were the topics which he most frequently heard discussed by the wise men of the day, and the inspiration thus caught gave form and pressure to his after life. Thus early imbued with the love of free institutions, educated by his father for the service of his country, and early led by WASHINGTON to its altar, he has stood before the world as one of its eminent statesmen. He has occupied, in turn, almost every place of honor which the country could give him, and for more than half a century, has been thus identified with its history. * * * * *

"It is believed to have been the earnest wish of his heart to die, like Chatham, in the midst of his labors. It was a sublime thought, that where he had toiled in the house of the nation, in hours of the day devoted to its service, the stroke of death should reach him, and there sever the ties of love and patriotism which bound him to earth. He fell in his seat, attacked by paralysis, of which he had before been a subject. To describe the scene which ensued would be impossible. It was more than the spontaneous gush of feeling which all such events call forth, so much to the honor of our nature. It was the expression of reverence for his moral worth, of admiration for his great intellectual endowments, and of veneration for his age and public services. All gathered round the sufferer, and the strong sympathy and deep feeling which were manifested, showed that the business of the House (which was instantly adjourned) was forgotten amid the distressing anxieties of the moment. He was soon removed to the apartment of the Speaker, where he remained surrounded by afflicted friends till the weary clay resigned its immortal spirit. 'This is the end of earth!' Brief but emphatic words They were among the last uttered by the dying Christian."

When Mr. Davis had concluded his remarks, Mr. Benton, of Missouri, delivered a most beautiful eulogy on the character of Mr. Adams. He said :—

"Mr. President: The voice of his native State has been heard, through one of the Senators of Massachusetts, announcing the death of her aged and most distinguished son. The voice of the other

Senator, (Mr. Webster,) is not heard, nor is his presence seen. A domestic calamity, known to us all, and felt by us all, confines him to the chamber of private grief, while the Senate is occupied with the public manifestations of a respect and sorrow which a national loss inspires. In the absence of that Senator, and as the member of this body longest here, it is not unfitting or unbecoming in me to second the motion which has been made for extending the last honors of the Senate to him who, forty-five years ago, was a member of this body, who, at the time of his death, was among the oldest members of the House of Representatives, and who, putting the years of his service together, was the oldest of all the members of the American Government.

" The eulogium of Mr. Adams is made in the facts of his life, which the Senator from Massachusetts (Mr. Davis) has so strikingly stated, that, from early manhood to octogenarian age, he has been constantly and most honorably employed in the public service. For a period of more than fifty years, from the time of his first appointment as Minister abroad under Washington, to his last election to the House of Representatives by the people of his native district, he has been constantly retained in the public service, and that, not by the favor of a Sovereign, or by hereditary title, but by the elections and appointments of republican Government. This fact makes the eulogy of the illustrious deceased. For what, except a union of all the qualities which command the esteem and confidence of man, could have ensured a public service so long, by appointments free and popular, and from sources so various and exalted ? Minister many times abroad ; member of this body ; member of the House of Representatives ; cabinet Minister ; President of the United States ; such has been the galaxy of his splendid appointments. And what but moral excellence the most perfect—intellectual ability the most eminent—fidelity the most unwavering—service the most useful, could have commanded such a succession of appointments so exalted, and from sources so various and so eminent ? Nothing less could have commanded such a series of appointments ; and accordingly we see the union of all these great qualities in him who has received them.

" In this long career of public service Mr. Adams was distinguished not only by faithful attention to all the great duties of his stations, but to all their less and minor duties. He was not the

Salaminian galley, to be launched only on extraordinary occasions, but he was the ready vessel, always launched when the duties of his station required it, be the occasion great or small. As President, as cabinet Minister, as Minister abroad, he examined all questions that came before him, and examined all in all their parts, in all the minutiæ of their detail, as well as in all the vastness of their comprehension. As Senator, and as a member of the House of Representatives, the obscure committee-room was as much the witness of his laborious application to the drudgery of legislation, as the halls of the two Houses were to the ever ready speech, replete with knowledge, which instructed all hearers, enlightened all subjects, and gave dignity and ornament to debate.

"In the observance of all the proprieties of life, Mr. Adams was a most noble and impressive example. He cultivated the minor as well as the greater virtues. Wherever his presence could give aid and countenance to what was useful and honorable to man, there he was. In the exercises of the school and of the college—in the meritorious meetings of the agricultural, mechanical, and commercial societies—in attendance upon Divine worship—he gave the punctual attendance rarely seen but in those who are free from the weight of public cares.

"Punctual to every duty, death found him at the post of duty; and where else could it have found him, at any stage of his career, for the fifty years of his illustrious public life? From the time of his first appointment by Washington to his last election by the people of his native town, where could death have found him but at the post of duty? At that post, in the fullness of age, in the ripeness of renown, crowned with honors, surrounded by his family, his friends, and admirers, and in the very presence of the national representation, he has been gathered to his fathers, leaving behind him the memory of public services which are the history of his country for half a century, and the example of a life, public and private, which should be the study and the model of the generations of his countrymen."

At the conclusion of Mr. Benton's address, the fol lowing resolutions, introduced by Mr. Davis, were passed by the Senate :—

" Resolved, That the Senate has received with deep sensibility
the message from the House of Representatives announcing the
death of the Hon. JOHN QUINCY ADAMS, a Representative from the
State of Massachusetts.

" Resolved, That, in token of respect for the memory of the deceased, the Senate will attend his funeral at the hour appointed by
the House of Representatives, and will wear the usual badge of
mourning for thirty days.

" Resolved, That, as a further mark of respect for the memory
of the deceased, the Senate do now adjourn until Saturday next, the
time appointed for the funeral."

President Polk issued a Proclamation announcing
to the nation its bereavement, and directing the suspension of all public business for the day. The public
offices were clothed in mourning. Orders were issued
from the War and Navy Departments, directing that
at every military and naval station, on the day after
the order should be received, the honors customary to
the illustrious dead should be paid.

At 12 o'clock on Saturday, the 26th of February,
the funeral took place in the capitol. It was a solemn,
an imposing scene. The Hall of Representatives was
hung in sable habiliments. The portraits of Washington and La Fayette, the beautiful statue of the Muse
of History in the car of Time, and the vacant chair
of the deceased, were wreathed in crape. In the
midst, and the most conspicuous of all, was the coffin
containing the remains of the illustrious dead, covered
with its velvet pall. The President of the United
States, and the Heads of Departments, the Members
of both Houses of Congress, the Judges of the Supreme

Court, the Foreign Ministers, Officers of the Army and
Navy, Members of State Legislatures, and an immense
concourse of the great, the wise, and the good, were
present, to bestow honor on all that remained of the
statesman, the philosopher, and the Christian.

A discourse was delivered on the occasion, by the
Rev. R. R. Gurley, chaplain to the House of Representatives, from Job xi. 17, 18—"And thine age shall be
clearer than the noon-day; thou shalt shine forth, thou
shalt be as the morning: and thou shalt be secure,
because there is hope." The following are extracts
from the sermon :—

"In some circumstances, on some occasions, we most naturally
express our emotions in silence and in tears. What voice of man
can add to the impressiveness and solemnity of this scene ? The
presence and aspect of this vast assembly, the Chief Magistrate,
Counsellors, Judges, Senators, and Representatives of the nation,
distinguished officers of the army and the navy, and the honored Ambassadors from foreign powers,—these symbols and badges of a universal mourning, darkening this hall into sympathy with our sorrow,
leave no place for the question, ' Know ye not that a prince and a
great man is fallen in Israel ?' Near to us, indeed, has come the in-
visible hand of the Almighty—that hand in which is the soul of every
living thing, and the breath of all mankind; in this very hall, from
yonder seat, which he so long occupied, in the midst of the representatives of the people, has it taken one full of years and honors,
eminent, for more than half a century, in various departments of the
public service ; who adorned every station, even the highest, by his
abilities and virtues ; and whose influence, powerful in its beneficence, is felt in many, if not in all the States of the civilized
world. * * * * *

"Not more certainly is the body invigorated and preserved by
suitable food, by manly exercises, by the vital air, than are the intellectual and moral faculties by the investigation and reception of

divine truths, by habits of obedience to the divine will, by cheerful submission to the order and discipline of Divine Providence. Nor let us ever distrust the Father of our spirits, who knows perfectly all the wants of our nature, but rest assured that his commandments in the sacred Scriptures are entirely in harmony with the decrees of his providence; and that as to fear Him and keep His commandments is the whole duty (because the highest duty, and comprehending all others), so will it prove the whole and eternal happiness of man. If the indissoluble and harmonious connection between the laws of nature, of Providence and the moral law, be not always obvious, it is always certain. Over all the darkness, disturbances, and evils of the world shines revealed, more or less clearly, like the serene and cheerful heavens, this immutable law, binding virtue, however obscure, persecuted, or forsaken, to reward; duty, however humble or arduous, to happiness. Hence the declaration, that all things shall work together for good to them who love God, and that all things are theirs—the past and future, things temporal and spiritual, prosperity and adversity, angels, and principalities, and powers, and God himself, in all the resources of his wisdom and all the eternity of his reign.

" How shone out, clear as the noonday, yet mild and gentle as the morning, even in age, in the life and character of that great and venerable man, around whose precious, but, alas! inanimate form we all press in gratitude, admiration, and love, those high virtues derived from faith in God, and nurtured by his revealed truth, this bereaved Congress, and, I may add, this nation witnesses. * * * * * *

" Truly emblematic of his moral integrity and strength of character would be the granite column from his native hills, one and entire, just in its proportions, towering in its height, immoveable in its foundations, and pointing to Heaven as the temple and throne of everlasting authority, the final refuge, the imperishable home of all regenerated and faithful souls.

" Independence of mere human authority in the use of his reason, on all subjects, was united with veneration most sincere and profound for the sacred Scriptures, as a supernatural revelation from God, ' whose prerogative extends not less to the reason than the will of man,' and from a daily perusal of the Divine Word, and a constant and devout attendance upon the public worship of the Sabbath, although differing on some points from common opinions, he cherished enlarged views of Christian communion, and recognized in most, if not all the religious denominations of this country, members of one and the same family and kingdom of Jesus Christ. * * * * * * *

"Alas, the sad and appalling ruins of death! 'This is the end of earth.' Approach! lovers of pleasure, seekers after wisdom, aspirants, by pre-eminence in station, and power, and influence among men, to fame; see the end of human distinctions and earthly greatness! Surely man walketh in a vain show; surely man in his best estate is altogether vanity. How pertinent to this scene the words of Job: 'He leadeth princes away spoiled, and overthroweth the mighty. He removeth away the speech of the trusty, and taketh away the understanding of the aged. He discovereth deep things out of darkness, and bringeth out to light the shadow of death!' How, indeed, is the mighty fallen, and the head of the wise laid low! All flesh is grass—all the glory of man as the flower of the field. And shall this vast congregation soon be brought to the grave—that house appointed for all the living? Hear, then, the great announcement of the Son of God: 'I am the resurrection and the life, and whosoever believeth in me, though he were dead yet shall he live, and whosoever liveth and believeth in me shall never die.' Is it strange that he who communed so much with the future as the great statesman to whose virtues and memory we now pay this sad, final, solemn tribute of honor and affection, should, in the last conversation I ever had with him, have expressed both regret and astonishment at the indifference among too many of our public men to the truths and ordinances of our holy religion? Is it to affect our hearts that he has been permitted to fall in the midst of us, to arouse us from this insensibility, and cause us to press towards the gates of the eternal city of God? Let us bless God for another great example to shine upon us, that another star (we humbly trust) is planted amid the heavenly constellations to guide us to eternity!"

At the conclusion of the exercises in the capitol, a vast procession, escorted by military companies, conveyed the remains to the Congressional burying ground, where they were to rest until preparations for their removal to Quincy should be completed.

> " Sad was the pomp that yesterday beheld,
>   As with the mourner's heart the anthem swelled;
> The rich-plumed canopy, the gorgeous pall,
> The sacred march, and sable vested wall!—
> These were not rites of inexpressive show,
> But hallowed as the types of real woe!
> Illustrious deceased! a NATION's sighs,
> A NATION's HEART, went with thine obsequies!"

The following letter of thanks from Mrs. Adams, addressed to the Speaker, was laid before the House of Representatives:—

> " *Washington, February* 29, 1848.

" SIR : The resolutions in honor of my dear deceased husband, passed by the illustrious assembly over which you preside, and of which he at the moment of his death was a member, have been duly communicated to me.

" Penetrated with grief at this distressing event of my life, mourning the loss of one who has been at once my example and my support through the trials of half a century, permit me nevertheless to express through you my deepest gratitude for the signal manner in which the public regard has been voluntarily manifested by your honorable body, and the consolation derived to me and mine from the reflection that the unwearied efforts of an old public servant have not even in this world proved without their reward in the generous appreciation of them by his country.

" With great respect, I remain, sir, your obedient servant,

"LOUISA CATHARINE ADAMS."

On the following week, the Committee of one from each State and Territory in the Union, appointed by the House of Representatives to take charge of the

remains of the deceased ex-President, and convey
them to Quincy for final interment, commenced their
journey.   It was a new, yet inexpressibly thrilling and
imposing spectacle.   The dead body of "the Old Man
Eloquent," surrounded and guarded by a son of each
of the States and Territories of that Union which he
had so largely assisted in consolidating and sustaining,
leaves the capitol of the nation, where for more than
thirty years he had acted the most conspicuous part
among the fathers of the land, to rest in the tomb of
its ancestors, amid the venerable shades of Quincy.
How solemn the progress of such a procession.   It
was indeed, "the Funeral March of the Dead!"
Wherever it passed, the people rose up and paid the
utmost marks of respect to the remains of one who
had occupied so large a space in the history of his
country.   In towns, in villages, in cities, as the mournful cortege swept through, business was suspended,
flags were displayed at half mast, bells were tolled,
minute guns were fired, civil and military processions
received the sacred remains, and watched over them
by night and by day, and passed them on from State
to State.

"What a progress was it which the dead patriot
thus made !   From the capitol of the nation, beneath
whose dome, and while at his post of duty, he was
seized by death—within sight almost of that Mount
Vernon where repose the ashes of him, the Father of
his Country, who first distinguished, encouraged and

employed the extraordinary capacity of the youthful
Adams—through cities that in his life time have grown
up from villages—passing, at Baltimore, almost beneath
the shadow of the monument which there testifies of
the valor of those who fell for country in the war of
1812—and in Philadelphia halting and reposing within
the hall where his great father, John Adams, had fearlessly stood for Independence, and where Independence
was proclaimed—the dead passed on, everywhere followed by the reverential gaze and the mourning heart,
till, reaching the great metropolis of New York, where
the same father had been sworn in and taken his seat,
as the first Vice President of the United States, with
George Washington for President! Thence away the
march was resumed, till it reached old Faneuil Hall—
the cradle of American liberty, the fitting final resting-
place, while yet unburied, of the body of one in whose
heart, at no moment of life, did the love of liberty, imbibed or strengthened in that hall, suffer the slightest
abatement."*

Faneuil Hall was clothed in the dark drapery of
mourning, fitting to receive the body of one of the
greatest of the many noble sons of the venerable Bay
State. Amid solemn dirges and appropriate ceremonies, the chairman of the Congressional Committee
surrendered to a Committee from the Legislature of
Massachusetts, the sacred remains they had accompanied from the capitol of the United States.—

* King's Eulogy.

" Throughout the journey," said the chairman, "there have been displayed manifestations of the highest admiration and respect for the memory of your late distinguished fellow-citizen. In the large cities through which we expected to pass, we anticipated such demonstrations; but in every village and hamlet, at the humblest cottage which we passed, and from the laborers in the field, the same profound respect was testified by their uncovered heads."

The Committee of the Massachusetts Legislature having thus received the body from its Congressional escort, in turn surrendered it to the keeping of the municipal authorities of Boston, for burial at Quincy. This ceremony was performed by Mr. Buckingham, chairman of the Legislative Committee, in these impressive words:—

" In the name and behalf of the Government and People of the Commonwealth of Massachusetts, whose honored but humble servant I this day am, I consign to your faithful keeping, Mr. Mayor, the remains of JOHN QUINCY ADAMS—all that was mortal of that venerable man, whose age and whose virtues had rendered him an object of intense interest and admiration to his country and to the world. We place these sacred remains in your possession, to be conveyed to their appointed home—to sleep in the sepulchre and with the dust of his fathers."

Mr. Quincy, the Mayor, in accepting the guardianship conferred upon him in behalf of the city of Boston, replied in the following terms:—

" There is something sublime in the scene that surrounds us. An honored son of Massachusetts—one who was educated by a signer of the Declaration of Independence—one who heard the thunder of the great struggle for liberty on yonder hill, has, after a life of unparalleled usefulness and fidelity, fallen in the capitol of the country he served. His remains were escorted here by delegates from every State in the Union. They have passed over spots ever memorable in history. They have everywhere been received with funeral honors. They have reposed in the hall of independence. They now lie in the cradle of liberty. As a citizen of Massachusetts, I cannot but acknowledge our sense of the honor paid to her distinguished son. Mourned by a nation at its capitol, attended by the representatives of millions to the grave, he has received a tribute to his memory unequalled among men.

"These remains now rest in the cradle of liberty. It is their last resting-place on their journey home. As a statesman's, 'this is to them the last of earth!' To-morrow they will be deposited in the peaceful church-yard of the village of his birth, there to be mourned, not as statesmen mourn for statesmen, but as friends mourn for friends.

"He will be 'gathered to his fathers!' And how great, in this case, is the significance of the expression! It is possible that other men may be attended as he will be to the grave. But when again shall the tomb of a President of the United States open its doors to receive a son who has filled the same office?"

On the following day, the body, under the charge of the municipal officers of Boston, was conveyed to Quincy. In the Unitarian church, in the presence of old neighbors and friends, the last funeral exercises were held, and the last sad burial service was performed.

By the side of the graves of his fathers, overshadowed by aged trees, which had sheltered his head in the days of boyhood, in a plain tomb, prepared under his own direction, and inscribed simply with his name, sleep the ashes of JOHN QUINCY ADAMS.

" Let no weak drops
Be shed for him. The virgin in her bloom
Cut off, the joyous youth, and darling child,
These are the tombs that claim the *tender* tear
And elegiac songs. But Adams calls
For other notes of gratulation high ;
That now he wanders thro' those endless worlds
He here so well descried ; and, wondering, talks
And hymns their Author with his glad compeers.
Columbia's boast ! whether with angels thou
Sittest in dread discourse, or fellow blest
Who joy to see the honor of their kind ;
Or whether, mounted on cherubic wing,
Thy swift career is with the whirling orbs,
Comparing things with things, in rapture lost,
And grateful adoration for that light
So plenteous ray'd into thy mind below
From Light himself—oh ! look with pity down
On human kind, a frail, erroneous race !
Exalt the spirit of a downward world !
O'er thy dejected country chief preside,
And be her Genius called ! her studies raise,
Correct her manners, and inspire her youth ;
For, though deprav'd and sunk, she brought thee forth,
And glories in thy name. She points thee out
To all her sons, and bids them eye thy star—
Thy star, which, followed steadfastly, shall lead
To wisdom, virtue, glory here, and joy
Unspeakable in worlds to come."

EULOGY.*

~~~~~~

WE are in the midst of extraordinary events. British-American Civilization and Spanish-American Society have come into collision, each in its fullest maturity. The armies of the North have penetrated the chapparels at Palo Alto and Resaca de la Palma—passed the fortresses of Monterey, and rolled back upon the heart of Mexico the unavailing tide of strong resistance from the mountain-side of Buena Vista. Martial colonists are encamped on the coasts of California, while San Juan d'Ulloa has fallen, and the invaders have swept the gorge of Cerro Gordo—carried Perote and Puebla, and planted the banner of burning stars and ever-multiplying stripes on the towers of the city of the Aztecs.

The thirtieth Congress assembles in this conjuncture, and the debates are solemn, earnest, and bewildering. Interest, passion, conscience, freedom, and humanity, all have their advocates. Shall new loans and levies be granted to prosecute still farther a war so glorious ? or shall it be abandoned ? Shall we be

---

* Delivered before the Legislature of New York, by Wm. H. Seward.

content with the humiliation of the foe? or shall we complete his subjugation? Would that severity be magnanimous, or even just? Nay, is the war itself just? Who provoked, and by what unpardonable offence, this disastrous strife between two eminent Republics, so scandalous to Democratic Institutions? Where shall we trace anew the ever-advancing line of our empire? Shall it be drawn on the shore of the Rio Grande, or on the summit of the Sierra Madre? or shall Mexican Independence be extinguished, and our eagle close his adventurous pinions only when he looks off upon the waves that separate us from the Indies? Does Freedom own and accept our profuse oblations of blood, or does she reject the sacrifice? Will these conquests extend her domain, or will they be usurped by ever-grasping slavery? What effect will this new-born ambition have upon ourselves? Will it leave us the virtue to continue the career of social progress? How shall we govern the conquered people? Shall we incorporate their mingled races with ourselves, or rule them with the despotism of pro-consular power? Can we preserve these remote and hostile possessions in any way, without forfeiting our own blood-bought heritage of freedom?

Steam and lightning, which have become docile messengers, make the American people listeners to this high debate, and anxiety, and interest, intense and universal, absorb them all. Suddenly the council is dissolved. Silence is in the capitol, and sorrow has thrown its pall over the land. What new event is this? Has some Cromwell closed the legislative chambers? or has some Cæsar, returning from his distant conquests, passed the Rubicon, seized the purple, and fallen in the Senate beneath the swords of self-appointed executioners of his country's vengeance? No! nothing of all this. What means, then, this abrupt and fearful silence? What unlooked for calamity has quelled the debates of the Senate and calmed the excitement of the people? An old man, whose tongue once indeed was eloquent, but now through age had well nigh lost its cunning, has fallen into the swoon of death. He was not an actor in the drama of conquest—nor had his feeble voice yet mingled in the lofty argument—

> "A grey-haired sire, whose eye intent
> Was on the visioned future bent."

And now he has dreamed out at last the troubled dream of life. Sighs of unavailing grief ascend to Heaven. Panegyric, fluent in long-stifled praise, performs its office. The army and the navy pay conventional honors, with the pomp of national woe, and then the hearse moves onward. It rests appropriately, on its way, in the hall where independence was proclaimed, and again under the dome where freedom was born At length the tomb of JOHN ADAMS opens to receive a son, who also, born a subject of a king, had stood as a representative of his emancipated country, before principalities and powers, and had won by merit, and worn without reproach, the honors of the Republic.

From that scene, so impressive in itself, and impressive because it never before happened, and can never happen again, we have come up to this place surrounded with the decent drapery of public mourning, on a day set apart by authority, to recite the history of the citizen, who, in the ripeness of age, and fulness of honors, has thus descended to his rest. It is fit to do so, because it is by such exercises that nations regenerate their early virtues and renew their constitutions. All nations must perpetually renovate their virtues and their constitutions, or perish. Never was there more need to renovate ours than now, when we seem to be passing from the safe old policy of peace and moderation into a career of conquest and martial renown. Never was the duty of preserving our free institutions in all their purity, more obvious than it is now, when they have become beacons to mankind in what seems to be a general dissolution of their ancient social systems.

The history of JOHN QUINCY ADAMS is one that opens no new truth in the philosophy of virtue; for there is no undiscovered truth in that philosophy. But it is a history that sheds marvellous confirmation on maxims which all mankind know, and yet are prone to undervalue and forget. The exalted character before us was formed by the combination of virtue, courage, assiduity, and modesty, under favorable conditions, with native talent and genius, and illustrates the truth, that in morals as in nature, simplicity is the chief element of the sublime.

John Quincy Adams was fortunate in his lineage; in the period, and in the place of his nativity; in all the circumstances of education; in the age and country in which he lived; in the incidents, as well as the occasions of his public service; and in the period and manner of his death. He was a descendant from one of the Puritan planters of Massachusetts, and a son of the most intrepid actor in the Revolution of Independence. Quincy, the place of his birth, is a plain, bounded on the west by towering granite hills, and swept without defence by every wind from the ocean. Its soil in ancient times was as sterile as its climate is always rigorous.

Born on the eleventh day of July, 1767, in the hour of the agitation of rebellion, and reared within sight and sound of gathering war, the earliest political ideas he received were such as John Adams then uttered— "We must fight." "Sink or swim—live or die—survive or perish with my country, is my unalterable determination." A mother fervently pious, and eminent in intellectual gifts, directed with more than maternal assiduity and solicitude the education of him who was to render her own name immortal. Never quite divorced from home, yet twice, and for long periods in his youth, a visitor in Europe, he enjoyed always the parental discipline of one of the founders of the Amer-

ican State, and often the daily conversation of Franklin
and Jefferson ; and combined travel in France, Spain,
England, Holland, Denmark, Sweden, and Russia,
and even diplomatic experience, with the instructions
of the schools of Paris, of the University at Leyden,
and of Harvard University at Cambridge ; and all
these influences fell upon him at a period when his
country, then opening the way to human liberty
through trials of fire, fixed the attention of mankind.

The establishment of the Republic of the United
States of America, is the most important secular event
in the history of the human race. It did not disen-
tangle the confused theory of the origin of Government, but cut through the bonds of power existing by
prescription, at a blow ; and thus directly and immediately affected the opinions and the actions of men in
every part of the civilized world. It animated them
everywhere to seek freedom from despotic power and
aristocratic restraint. Whenever and wherever they
have since moved, either by peaceful agitation or by
physical force, to meliorate systems of government,
whether in France at the close of the last century, or
afterward on the second subversion of the elder branch
of the Bourbons, or in the recent overthrow of the
constitutional king, or in Ireland, or in England, or in
Italy, or in Greece, or in South America, whether they
succeeded or failed, there, in the tumult or in the strife,
was the spirit of the American Revolution. " It gave
an example of a great people, not merely emancipating

themselves, but governing themselves, without either a monarch to control, or an aristocracy to restrain them ; and it demonstrated, for the first time in the history of the world, contrary to the predictions and theories of speculative philosophy, that a great nation, when duly prepared, is capable of self-government by purely republican institutions."

But the establishment of the American Republic was too great an achievement to be made all at once. It was a drama of five grand acts, each of which filled a considerable period, and called upon the stage actors of peculiar powers and distinguished virtues. Those acts were, colonization, preparation, revolution, organization, consolidation.

Two of these acts were closed before John Quincy Adams was born. The third, the revolution, the shortest of them all, dazzles the contemplation by the rapidity and the martial character of its incidents. The fourth, the organization of the Government, by the splendors of genius elicited, and the felicity of the new form of government presented, satisfies the superficial inquirer that, when the Constitution had been adopted, nothing remained to perfect the great achievement. But other nations have had successful revolutions, and have set up free constitutions, and have yet sunk again under reinvigorated despotism. The CONSOLIDATION of the American Republic—the crowning act—occupied forty years, reaching from 1789 to 1829. During that period, John Quincy Adams participated continually in public affairs, and ultimately became the principal actor.

The new Government was purely an experiment. In opposition to the fixed habits of mankind, it established suffrage practically universal, and representation so perfect that not one Legislative House only, but both Houses; not legislative officers only, but all officers, executive, ministerial, and even judicial, were directly or indirectly elected by the people. The longest term of the senatorial trust was but six years, and the shortest only two, and even the tenure of the executive power was only four years. This Government, betraying so much popular jealousy, was invested with only special and limited sovereignty. The conduct of merely municipal affairs was distributed within the States, among Governments even more popular than the federal structure, and without whose ever-renewed support that structure must fall.

The Government thus constituted, so new, so complex and artificial, was to be consolidated, in the midst of difficulties at home, and of dangers abroad. The constitution had been adopted only upon convictions of absolute necessity, and with evanescent dispositions of compromise. By nearly half of the people it was thought too feeble to sustain itself, and secure the rights for which governments are instituted among men. By as many it was thought liable to be converted into an over-shadowing despotism, more formidable and more odious than the monarchy which had been subverted. These conflicting opinions revealed themselves in like discordance upon every important question of administration, and were made the basis of parties, which soon became jealous and irreconcilable, and ultimately inveterate, and even in some degree disloyal.

These domestic feuds were aggravated by pernicious influences from Europe. In the progress of western civilization, the nations of the earth had become social. The new Republic could not, like the Celestial Empire, or that of Japan, confine itself within its own boundaries, and exist without national intercourse. It had entered the family of nations. But the position it was to assume, and the advantages it was to be allowed to enjoy, were yet to be ascertained and fixed. Its independence, confessed to be only a doubtful experiment at home, was naturally thought ephemeral in Europe. Its example was ominous, and the European Powers willingly believed that, if discountenanced and baffled, America would soon relapse into colonial subjugation. Such prejudices were founded in the fixed habits of society. Not only the thirteen colonies, but the whole American hemisphere, had been governed by European States from the period of its discovery. The very soil belonged to the trans-atlantic monarchs by discovery, or by ecclesiastical gift. Dominion over it attached by divine right to their persons, and drew after it obligations of inalienable allegiance upon those who became the inhabitants of the new world. The new world was indeed divided between different powers, but the system of government was the same. It was administered for the benefit of the parental State alone. Each power prohibited all foreign trade with its Colonies, and all intercourse between them and other plantations, supplied its Colonies with what they needed from abroad, interdicted their manufactures, and monopolized their trade. The prevalence of this system over the whole continent of America and the adjacent islands prevented all enterprize in the colonies, discouraged all improvement, and retarded their progress to independence.

The American Revolution sundered these bonds only so far as they confined thirteen of the British Colonies, and left the remaining British dominions, and the continent, from Georgia around Cape Horn to the Northern Ocean, under the same thraldom as before. Even the United States had attained only physical independence. The moral influences of the colonial system oppressed them still. Their trade, their laws, their science, their literature, their social connections, their ecclesiastical relations, their manners and their habits, were still colonial; and their thoughts continually clung around the ancient and majestic States of the Eastern Continent.

The American Revolution, so happily concluded here, broke out in France simultaneously with the beginning of Washington's administration. The French nation passed in fifteen years from absolute despotism under

Louis XVI., through all the phases of democracy to a military despotism under Napoleon Bonaparte; and retained, through all these changes, only two characteristics—unceasing ferocity of faction, and increasing violence of aggression against foreign States. The scandal of the French Revolution fell back upon the United States of America, who were regarded as the first disturbers of the ancient social system. The principal European monarchs combined, under the guidance of England, to arrest the presumptuous career of France and extirpate democracy by the sword. Nevertheless, the republican cause, however odious in Europe, was our national cause. The sympathies of a large portion of the American people could not be withdrawn from the French nation, which always claimed, even when marshalled into legions under the Corsican conqueror, to be fighting the battles of freedom; while, on the other side, the citizens who regarded innovation as worse than tyranny, considered England and her allies as engaged in sustaining the cause of order, of government, and of society itself.

The line already drawn between the American people in regard to their organic law, naturally became the dividing line of the popular sympathies in the great European conflict. Thus deeply furrowed, that line became "a great gulf fixed." The Federal party unconsciously became an English party, although it indignantly disowned the epithet; and the Republican party became a French party, although with equal sincerity it denied the gross impeachment. Each belligerent was thus encouraged to hope for aid from the United States, through the ever-expected triumph of its friends; while both conceived contemptuous opinions of a people who, from too eager interest in a foreign fray, suffered their own national rights to be trampled upon with impunity by the contending States.

Washington set the new machine of government in motion. He formed his cabinet of recognized leaders of the adverse parties. Hamilton and Knox of the Federal party were balanced by Jefferson and Randolph of the adverse party. "Washington took part with neither, but held the balance between them with the scrupulous justice which marked his lofty nature." On the 25th of April, 1793, he announced the neutrality of the United States between the belligerents, and his decision, without winning the respect of either, exasperated both. Each invaded our national rights more flagrantly than before, and excused the injustice by the plea of necessary retaliation against its adversary, and each found willing apologists in a sympathizing faction in our own country.

Commercial and political relations were to be established between the United States and the European Powers in this season of conflict. Ministers were needed who could maintain and vindicate abroad the same impartiality practised by Washington at home. There was one citizen eminently qualified for such a trust in such a conjuncture. Need I say that citizen was the younger Adams, and that Washington had the sagacity to discover him?

John Quincy Adams successively completed missions at the Hague and at Berlin, in the period intervening between 1794 and 1801, with such advantage and success, that in 1802 he was honored by his native commonwealth with a seat as her representative in the Senate of the United States. The insults offered to our country by the belligerents increased in aggravation as the contest between them became more violent and convulsive. France, in 1804, laid aside even the name and forms of a Republic, and the first consul, dropping the emblems of popular power, placed the long-coveted diadem upon his brow, where its jewels sparkled among the laurels he had won in the conquest of Italy. Washington's administration had passed away, leaving the American people in sullen discontent. John Adams had succeeded, and had atoned by the loss of power for the offence he had given by causing a just but unavailing war to be declared against France. Jefferson was at the head of the Government; he thought the belligerents might be reduced to forbearance by depriving them of our commercial contributions of supplies, and recommended, first an embargo, and then non-intercourse. Britain was an insular and France a continental power. The effects of these measures would therefore be more severe on the former than on the latter, and, unhappily, they were more severe on our own country than on either of the offenders.

Massachusetts was the chief commercial State in the Union. She saw the ruin of her commerce involved in the policy of Jefferson, and regarded it as an unworthy concession to the usurper of the French throne. In this emergency John Quincy Adams turned his back on Massachusetts, and threw into the uprising scale of the administration, the weight of his talents and of his already eminent fame. Massachusetts instructed the recusant to recant. He refused to obey, and resigned his place. His change of political relations astounded the country, and, with the customary charity of partisan zeal, was attributed to venality. It is now seen by us in the light reflected upon it by the habitual independence, unquestioned purity, and lofty patriotism of his whole life ; and thus seen, constitutes only the first marked one of many instances wherein he broke the green withes which party fastened upon him, and maintained the cause of his country, referring the care of his fame to God and to an impartial posterity. Like Decimus Brutus, whom Julius Cæsar saluted among his executioners with the exclamation *" Et tu, Brute !"* John Quincy Adams was not unfaithful, but he could not be obliged where he was not left free.

Jefferson retired in 1809, leaving to his successor, the scholastic and peace-loving Madison, the perilous legacy of perplexed foreign relations, and embittered domestic feuds. Great Britain now filled the measure of exasperation by insolently searching our vessels on the high seas, and impressing into her marine all whom she chose to suspect of having been born in her allegiance, even though they had renounced it and had assumed the relations of American citizens. War was therefore imminent and inevitable. Russia was then coming forward to a position of commanding influence in Europe, and her youthful Emperor Alexander had won, by his chivalrous bearing, the respect of mankind. John Quincy Adams was wisely sent by the United States, to establish relations of amity with the great power of the North; and while he was thus engaged, the flames of European war, which had been so long averted, involved his own country. War was declared against Great Britain.

It was just. It was necessary. Yet it was a war that dared Great Britain to re-assert her ancient sovereignty. It was a war with a power whose wealth and credit were practically inexhaustible, a power whose navy rode unchecked over all the seas, and whose impregnable garrisons encircled the globe.

Against such a power the war was waged by a nation that had not yet accumulated wealth, nor established credit, nor even opened avenues suitable for transporting munitions of war through its extended territories—that had only the germ of a navy, an inconsiderable army, and not one substantial fortress. Yet such a war, under such circumstances, was denounced as unnecessary and unjust, though for no better reason than because greater contumelies haa been endured at the hands of France. Thus a domestic feud, based on the very question of the war itself, enervated the national strength, and encouraged the mighty adversary.

The desperate valor displayed at Chippewa and Lundy's Lane, at Fort Erie and Plattsburgh, and the brilliant victories won in contests between single ships of war on the ocean and armed fleets on the lakes, vindicated the military prowess of the United States, but brought us no decisive advantage. A suspension of the conflict in Europe followed Napoleon's disastrous invasion of Russia, and left America alone opposed to her great adversary. Peace was necessary, because the national credit was exhausted—because the fortunes of the war were inclining against us—and because the opposition to it was ripening into disorganizing councils. Adams had prepared the way by securing the mediation of Alexander. Then, in that critical period, associated with Russell, Bayard, the learned and versatile Gallatin, and the eloquent and chivalric Clay, he negotiated with firmness, with assiduity, with patience, and with consummate ability, a definitive treaty of peace—a treaty of peace which, although it omitted the causes of the war already obsolete, saved and established and confirmed in its whole integrity the independence of the Republic—a treaty of peace that yet endures, and, we willingly hope, may endure forever.

After fulfilling a subsequent mission at the Court of St. James, the pacificator entered the domestic service of the country as Secretary of State in the administration of James Monroe; and at the expiration of that administration became President of the United States. He attained the honors of the Republic at the age of fifty-seven, in the forty-ninth year of independence. He was sixth in the succession, and with him closed the line of Chief Magistrates who had rendered to their country some tribute of their talents in civil or military service in the war of independence.

John Quincy Adams, on entering civil life, had found the Republic unstable. He retired in 1829, leaving it firmly established. It was thus his happy fortune to preside at the completion of that work of consolidation the beginning of which was the end of the labors of Washington.

John Quincy Adams engaged in this great work while yet in private life, in 1793. He showed to his fellow-citizens, in a series of essays, the inability of the French people to maintain free institutions at that time, and the consequent necessity of American neutrality in the European war. These publications aided Washington so much the more because they anticipated his own decision. Adams sustained the same great cause when he strengthened the administration of Jefferson against the preponderating influence of

Great Britain. His diplomatic services in Holland and Russia secured, at a critical period, a favorable consideration in the Courts of those countries, which conduced to the same end; and his brilliant success in restoring peace to the country so sorely pressed, relieved her from her enemies, reassured her, and gave to sceptical Europe conclusive proof that her republican institutions were destined to endure.

The administration of John Quincy Adams blends so intimately with that of Monroe, in which he was chief Minister, that no dividing line can be drawn between them. Adams may be said, without derogation from the fame of Monroe, to have swayed the Government during his presidency; and with equal truth, Monroe may be admitted to have continued his administration through that of his successor.

The consolidation of the Republic required that faction should be extinguished. Monroe began this difficult task cautiously, and pursued it with good effect. John Quincy Adams completed the achievement. The dignity and moderation which marked his acceptance of the highest trust which a free people could confer, beautifully foreshadowed the magnanimity with which it was to be discharged. He confessed himself deeply sensible of the circumstances under which it had been conferred :—

All my predecessors (he said) have been honored with majorities of the electoral voices, in the primary colleges. It has been my fortune to be placed, by the divisions of sentiment prevailing among our countrymen, on this occasion, in competition, friendly and honorable, with three of my fellow-citizens, all justly enjoying, in eminent degrees, the public favor; and of whose worth, talents and services, no one entertains a higher and more respectful sense than myself. The names of two of them were, in the fulfilment of the provisions of the constitution, presented to the selection of the House of Representatives, in concurrence with my own, names closely associated with the glory of the nation, and one of them farther recommended by a larger majority of the primary electoral suffrages than mine. In this state of things, could my refusal to accept the trust thus delegated to me give an opportunity to the people to form and to express, with a nearer approach to unanimity, the object of their preference, I should not hesitate to decline the acceptance of this eminent charge, and to submit the decision of this momentous question again to their determination.

It argued a noble consciousness of virtue to express, on such an occasion, so ingenuously, the emotions of a generous ambition.

He displayed the same great quality no less when he called to the post of chief Minister, in spite of clamors of corruption, Henry Clay, that one of his late rivals who alone among his countrymen had the talents and generosity which the responsibilities of the period exacted.

John Quincy Adams signalized his accession to the post of dangerous elevation by avowing the sentiments concerning parties by which he was inflexibly governed throughout his administration :—

Of the two great political parties [he said] which have divided the opinions and feelings of our country, the candid and the just will now admit, that both have contributed splendid talents, spotless integrity, ardent patriotism, and disinterested sacrifices, to the formation and administration of the Government, and that both have required a liberal indulgence for a portion of human infirmity and error. The revolutionary wars of Europe, commencing precisely at the moment when the Government of the United States first went into operation under the constitution, excited collisions of sentiments, and of sympathies, which kindled all the passions and embittered the conflict of parties, till the nation was involved in war, and the Union was shaken to its centre. This time of trial embraced a period of five-and-twenty years, during which the policy of the Union in its relations with Europe constituted the principal basis of our own political divisions, and the most arduous part of action of the Federal Government. With the catastrophe in which the wars of the French Revolution terminated, and our own subsequent peace with Great Britain, this baneful weed of party strife was uprooted. From that time no difference of principle, connected with the theory of government, or with our intercourse with foreign nations, has existed or been called forth in force sufficient to sustain a continued combination of parties, or given more than wholesome animation to public sentiment or legislative debate. Our political creed, without a dissenting voice that can be heard, is that the will of the people is the source, and the happiness of the people is the end, of all legitimate government upon earth—that the best security for the beneficence, and the best guaranty against the abuse of power, consists in the freedom, the purity, and the frequency of popular elections. That the General Government of the Union, and the separate Governments of the States, are all sovereignties of legitimate powers; fellow servants of the same masters, uncontrolled within their respective spheres—uncontrollable by encroachments on each other. If there have been those who doubted whether a confederated representative democracy was a government competent to the wise and orderly management of the common concerns of a mighty nation, those doubts have been dispelled. If there have been projects of partial confederacies to be erected upon the ruins of the Union, they have been scattered to the winds. If there have been dangerous attachments to one foreign nation, and antipathies against another, they have been extinguished. Ten years of peace at home and abroad have assuaged the animosities of political contention and blended into harmony the most discordant elements of public opinion. There still remains one effort of magnanimity, one sacrifice of prejudice and passion, to be made by the individuals throughout the nation who have heretofore followed the standards of political party. It is that of discarding every remnant of rancor against each other, of embracing, as countrymen and friends, and of yielding to talents and virtue alone that confidence which, in times of contention for principle, was bestowed only upon those who bore the badge of party communion.

During the administration of John Quincy Adams, he was really the Chief Magistrate. He submitted neither his reason nor his conscience to the control of any partisan cabal. No man was appointed to office in obedience to political dictation, and no faithful public servant was proscribed. The result rewarded his magnanimity. Faction ceased to exist. When South Carolina, a few years afterward, assumed the very ground that the ancient republican party had indicated as lawful and constitutional, and claimed the right and power to set aside, within her own limits, acts of Congress which she pronounced void, because they transcended the Federal authority, she called on the republican party throughout the Union in vain. The dangerous heresy had been renounced forever. Since that time there has been no serious project of a combination to resist the laws of the Union, much less of a conspiracy to subvert the Union itself.

What though the elements of political strife remain? They are necessary for the life of free States. What though there still are parties, and the din and turmoil of their contests are ceaselessly heard? They are founded now on questions of mere administration, or on the more ephemeral questions of personal merit.

Such parties are dangerous only in the decline, not in the vigor of Republics. Rome was no longer fit for freedom, and needed a Dictator and a Sovereign, when Pompey and Cæsar divided the citizens. What though the magnanimity of Adams was not appreciated, and his contemporaries preferred his military competitor in the subsequent election? The sword gathers none but ripe fruits, and the masses of any people will sometimes prefer them to the long maturing harvest, which the statesmen of the living generations sow, to be reaped by their successors. For all this Adams cared not. He had extinguished the factions which for forty years had endangered the State. He had left on the records of history instructions and an example teaching how faction could be overthrown, and his country might resort to them when danger should recur. For himself he knew well, none knew better, that

"He who ascends to mountain-tops shall find
   The loftiest peaks most wrapt in clouds and snow.
He who surpasses or subdues mankind,
   Must look down on the hate of those below.
Though high *above* the sun of glory glow,
   And far *beneath* the earth and ocean spread,
Round him are icy rocks, and loudly blow
   Contending tempests on his naked head,
And thus reward the toils which to their summits led."

The federal authority had so long been factiously opposed, that the popular respect for its laws needed to be renewed. The State of Georgia presented the fit occasion. She insisted on expelling, forcibly, remnants of Indian tribes, within her limits, in virtue of a treaty which was impeached for fraud, and came for revision before the Supreme Court and the Senate. The President met the emergency with boldness and decision. The demonstration thus given that good faith should be practised, and the law have its way, no matter how unequal the litigating parties, operated favorably toward restoring the moral influence of the Government. That influence, although sometimes checked, has recently increased in strength, until the federal authority is universally regarded as final, and liberty again walks confidently hand in hand with law.

John Quincy Adams "loved peace and ensued it." He loved peace as a Christian, because war was at enmity with the spirit and precepts of a religion which he held to be divine. As a statesman and magistrate, he loved peace, because war was not merely injurious to national prosperity, but because, whether successful or adverse, it was subversive of liberty. Democracies are prone to war, and war consumes them. He favored, therefore, all the philanthropic efforts of the age to cultivate the spirit of peace, and looked forward with benevolent hope to the ultimate institution of a General Congress of nations for the adjustment of their controversies. But he was no visionary and no enthusiast. He knew that as yet war was often inevitable— that pusillanimity provoked it, and that national honor was national property of the highest value ; because it was the best national defence. He admitted only de

fensive war—but he did not narrowly define it. He
held *that* to be a defensive war, which was waged to
sustain what could not be surrendered or relinquished
without compromising the independence, the just influence, or even the proper dignity of the State. Thus
he had supported the war with Great Britain—thus in
later years he sustained President Jackson in his bold
demonstration against France, when that power wan-
tonly refused to perform the stipulations it had made
in a treaty of indemnity; and thus he yielded his support to what was thought a warlike measure of the
present administration in the diplomatic controversy
with Great Britain concerning the Territory of Oregon.
The living and the dead have mutual rights, and therefore it must be added that he considered the present
war with Mexico as unnecessary, unjust, and criminal.
His opinion on this exciting question is among those
on which he referred himself to that future age which
he so often constituted the umpire between himself and
his contemporaries.

With such principles on the subject of war, he
regarded the establishment of a system of national
defence as a necessary policy for consolidating the
Republic. He prosecuted, therefore, on a large scale,
the work of fortification, and defended against popular
opposition the institution for the cultivation of military science, which has so recently vindicated that
early favor through the learning, valor, patriotism and
humanity exhibited by its pupils on the fields of Mexico.

But with that jealousy of the military spirit which never forsakes the wise republican statesman, he co-operated in reducing the army to the lowest scale commensurate with its necessary efficiency:

It was a vain and dangerous delusion (he said) to believe that in the present or any probable condition of the world, a commerce so extensive as ours could exist without the continual support of a military marine — the only arm by which the power of a confederacy could be estimated or felt by foreign nations, and the only standing force which could never be dangerous to our own liberties.

The enlargement of our navy, under the influence of these opinions, is among the measures of national consolidation we owe to him; and the institution for naval education we enjoy, is a recent result of his early suggestions.

But John Quincy Adams relied for national security and peace mainly on an enlightened and broad system of civil policy. He looked through the future combinations of States, and studied the accidents to which they were exposed, that he might seasonably remove causes of future conflict. His genius, when exercised in this lofty duty, played in its native element. He had cordially approved the measures by which Washington had secured the free navigation of the Mississippi. He approved the acquisition of Louisiana, although with Jefferson he insisted on a preliminary amendment of the constitution for that purpose. He had no narrow bigotry, concerning the soil to which the institutions of our fathers should be confined, and no local prejudice against their extension in any direction required by the public security, if the extension should be made with justice, honor, and humanity.

The acquisition of Louisiana had only given us additional territory, fruitful in new commerce, to be exposed to dangers which remain to be overcome. Spain still possessed, beside the Island of Cuba, the Peninsula of the Floridas, and thus held the keys of the Mississippi. The real independence, the commercial and the moral independence, of the United States, remained to be effected at the close of the European wars, and of our own war with England. Our political independence had been confirmed, and that was all. John Quincy Adams addressed himself, as Secretary of State, to the subversion of what remained of the colonial system. He commenced by an auspicious purchase of the Floridas, which gave us important maritime advantages on the Gulf of Mexico, while it continued our Atlantic sea-board unbroken from the Bay of Fundy to the Sabine.

The ever-advancing American Revolution was at the same time opening the way to complete disinthralment. The Spanish-American Provinces revolted, and seven new Republics, with constitutions not widely differing from our own—Buenos Ayres, Guatemala, Colombia, Mexico, Chili, Central America, and Peru—suddenly claimed audience and admission among the nations of the earth. The people of those countries were but doubtfully prepared to maintain their contest for independence, or to support republican institutions. But on the other side Spain was enervated and declining. She applied to the Holy League of Europe for their aid, and the new Republics applied to the United States for that recognition which could not fail to impart strength. The question was momentous. The ancient colonial system was at stake. All Europe was interested in maintaining it. The Holy League held Europe fast bound to the rock of despotism, and were at liberty to engage the United States in a war for the subversion of their independence, if they should dare to extend their aid or protection to the rebellious Colonies in South America.

Such a war would be a war of the two continents— an universal war. Who could foretell its termination, or its dread results? But the emancipation of Spanish America was necessary for our own larger freedom, and our own complete security. That freedom and that security required that the nations of Europe should relax their grasp on the American Continent. The question was long and anxiously debated. The American people hesitated to hazard, for speculative advantages, the measures of independence already obtained. Monroe and Adams waited calmly and firmly. The impassioned voice of Henry Clay rose from the Chamber of Representatives. It rang through the continent like the notes of the clarion, inspiring South America with new resolution, and North America with the confidence the critical occasion demanded. That noble appeal was answered. South America stood firm, and North America was ready. Then it was that John Quincy Adams, with those generous impulses which the impatient blood of his revolutionary sire always prompted, and with that enlightened sagacity which never misapprehended the interests of his country, nor mistook the time nor the means to secure them, obtained from the administration and from Congress the acknowledgment of the independence of the young American nations. To give decisive effect to this great measure, Monroe, in 1823, solemnly declared to the world, that thenceforth any attempt by any foreign power to establish the colonial system in any part of this continent, already emancipated, would be resisted as an aggression against the independence of the United States. On the accession of Adams to the administration of the Government, the vast American continental possessions of Brazil separated themselves from the crown of Portugal and became an independent State. Adams improved these propitious and sublime events by negotiating treaties of reciprocal trade with the youthful nations; and, concurring with Monroe, accepted, in behalf of the United States, their invitation to a General Congress of American States to be held at Panama, to cement relations of amity among themselves, and to consider, if it should become necessary, the proper means to repel the apprehended interference of the Holy League of Europe.

The last measure transcended the confidence of a

large and respectable portion of the American people. But its moral effect was needed to secure the stability of the South American Republics. Adams persevered, and, in defending his course, gave notice to the powers of Europe, by this bold declaration, that the determination of the United States was inflexible :—

" If it be asked, whether this meeting, and the principles which may be adjusted and settled by it, as rules of intercourse between American nations, may not give umbrage to European powers, or offence to Spain, it is deemed a sufficient answer, that our attendance at Panama can give no just cause of umbrage or offence to either, and that the United States will stipulate nothing there, which can give such cause. Here the right of inquiry into our purposes and measures must stop. The Holy League of Europe, itself, was formed without inquiring of the United States, whether it would or would not give umbrage to them. The fear of giving umbrage to the Holy League of Europe was urged as a motive for denying to the American nations the acknowledgment of their independence. The Congress and the administration of that day consulted their rights and their duties, not their fears. The United States must still, as heretofore, take counsel from their duties, rather than their fears."

Contrast, fellow-citizens, this declaration of John Quincy Adams, President of the United States in 1825, with the proclamation of neutrality, between the belligerents of Europe, made by Washington in 1793, with the querrulous complaints of your Ministers against the French Directory and the British Ministry at the close of the last century, and with the acts of embargo and non-intercourse at the beginning of the present century, destroying our own commerce to conquer forbearance from the intolerant European powers.

Learn from this contrast, the epoch of the consolidation of the Republic. Thus instructed, do honor to the statesman and magistrate by whom, not forgetting the meed due to his illustrious compeers, the colonial system was overthrown throughout Spanish America, and the independence of the United States was completely and finally consummated.

The intrepid and unwearied statesman now directed his attention to the remnants of the colonial system still preserved in the Canadas and West Indies. Great Britain, by parliamentary measures, had undermined our manufactures, and, receiving only our raw materials, repaid us with fabrics manufactured from them, while she excluded us altogether from the carrying trade with her colonial possessions. John Quincy Adams sought to counteract this injurious legislation, by a revenue system, which should restore the manufacturing industry of the country, while he offered reciprocal trade as a compromise. His administration ended during a beneficial trial of this vigorous policy. But it taxed too severely the patriotism of some of the States, and was relinquished by his successors.

Indolence begets degeneracy, and immobility is the first stage of dissolution. John Quincy Adams sought not merely to consolidate the Republic, but to perpetuate it. For this purpose he bent vast efforts, with success, to such a policy of internal improvement as would increase the facilities of communication and intercourse between the States, and bring into being that great internal trade which must ever constitute the strongest bond of federal union. Wherever a lighthouse has been erected, on our sea-coast, on our lakes, or on our rivers—wherever a mole or pier has been constructed or begun—wherever a channel obstructed by shoals or sawyers has been opened, or begun to be opened—wherever a canal or railroad, adapted to national uses, has been made or projected—there the engineers of the United States, during the administration of John Quincy Adams, made explorations, and opened the way for a diligent prosecution of his designs by his successors. This policy, apparently so stupendous, was connected with a system of fiscal economy so rigorous, that the treasury augmented its stores, while the work of improvement went on; the public debt, contracted in past wars, dissolved away, and the nation flourished in unexampled prosperity. John Quincy Adams administered the Federal Government, while De Witt Clinton was presiding in the State of New York. It is refreshing to recall the noble emulation of these illustrious benefactors—an emulation that shows how inseparable sound philosophy is from true patriotism.

If [said Adams, in his first annual message to the Congress of the United States,] the powers enumerated may be effectually brought into action by laws promoting the improvement of agriculture, commerce and manufactures, the cultivation and encouragement of the mechanic arts, and of the elegant arts, the advancement of literature, and the progress of the sciences, ornamental and profound, to refrain from exercising them for the benefit of the people would be to hide in the earth the talent committed to our charge, would be treachery to the most sacred of trusts. The spirit of improvement is abroad upon the earth. It stimulates the hearts, and sharpens the faculties, not of our fellow-citizens alone, but of the nations of Europe, and of their rulers. While dwelling with pleasing satisfaction upon the superior excellence of our political institutions, let us not be unmindful that liberty is power, that the nation blessed with the largest portion of liberty, must in proportion to its numbers be the most powerful nation upon earth, and that the tenure of power by man is, in the moral purposes of his Creator, upon condition that it shall be exercised to ends of beneficence, to improve the condition of himself, and his fellow men. While foreign nations, less blessed with that freedom which is power than ourselves, are advancing with gigantic strides in the career of public improvement, were we to slumber in indolence, or fold our arms and proclaim to the world that we are palsied by the will of our constituents, would it not be to cast away the bounties of Providence and doom ourselves to perpetual inferiority ? In the course of the year now drawing to its close, we have beheld, under the auspices, and at the expense of one State of this Union, a new university unfolding its portals to the sons of science, and holding up the torch of human improvement to eyes that seek the light.* We have seen, under the persevering and enlightened enterprise of another State, the waters of our Western lakes mingle with those of the ocean. If undertakings like these have been accomplished in the compass of a few years, by the authority of single members of our confederacy, can we, the representative authorities of the whole Union, fall behind our fellow servants in the exercise of the trust committed to us for the benefit of our common sovereign, by the accomplishment of works important to the whole and to which neither the authority nor the resources of any one State can be adequate ?

The disastrous career of many of the States, and the absolute inaction of others, since the responsibilities of internal improvement have been cast off by the

* The University of Virginia.

federal authorities, and devolved upon the States, without other sources of revenue than direct taxation, and with no other motives to stimulate them than their own local interests, are a fitting commentary on the error of that departure from the policy of John Quincy Adams. If other comment were necessary, it would be found in the fact that States have revised and amended their constitutions, so as to abridge the power of their Legislatures to prosecute the beneficent enterprises which the Federal Government has devolved upon them. The Smithsonian Institute, at the seat of Government, founded by the liberality of a cosmopolite, is that same university so earnestly recommended by Adams for the increase and diffusion of knowledge among men. The exploration of the globe, for purposes of geographical and political knowledge, which has so recently been made under the authority of the Union, and with such noble results, was an enterprize conceived and suggested by the same statesman. The National Observatory at the capital, which is piercing the regions nearest to the throne of the eternal Author of the universe, is an emanation of the same comprehensive wisdom.

Such was the administration of John Quincy Adams. Surely it exhibits enough done for duty and for fame—if the ancient philosopher said truly, that the duty of a statesman was to make the citizens happy, to make them firm in power, rich in wealth, splendid in glory, and eminent in virtue, and that such achievements were the greatest and best of all works among men.

But the measure of duty was not yet fulfilled. The Republic thought it no longer had need of the services of Adams, and he bowed to its command. Two years elapsed, and lo! the priest was seen again beside the deserted altar, and a brighter, purer, and more lasting flame arose out of the extinguished embers.

> " He looked in years. But in his years were seen
> A youthful vigor, an autumnal green."

The Republic had been extended and consolidated; but human slavery, which had been incorporated in it, was extended and consolidated also, and was spreading, so as to impair the strength of the great fabric on which the hopes of the nations were suspended. Slavery therefore must be restrained, and, without violence or injustice, must be abolished. The difficult task of removing it had been postponed by the statesmen of the Revolution, and had been delayed and forgotten by their successors. There were now resolute hearts and willing hands to undertake it, but who was strong enough, and bold enough to lead? Who had patience to bear with enthusiasm that overleaped its mark, and with intolerance that defeated its own generous purposes? Slaveholders had power, nay, the national power; and strange to say, they had it with the nation's consent and sympathy. Who was bold enough to provoke them, and bring the execration of the nation down upon his own head? Who would do this, when even abolitionists themselves, rendered implacable by the manifestation of those sentiments of justice and moderation, without which the most humane cause, depending on a change of public opinion, cannot be conducted safely to a prosperous end, were ready to betray their own champion into the hands of the avenger? That leader was found in the person of John Quincy Adams. He took his seat in the House of Representatives in 1831, without assumption or ostentation. Abolitionists placed in his hand petitions for the suppression of slavery in the District of Columbia, the seat of the federal authorities. He offered them to the House of Representatives, and they were rejected with contumely and scorn. Suddenly the alarm went forth, that the aged and venerable servant was retaliating upon his country by instigating a servile war, that such a war must be avoided, even at the cost of sacrificing the freedom of petition and the freedom of debate, and that if the free States would not consent to make that sacrifice, then the Union should be dissolved. This alarm had its desired effect. The House of Representatives, in 1837, adopted a rule of discipline, equivalent to an act, ordaining that no petition relating to slavery, nearly or remotely, should be read, debated or considered. The Senate adopted a like edict. The State authorities approved. Slavery was not less strongly entrenched behind the bulwark of precedents in the courts of law than in the fixed habits of thought and action among the people. The people even in the free States denounced the discussion of slavery, and suppressed it by unlawful force. John Quincy Adams stood unmoved amid the storm. He knew that the only danger incident to political reform, was the danger of delaying it too long. The French Revolution had made this an axiom of political science. If, indeed, the discussion of slavery was so hazardous as was pretended, it had been deferred too long already. The advocates of slavery had committed a fatal error. They had abolished freedom of speech and freedom of petition to save an obnoxious institution. As soon as the panic should subside, the people would demand the restoration of those precious rights, and would scrutinize with fearless fidelity the cause for which they had been suppressed. He offered petition after petition, each bolder and more importunate than the last. He debated questions, kindred to those which were forbidden, with the firmness and fervor of his noble nature. For age

> Had not quenched the open truth
> And fiery vehemence of youth.

Soon he gained upon his adversaries. District after district sent champions to his side. States reconsidered, and resolved in his behalf. He saw the tide was turning, and then struck one bold blow, not now for freedom of petition and debate, but a stroke of bold and retaliating warfare. He offered a resolution declaring that the following amendments of the constitution of the United States be submitted to the people of the several States for their adoption :

From and after the fourth day of July, 1842, there shall be, throughout the United States, NO HEREDITARY SLAVERY, but on and after that day every child born within the United States shall be FREE.

With the exception of the Territory of Florida, there shall, henceforth, never be admitted into this Union, any STATE the constitution of which shall tolerate within the same the existence of SLAVERY.

In 1845, the obnoxious rule of the House of Representatives was rescinded. The freedom of debate and petition was restored, and the unrestrained and irrepressible discussion of slavery by the press and political parties began. For the rest, the work of emancipation abides the action, whether it be slow or fast, of the moral sense of the American people. It depends not on the zeal and firmness only of the reformers, but on their wisdom and moderation also. Stoicism, that had no charity for error, never converted any human society to virtue; Christianity, that remembers the true nature of man, has encompassed a large portion of the globe. How long emancipation may be delayed, is among the things concealed from our knowledge, but not so the certain result. The perils of the enterprize are already passed—its difficulties have already been removed—when it shall have been accomplished it will be justly regarded as the last noble effort which rendered the Republic imperishable.

Then the merit of the great achievement will be awarded to John Quincy Adams; and by none more gratefully than by the communities on whom the institution of slavery has brought the calamity of premature and consumptive decline, in the midst of free, vigorous, and expanding States.

If this great transaction could be surpassed in dramatic sublimity, it was surpassed when the same impassioned advocate of humanity appeared, at the age of seventy-four, with all the glorious associations that now clustered upon him, at the bar of the Supreme Court of the United States, and pleaded, without solicitation or reward, the cause of Cinque and thirty other Africans, who had been stolen by a Spanish slaver from their native coast, had slain the master and crew of the pirate vessel, floated into the waters of the United States, and there been claimed by the President, in behalf of the authorities of Spain. He pleaded this great cause with such happy effect, that the captives were set at liberty. Conveyed by the charity of the humane to their native shores, they bore the pleasing intelligence to Africa, that justice was at last claiming its way among civilized and Christian men!

The recital of heroic actions loses its chief value, if we cannot discover the principles in which they were born. The text of John Quincy Adams, from which he deduced the duties of citizens, and of the republic, was the address of the Continental Congress to the people of the United States, on the occasion of the

successful close of the American Revolution. He
dwelt often and emphatically on the words :

Let it be remembered, that it has ever been the pride and the
boast of America, that the rights for which she contended were
the rights of human nature. By the blessing of the Author of
those rights, they have prevailed over all opposition, and form the
basis of thirteen independent States. No instance has heretofore
occurred, nor can any instance be expected hereafter to occur, in
which the unadulterated forms of republican government can pretend to so fair an opportunity of justifying themselves by their fruits.
In this view, the citizens of the United States are responsible for
the greatest trust ever confided to a political society. If JUSTICE,
GOOD FAITH, HONOR, GRATITUDE, and all the other qualities which
ennoble the character of a nation and fulfil the ends of government, be the fruits of our establishments, the cause of liberty will
acquire a dignity and lustre which it has never yet enjoyed, and an
example will be set which cannot but have the most favorable influence on mankind. If, on the other side, our Governments should
be unfortunately blotted with the reverse of these cardinal virtues,
the great cause which we have engaged to vindicate will be dishonored and betrayed ; the last and fairest experiment in favor of
the rights of human nature will be turned against them, and their
patrons and friends exposed to the insults, and silenced by the votaries of tyranny and usurpation.

Senators and Representatives of the People of the
State of New York : I had turned my steps away from
your honored halls, long since, as I thought forever.
I come back to them by your command, to fulfil a
higher duty and more honorable service than ever
before devolved upon me. I repay your generous
confidence, by offering to you this exposition of the
duties of the magistrate and of the citizen. It is the
same which John Quincy Adams gave to the Congress

of the United States, in his oration on the death of James Madison. It is the key to his own exalted character, and it enables us to measure the benefits he conferred upon his country. If then you ask what motive enabled him to rise above parties, sects, combinations, prejudices, passions, and seductions, I answer that he served his country, not alone, or chiefly because that country was his own, but because he knew her duties and her destiny, and knew her cause was the cause of human nature.

If you inquire why he was so rigorous in virtue as to be often thought austere, I answer it was because human nature required the exercise of justice, honor, and gratitude, by all who were clothed with authority to act in the name of the American people. If you ask why he seemed, sometimes, with apparent inconsistency, to lend his charities to the distant and the future rather than to his own kindred and times, I reply, it was because he held that the tenure of human power is on condition of its being beneficently exercised for the common welfare of the human race. Such men are of no country. They belong to mankind. If we cannot rise to this height of virtue, we cannot hope to comprehend the character of John Quincy Adams, or understand the homage paid by the American people to his memory.

Need it be said that John Quincy Adams studied justice, honor and gratitude, not by the false standards of the age, but by their own true nature? He general-ized truth, and traced it always to its source, the bosom of God. Thus in his defence of the Amistad captives he began with defining justice in the language of Justinian, " Constans et perpetua voluntas jus suum cuique tribuendi." He quoted on the same occasion from the Declaration of Independence, not by way of rhetorical embellishment, and not even as a valid human ordinance, but as a truth of nature, of universal application, the memorable words, " We hold these truths to be self-evident, that all men are created equal, and that they are endowed by their Creator with certain inalienable rights, and that among these rights are life, liberty, and the pursuit of happiness." In his vindication of the right of debate, he declared that the principle that religious opinions were altogether beyond the sphere of legislative control, was but one modification of a more extensive axiom, which included the unbounded freedom of the press, and of speech, and of the communication of thought in all its forms. He rested the inviolability of the right of petition, not on constitutions, or charters, which might be glossed, abrogated or expunged, but in the inherent right of every animate creature to pray to its superior.

The model by which he formed his character was Cicero. Not the living Cicero, sometimes inconsistent; often irresolute; too often seeming to act a studied part; and always covetous of applause. But Cicero, as he aimed to be, and as he appears revealed in those immortal emanations of his genius which have been the

delight and guide of intellect and virtue in every succeeding age.   Like the Roman, Adams was an orator,
but he did not fall into the error of the Roman, in practically valuing eloquence more than the beneficence to
which it should be devoted.   Like him he was a statesman and magistrate worthy to be called " The second
founder of the Republic,"—like him a teacher of didac-
tic philosophy, of morals, and even of his own peculiar
art; and like him he made all liberal learning tributary
to that noble art, while poetry was the inseparable
companion of his genius in its hours of relaxation from
the labors of the forum and of the capitol.

Like him he loved only the society of good men, and
by his generous praise of such, illustrated the Roman's
beautiful aphorism, that no one can be envious of good
deeds, who has confidence in his own virtue.   Like
Cicero he kept himself unstained by social or domestic
vices; preserved serenity and cheerfulness; cherished
habitual reverence for the Deity, and dwelt continually,
not on the mystic theology of the schools, but on the
hopes of a better life.   He lived in what will be regarded as the virtuous age of his country, while Cicero
was surrounded by an overwhelming degeneracy.   He
had the light of Christianity for his guide; and its sublime motives as incitements to virtue: while Cicero
had only the confused instructions of the Grecian
schools, and saw nothing certainly attainable but
present applause and future fame.   In moral courage,
therefore, he excelled his model and rivalled Cato

But Cato was a visionary, who insisted upon his right to act always without reference to the condition of mankind, as he should have acted in Plato's imaginary Republic. Adams stood in this respect midway between the impracticable stoic and the too flexible academician. He had no occasion to say, as the Grecian orator did, that if he had sometimes acted contrary to himself, he had never acted contrary to the Republic; but he might justly have said, as the noble Roman did, "I have rendered to my country all the great services which she was willing to receive at my hands, and I have never harbored a thought concerning her that was not divine."

More fortunate than Cicero, who fell a victim of civil wars which he could not avert, Adams was permitted to linger on the earth, until the generations of that future age, for whom he had lived and to whom he had appealed from the condemnation of contemporaries, came up before the curtain which had shut out his sight, and pronounced over him, as he was sinking into the grave, their judgment of approval and benediction.

The distinguished characteristics of his life were BE-NEFICENT LABOR and PERSONAL CONTENTMENT. He never sought wealth, but devoted himself to the service of mankind. Yet, by the practice of frugality and method, he secured the enjoyment of dealing forth continually no stinted charities, and died in affluence. He never solicited place or preferment, and had no partizan combinations or even connections; yet he received honors which eluded the covetous grasp of those who formed parties, rewarded friends and proscribed enemies; and he filled a longer period of varied and distinguished service than ever fell to the lot of any other citizen. In every stage of this progress he was CONTENT. He was content to be president, minister, representative, or citizen.

Stricken in the midst of this service, in the very act of rising to debate, he fell into the arms of conscript fathers of the Republic. A long lethargy supervened and oppressed his senses. Nature rallied the wasting powers, on the verge of the grave, for a very brief period. But it was long enough for him. The re-kindled eye showed that the re-collected mind was clear, calm, and vigorous. His weeping family, and his sorrowing compeers were there. He surveyed the scene and knew at once its fatal import. He had left no duty unperformed; he had no wish unsatisfied; no ambition unattained; no regret, no sorrow, no fear, no remorse. He could not shake off the dews of death that gathered on his brow. He could not pierce the thick shades that rose up before him. But he knew that eternity lay close by the shores of time. He knew that his Redeemer lived. Eloquence, even in that hour, inspired him with his ancient sublimity of utterance. "THIS," said the dying man, "THIS IS THE END OF EARTH." He paused for a moment, and then added, "I AM CONTENT." Angels might well draw aside the curtains of the skies to look down on such a scene—a scene that approximated even to that scene of unapproachable sublimity, not to be recalled without reverence, when, in mortal agony, ONE who spake as never man spake, said, "IT IS FINISHED !"

Only two years after the birth of John Quincy Adams, there appeared on an island in the Mediterranean sea, a human spirit newly born, endowed with equal genius, without the regulating qualities of justice and benevolence which Adams possessed in an eminent degree. A like career opened to both—born like Adams, a subject of a king—the child of more genial skies, like him, became in early life a patriot and a citizen of a new and great Republic. Like Adams he lent his service to the State in precocious youth, and in its hour of need, and won its confidence. But unlike Adams he could not wait the dull delays of slow and laborious, but sure advancement. He sought power by the hasty road that leads through fields of carnage, and he became, like Adams, a supreme magistrate, a Consul. But there were other Consuls. He was not content. He thrust them aside, and was Consul alone. Consular power was too short. He fought new battles, and was Consul for life. But power, confessedly derived from the people, must be exercised in obedience to their will, and must be resigned to them again, at least in death. He was not content. He desolated Europe afresh, subverted the Republic, imprisoned the patriarch who presided over Rome's comprehensive See, and obliged him to pour on his head the sacred oil that made the persons of kings divine, and their right to reign indefeasible. He was an Emperor. But he saw around him a mother, brothers and sisters, not ennobled ; whose humble state reminded him, and the world, that he was born a plebeian ; and he had no heir to wait impatient for the imperial crown. He scourged the earth again, and again fortune smiled on him even in his wild extravagance. He bestowed kingdoms and principalities upon his kindred—put away the devoted wife of his youthful days, and another, a daughter of Hapsburgh's imperial house, joyfully accepted his proud alliance. Offspring gladdened his anxious sight ; a diadem was placed on its infant brow, and it received the homage of princes, even in its cradle. Now he was indeed a monarch—a legitimate monarch—a monarch by divine appointment—the first of an endless succession of monarchs. But there were other monarchs who held sway in the earth. He was not content. He would reign with his kindred alone. He gathered new and greater armies—from his own land —from subjugated lands. He called forth the young and brave—one from every household—from the Pyrenees to Zuyder Zee—from Jura to the ocean. He marshalled them into long and majestic columns, and went forth to seize that universal dominion, which seemed almost within his grasp. But ambition had tempted fortune too far. The nations of the earth resisted, repelled, pursued, surrounded him. The pageant was ended The crown fell from his presumptuous head. The wife who had wedded him in his pride, forsook him when the hour of fear came upon him. His child was ravished from his sight. His kinsmen were degraded to their first estate, and he was no longer Emperor, nor Consul, nor General, nor even a citizen, but an exile and a prisoner, on a lonely island, in the midst of the wild Atlantic. Discontent attended him there. The wayward man fretted out a few long years of his yet unbroken manhood, looking off at the earliest dawn and in evening's latest twilight, towards that distant world that had only just eluded his grasp. His heart corroded. Death came, not unlooked for, though it came even then unwelcome. He was stretched on his bed within the fort which constituted his prison. A few fast and faithful friends stood around, with the guards who rejoiced that the hour of relief from long and wearisome watching was at hand. As his strength wasted away, delirium stirred up the brain from its long and inglorious inactivity. The pageant of ambition returned. He was again a Lieutenant, a General, a Consul, an Emperor of France. He filled again the throne of Charlemagne. His kindred pressed around him again, re-invested with the pompous pageantry of royalty. The daughter of the long line of kings again stood proudly by his side, and the sunny face of his child shone out from beneath the diadem that encircled its flowing locks. The marshals of the Empire awaited his command. The legions of the old guard were in the field, their scarred faces rejuvenated, and their ranks, thinned in many battles, replenished, Russia, Prussia, Austria, Denmark and England, gathered their mighty hosts to give him battle. Once more he mounted his impatient charger, and rushed forth to conquest. He waved his sword aloft, and cried "TETE D'ARMEE." The feverish vision broke— the mockery was ended. The silver cord was loosed, and the warrior fell back upon his bed a lifeless corpse. THIS was the END OF EARTH. THE CORSICAN WAS NOT CONTENT.

STATESMEN AND CITIZENS! the contrast suggests its own impressive moral.

THE END.